ST. TERESA OF JESUS

and

ST. JOHN OF THE CROSS

on

THE BEATITUDES

By THOMAS M. REID, OCDS

Published by The Little Flower Press

Cover: The Sermon on the Mount by Carl Heinrich Bloch

ST. TERESA OF JESUS and ST. JOHN OF THE CROSS on
THE BEATITUDES

© 2010 by Thomas M. Reid. All rights reserved.
Published by **The Little Flower Press**
Rochester Hills, Michigan
www.TheLittleFlowerPress.com
Printed in the United States of America

ISBN-13: 978-0-9842372-1-0
ISBN-10: 0-9842372-1-6

<u>Other works by Thomas M. Reid, OCDS</u>

Ascent of Mt. Carmel - St. John of the Cross – Study Guide
The Dark Night - St. John of the Cross – Study Guide
The Spiritual Canticle - St. John of the Cross – Study Guide
The Living Flame of Love - St. John of the Cross – Study Guide
Carmelite Spirituality and the Catholic Charismatic Renewal

Second Printing, February 2011
Third Printing, January 2012

The Little Flower Press

TABLE OF CONTENTS

ABBREVIATIONS vi

ACKNOWLEGEMENTS vii

INTRODUCTION viii

CHAPTER 1 1

**Blessed are the poor in spirit
for theirs is the Kingdom of Heaven**

A. St. Teresa of Jesus: The Way of Perfection 4
B. St. Teresa of Jesus: The Interior Castle 14
C. St. John of the Cross: The Ascent of Mt. Carmel 31
D. St. John of the Cross: The Dark Night 40
E. St. John of the Cross: The Spiritual Canticle 45
F. St. John of the Cross: The Living Flame of Love 50

CHAPTER 2 55

**Blessed are the meek
for they shall possess the earth**

A. St. Teresa of Jesus: The Way of Perfection 56
B. St. Teresa of Jesus: The Interior Castle 59
C. St. John of the Cross: The Ascent of Mt. Carmel 62
D. St. John of the Cross: The Dark Night 65
E. St. John of the Cross: The Spiritual Canticle 67
F. St. John of the Cross: The Living Flame of Love 69

CHAPTER 3 71

**Blessed are they who mourn
for they shall be comforted**

A. St. Teresa of Jesus: The Way of Perfection 72
B. St. Teresa of Jesus: The Interior Castle 76
C. St. John of the Cross: The Ascent of Mt Carmel 89
D. St. John of the Cross: The Dark Night 93
E. St. John of the Cross: The Spiritual Canticle 98
F. St. John of the Cross: The Living Flame of Love 101

CHAPTER 4 104

Blessed are they who hunger and thirst
for justice for they shall be satisfied

A. St. Teresa of Jesus: The Way of Perfection 105
B. St. Teresa of Jesus: The Interior Castle 108
C. St. John of the Cross: The Ascent of Mt. Carmel 115
D. St. John of the Cross: The Dark Night 119
E. St. John of the Cross: The Spiritual Canticle 124
F. St. John of the Cross: The Living Flame of Love 129

CHAPTER 5 136

Blessed are the merciful
for they shall obtain mercy

A. St. Teresa of Jesus: The Way of Perfection 137
B. St. Teresa of Jesus: The Interior Castle 141
C. St. John of the Cross: The Ascent of Mt. Carmel 151
D. St. John of the Cross: The Dark Night 155
E. St. John of the Cross: The Spiritual Canticle 161
F. St. John of the Cross; The Living Flame of Love 167

CHAPTER 6 173

Blessed are the clean of heart
for they shall see God

A. St. Teresa of Jesus: The Way of Perfection 174
B. St. Teresa of Jesus: The Interior Castle 177
C. St. John of the Cross: The Ascent of Mt. Carmel 185
D. St. John of the Cross: The Dark Night 193
E. St. John of the Cross: The Spiritual Canticle 200
F. St. John of the Cross: The Living Flame of Love 208

CHAPTER 7 212

**Blessed are the peacemakers
for they shall be called children of God**

A. St. Teresa of Jesus: The Way of Perfection 213
B. St. Teresa of Jesus: The Interior Castle 217
C. St. John of the Cross: The Ascent of Mt. Carmel 233
D. St. John of the Cross: The Dark Night 238
E. St. John of the Cross: The Spiritual Canticle 244
F. St. John of the Cross: The Living Flame of Love 258

CHAPTER 8 258

**Blessed are those who suffer persecution for justice sake
for theirs is the Kingdom of Heaven.**

**Blessed are you when men reproach you
and persecute you and speak falsely,
say all manner of evil against you for my sake.**

**Rejoice and exult because your reward is great in heaven;
for so did they persecute the prophets who were before you.**

A. St. Teresa of Jesus: The Way of Perfection 260
B. St. Teresa of Jesus: The Interior Castle 263
C. St. John of the Cross: The Ascent of Mt. Carmel 271
D. St. John of the Cross: The Dark Night 277
E. St. John of the Cross: The Spiritual Canticle 284
F. St. John of the Cross: The Living Flame of Love 289

ABREVIATIONS

In the course of this work, the following abbreviations will be used to designate sources of commentary, quoted statements from either, Sacred Scripture, our Carmelite Saints, the Constitutions of the Secular Order of Discalced Carmelites, or my previously published Study Guides to the major works of St. John of the Cross.

Mt. - *The Gospel of St. Matthew.*

AS - *The Ascent of Mt. Carmel,* by St. John of the Cross, OCD.
(Kavanaugh & Rodriguez edition of *Collected Works of St. John of the Cross.*)

DN - *The Dark Night* by St. John of the Cross, OCD.
(Kavanaugh & Rodriguez edition of *Collected Works of St. John of the Cross.*)

SC - *The Spiritual Canticle* by St. John of the Cross, OCD.
(Kavanaugh & Rodriguez edition of *Collected Works of St. John of the Cross.*)

LF - *The Living Flame of Love* by St. John of the Cross, OCD.
(Kavanaugh & Rodriguez edition of *Collected Works of St. John of the Cross.*)

IC - *The Interior Castle* by St. Teresa of Jesus (Avila), OCD.
(Kavanaugh & Rodriguez edition of *Collected Works of St. John of the Cross.*)

WP - *The Way of Perfection* by St. Teresa of Jesus (Avila), OCD.
(E. Allison Peer's edition of *The Way of Perfection.*)

SG - After any other abbreviation to designate the Study Guides for the works by St. John of the Cross, OCD by Thomas M. Reid, OCDS.

ACKNOWLEGEMENTS

In the course of preparing a book, the author never walks alone from concept to *ready for publication.* There are proof-readings to be accomplished and a knowledgeable computer and publishing assistant, to move the work from manuscript to formatted book form. I have been very fortunate to have among my friend's two women who possess the necessary skills to fulfill these tasks willingly and promptly.

The proofreading was done by Jennifer Heasley, OCDS, who is a member of the same Secular Discalced Carmelite community of which I am a member: The Assumption of the Blessed Virgin Mary Secular Discalced Carmelite Community of Detroit, Michigan. Her suggestions and corrections were first rate and improved this work considerably. I am very grateful to her for her unselfish expenditure of time on this book

The necessary work to bring this book to publication was performed by Patricia (Patty) Palmer of Port Huron, Michigan, also a member of The Assumption of the Blessed Virgin Mary Secular Carmelite community. This included setting up the web site for *The Little Flower Press*, formatting this manuscript into book form, and designing the cover. All of this was done while she was attending college, seeking a degree in accounting. If you want something done, give it to a busy person. Never was this little adage demonstrated to be truer than in the case of the work by Patty for this book. She has my unfailing gratitude for this and many other favors in the preparation of other books and Study Guides I have written. May God bless her generosity.

INTRODUCTION

The Promises, both Temporary and Permanent, that are taken by the Secular Discalced Carmelite, read in part as follows: *"...to tend toward evangelical perfection in the spirit of the evangelical counsels of chastity, poverty, obedience and of the Beatitudes, according to the Rule of the Secular Order of Discalced Carmelites."* The meaning of the evangelical counsels and how they are to apply to the life of the Secular Carmelite is easily understood by the one making the Promise. If formation in the Carmelite charism has been adequate, one has been instructed in what is expected of the candidate by the Order and the other members of the community when promising to live these counsels according to one's state in life. The candidate approaching the Promise, either Temporary (for three years) or Permanent (for the rest of one's life) realizes that they have been given an invitation by God to approach closer to Him, and that the means to that end are the evangelical counsels and the Rule of Carmel. But there is more: *"...to tend toward evangelical perfection in the spirit...of the Beatitudes."* What does this add to the spiritual life and endeavors of the Secular Carmelite? What duties and burdens do these place on the serious Secular Carmelite who is seeking that elusive goal of union with God? How does living in the spirit of the *Beatitudes* help the soul seeking union with God to achieve that union? Can this *spirit of the Beatitudes* be found in the spiritual doctrine of the great Carmelite saints, and if so, where?

The *Beatitudes*, announced by Christ in the *Sermon on the Mount*, are found in the synoptic Gospels, and most completely in chapter 5:3-12 of *The Gospel of St. Matthew*. They are nine in number. Each one begins with the word *blessed* from which comes the designation, *Beatitudes*. These admonitions come from the mouth of Christ, and it is this fact that requires us to attach great importance to their content. If these admonitions of Christ are true for every Christian, how much more so for the Secular Discalced Carmelite who is answering the invitation of God to come closer and seek union with Him.

The *Beatitudes* are the antithesis of the values of the world, and especially of the values of our modern society that we observe everywhere around us daily. These admonitions of Christ are folly to the world and those enamored of what the world offers. If one follows the *Beatitudes* seriously in daily life, and lives them in such a way as to be observable by others around them, the observers merely scratch their heads and dismiss the faithful Christian as eccentric, a fanatic, or perhaps a little crazy. They console themselves by saying that no one can live this way in the modern world and be successful. Christ must have meant them either only for His hearers in Palestine, or for only a few fervent souls destined for religious life in a secluded monastery or convent far from the life of commerce in the world. In one sense, it is true that one caught up in the commerce of the modern world is probably living in opposition to the *Beatitudes*. But Christ attaches no such limitation to His pronouncement of the *Beatitudes*. On the contrary, He is quite clear that they apply to anyone who seeks to be *blessed,* in the eyes of God, anyone who seeks *the one thing necessary.* However, we know from our own experience that not everyone seeks this goal. We are frequently led to the conclusion that some Christians are further from the *Beatitudes* than many who do not know Christ, or who have chosen to follow some other religious and moral paradigm. In the *Beatitudes*, we see in bold relief the conflict between Christ and the evil one, contesting for the souls of mankind. The *Beatitudes* form the core of Christ's message to the world. Everything He said and did, can be found in one of the *Beatitudes*. They stand opposed to the values the world holds dear; the values of the *prince of this world*, who daily strives to lead souls far from the *Beatitudes* by deceptions and lies. If we recognize that the devil's wiles and methods are in opposition to the *Beatitudes*, we can see the central position of importance these admonitions occupy in the teaching of Christ. There is no gray here: black and white are the only hues of these two opponents, Christ and the devil, *prince of this world.*

If the *Beatitudes* are so basic to the life of the spirit of all true followers of Christ, how much more so for the Secular Carmelite who is seeking a complete, and profoundly deeper union with God. In paragraph 16 of the *O.C.D.S. Constitutions*, the order calls our attention to the importance of the *Beatitudes* to the life of the Secular Carmelite. They are called, " a plan of action for life and a way to enter into relationship with the world, neighbors, and co-workers, families and friends," and from *The Way of Perfection*, "prayer and comfortable living are incompatible" (WP 4:2). If it is union with God that we seek, our saints tell us clearly that the way is narrow and the road is rough. We can only enter by the narrow gate if the ways of the world are rejected and the ways of Christ are accepted: by *The Beatitudes*.

If the spirit of the *Beatitudes* are promised by the Secular Carmelite as their new way of life, then we must be able to find this spirit in the spiritual doctrines of the seminal saints of our order: St. Teresa of Jesus, our mother, and St. John of the Cross, our father. It is the purpose of this book to locate the *Beatitudes* in the major works of these saints so that the Gospel can be seen to connect well to their spiritual doctrines. We will look into the major works of these saints in order to find the *Beatitudes* that come alive in their doctrines in a very practical way. We will apply them to the journey of the soul toward union with God as expressed in those works. In this way, this book will attempt to bring into greater focus the place the *Beatitudes* occupy in the spiritual life of the Secular Carmelite and why they are perfectly compatible with the path to union with God, so well expressed by our two foundational saints. With God's help, I will succeed in that endeavor. In the works of St. Teresa of Jesus, I will first make reference to the material in *The Way of Perfection* in which we find a particular *Beatitude* reflected, and then make reference to *The Interior Castle* to find the same *Beatitude* reflected in the various mansions of that work.

In the case of St. John of the Cross, I will follow the customary sequencing of his major works to find the same *Beatitude* reflected: *The Ascent of Mt. Carmel, The Dark Night, The Spiritual Canticle,* and then *The Living Flame of Love.* We will find, not to our surprise I am sure, that the spiritual doctrines of St. Teresa and St. John contain the *Beatitudes* as their foundation.

It is my suggestion that this book be used as material for meditation and mental prayer. It has been prepared with that use in mind, and therefore is not a work that should be read as a dissertation on a hypothesis that comes to some ultimate conclusion based on the arguments presented. The division into sections should facilitate the use of this book as material to prepare the soul for reflective thought on the content.

CHAPTER 1

BLESSED ARE THE POOR IN SPIRIT, FOR THEIRS IS THE KINGDOM OF HEAVEN

Let us begin by exploring the meaning of the words *the Kingdom of heaven*, (herein called the Kingdom of God) used by Christ in this *Beatitude*. In doing so, I am departing from the form of the other chapters by exploring the goal before the means to achieve it. In this chapter, we will give greater emphasis to this concept of the Kingdom of God than to the other consequential words used by our Lord in the other *Beatitudes* because this concept is foundational to all the other effects of the *Beatitudes*. We may ask, "Is the Kingdom of God something to be realized in the future after the end of time? Is it a process extending until the end of time to be realized only then? Is it a state of being that is a composite of all the souls who are saved, or can it be applied to each individual soul as a reality potentially within each soul irrespective of the inclusion of any other soul in that Kingdom?" Lastly, can we relate the expression *Kingdom of God* to St. John's and St. Teresa's goal of *union with God*, as amounting to substantially the same thing?

The Kingdom of God

All ages have understood the word *kingdom* as a description of absolute sovereignty over a place, and everyone and everything within that place. In earthly terms, we understand this concept as something imposed by law or power without regard to the free will choice of those subjected to, or subdued by this sovereignty. The only way to remove the burden of this sovereignty is to escape from it. Therefore, when Christ uses the word *kingdom,* His hearers form a common concept of the meaning of that word. In so many of Christ's efforts to make His teachings understood by His listeners, He uses concepts understood not only by the people of His time, but by people of all ages. These words keep that meaning through future generations, and that is precisely why He chooses them, so that all may understand what He is communicating to souls.

However, when Christ uses the word *kingdom* there is a different meaning introduced by Him to the usual understanding alluded to above: He introduces an element of choice on the part of those who would become subject to the sovereignty of His Kingdom, the Kingdom of God. The opportunity to reject the sovereignty of God and His Kingdom is available to all. God invites rather than coerces souls into His Kingdom. Further, His Kingdom does not spring into immediate existence in a soul, as a kingdom established by force. Instead, He tells us that this Kingdom grows gradually in souls. We all know well the parables Christ employs to describe the Kingdom of God. The mustard seed that grows from the smallest of seeds to the largest of shrubs and the leaven that rises gradually from the yeast added to it (Mt. 13:31, 33). But then He adds the element of choice when He describes the man who finds a treasure in a field and goes and sells all that he owns to purchase that field. This is followed by the story of the merchant who finds a pearl of great price and also sells all he has to purchase that pearl (Mt. 13:44, 45). Notice the choice of these two searchers. The choice consists in selling all they have after a correct evaluation of the value of the sought-after goal; the treasure and the pearl are worth more than all their other possessions. Christ describes the manner of establishing the Kingdom of God gradually, and that the Kingdom must be chosen. That choice can only follow on the accurate evaluation of the Kingdom as the most desirable goal of all. But notice that the requirement to obtain that pearl or treasure is to *sell all* to acquire it. If one sells all, he cannot easily turn back from this decision. The complete divestment of all, in this sense, only occurs gradually like the gradual growth of the mustard seed.

Eventually, if one continues the journey to spiritual perfection and the acquisition of the Kingdom of God, everything else contrary to the Kingdom is forsaken. The treasure and the pearl therefore, replace every attachment of the heart. On the other hand, one who chooses not to acquire these treasures reminds us of the rich young man who wanted to discover how he could gain the Kingdom of God, but went away sad because he could not part with his possessions, of which he had many. In Mt. 13:47-50 we see another aspect of the Kingdom of God described by Christ. The net gathers fish of every kind that are laid on the beach for separation, the good placed in vessels and the bad thrown away. He likens this separation to the angels separating the just from the wicked. The wicked will then be cast into the eternal fire. Therefore, the Kingdom of God is limited to the *just,* those who have successfully chosen and sought to acquire the treasure of infinite value.

Now we have seen that there are three essential elements involved with Christ's teaching on the Kingdom of God: God's sovereignty, our choice to give everything to acquire it, and that not all choose to enter that Kingdom. Pope Benedict XVI, in his recent book, *Jesus of Nazareth* describes several opinions regarding the Kingdom of God. He states that one writer has equated the Kingdom of God with Christ himself; that it is into Him that we must enter to possess the Kingdom of God. Therefore, according to this theory, those who have entered the Kingdom of God are the members of the mystical body of Christ. We are reminded of Christ's declaration in the Synagogue that "the Kingdom of God has come upon you."

Poor in Spirit

The great foundational concept of the Kingdom of God has been treated first, because each *Beatitude,* in one way or another involves participation in this concept of God's Kingdom. Let us then examine what it means to be poor in spirit, and how the concept of poverty of spirit is treated by the great saints of the Discalced Carmelite Order.

There are several ways to look at being poor in spirit. The words *in spirit* aim us in the right direction. Our Lord is not saying that abject privation of the means to maintain life in this world is a blessing. These needs of the human being in this life are created by God and must be met if life is to be sustained. If a cruel ruler starves his population or denies them shelter and adequate clothing, we do not say that he has granted them a blessing by doing so. Rather, our Lord is presenting a frame of mind and heart necessary to gain the eventual gift of eternal life. There are two aspects of this frame of mind that we need to examine in our search through the writings of our saints: first, the attitude of poverty toward this world's goods, and second, the attitude of humility in our relationship to God. The first results in holy detachment from all that is not God and the second in the virtue of humility, which recognizes the truth of the creature's relationship to its Creator, and its utter dependence upon Him in all things corporeal and spiritual.

It is now possible to examine the works of our two Carmelite saints to see how they treat these elements of the Kingdom of God. The inquiry is: do the writings and doctrines of these saints regarding the dynamics and goals of the specifically Carmelite path to holiness, reflect the elements of sovereignty, choice to enter and choice not to enter, in the teachings of Christ regarding the Kingdom of God?

A. St. Teresa of Jesus: The Way of Perfection

This work by St. Teresa is the first exposition of her spiritual doctrine. While the story of her life contains much of her spiritual history, this work presents in its first form and as its primary subject, her spiritual doctrine. Later, *The Interior Castle* presents that doctrine in a different and more matured form that we will examine later with the same goal in mind: Where are the *Beatitudes* reflected in her words?

Sovereignty of God over His Kingdom

We know from reading the works of St. Teresa that she continually refers to Christ as *His Majesty*. This expression discloses to us that her image of Christ is as a king. In her reflections on the words of the *Pater Noster*, she repeatedly uses terms to identify the Father as *King* and *Emperor of Heaven*. In doing so, she seeks to express the immense sovereignty of God over His creation, and the distance between the lowliness of man and the great holiness of God. She then examines the great humility of God in listening to our poor petitions, and His desire to grant them. Most importantly, in relation to our subject, she emphasizes God's ability and willingness to grant any petition we present to Him. In the *Pater Noster,* we beg God that His kingdom comes, in the world and in our soul.

> His Majesty, knowing of how little we are capable, saw that, unless He provided for us by giving us His Kingdom here on earth, we could neither hallow nor praise nor magnify nor glorify *nor exalt* this holy name of the Eternal Father in a way befitting it (WP 30).

St. Teresa states that the only way this Kingdom will come into our souls is to dispose ourselves humbly to ask for it to come. She asks us to realize that this Kingdom cannot be taken by storm at our choice, but can only be received when given by God in response to our petition. In this connection, she engages in a lengthy discussion of the prayer of quiet as necessary for the soul to be receptive to the giving of His Kingdom by God, after we have asked for it. This supernatural form of prayer is discussed by her in much greater detail in *The Interior Castle,* especially in the fifth and sixth dwelling places. This prayer of quiet creates the proper passive receptiveness to the gifts God wishes to give in prayer and the humility to wait for God to respond. This prayer is one in which the soul wishes to enter into itself, and proceeds to close the door of its soul to everything outside, in order to dwell in Paradise with God during this time.

The prayer of quiet, which disposes the soul humbly, passively, and in solitude to receive the giving of His Kingdom by God, is a supernatural state. As she explains in chapter 31 of *The Way of Perfection*, the prayer of quiet is a state of peace and presence given by God as a result of His entry into the soul. It cannot be produced by the soul itself, but must be given by God as a participation in His Kingdom. His sovereignty is therefore exercised here by the fact that only He can grant the soul this state of prayer, when and how He pleases, and it is precisely this intimate divine touch that constitutes the soul's entry into God's Kingdom, which Christ tells us is within us. She gives us a vivid description of the interior effect of the prayer of quiet:

> There seems nothing left for it (the soul) to desire. The faculties are stilled and have no wish to move, for any movement they may make appears to hinder the soul from loving God...They are in the Palace, near to their King, and they see that He is already beginning to give them His Kingdom on earth...They seem not to be in the world, and have no wish to see or hear anything but their God; nothing distresses them, nor does it seem that anything can possibly do so (WP 31).

St. Teresa goes on to say that, dominion over the whole world with all its happiness would not bring the soul this satisfaction experienced while in God's Kingdom in the prayer of quiet. The happiness of the world touches only the outside of the soul, the rind she calls it; but the prayer of quiet allows the soul to enter into the Kingdom of God in the interior depths of the soul. These depths are where God dwells in the soul, and where the power of evil cannot reach, for here it is that God and God alone is King, the Sovereign Master.

In chapter 6 of *The Way of Perfection,* St. Teresa sets forth the following statement that gets us into the elements of the Kingdom of God very nicely:

> It should be noted here that when we desire anyone's affection, we always seek it because of some interest profit or pleasure of our own. Those who are perfect, however, have trodden all these things beneath their feet (and have despised) the blessings which may come to them in this world, and its pleasures and delights- in such a way that even if they wanted to, so to say, they could not love anything outside God, or unless it had to do with God. What profit then can come to them from being loved themselves (WP 6)?

She here describes the soul that has sold all it has to acquire the field containing the great treasure, or the merchant who does the same to acquire the pearl of great price. Even if they wanted to, they "could not love anything outside God…" This lack of resistance and inability to love anything outside God follows on the choice first made to allow God to grant the soul the immense benefits of His Kingdom. This choice is not made once for all time, but is repeated over and over again, as the soul is gradually brought nearer to God as it progresses in spiritual growth. Each stage of the spiritual journey toward union with God presents the soul with new and increasingly difficult paths to negotiate. Many times the soul is immersed in severe suffering brought on by the detachments required to advance. The most severe suffering we experience is brought on by the necessary detachment from the self, required for spiritual growth, so that room for God is provided in the soul. We say, "Can I do this? Is this too hard for me? Can I bear the suffering I see ahead if I continue?" These sufferings are experienced with increasing severity until the final choice is made; "I can no longer live without this intimate closeness to God, and therefore, nothing will hold me back from pursuing it, regardless of what it requires of me to receive it."

In chapter 8 of *The Way of Perfection,* St. Teresa treats the importance of self-detachment. She says in addressing her community of Nuns of the Reform:

> Do you suppose, daughters, that it is a small benefit to obtain for ourselves this blessing of giving ourselves wholly to Him, and keeping nothing for ourselves? Since, as I say, all blessings are in Him, let us give Him hearty praise, sisters, for having brought us together here, where we are occupied in this alone (WP 8).

Her reference to "giving ourselves wholly to Him, and keeping nothing for ourselves," reflects the choice of the merchant who sells all to acquire the pearl of great price and the one who finds the treasure in the field, and sells all he has to acquire that field. The Kingdom of God is everything and allows no competitors. How different this is from the rich young man who goes away sad because he is not willing to part from his many possessions? How difficult it is for us to part from ourselves and what pleases us on the natural level: the honors, praise, profits and comforts available to us in this life, which we treasure so much. What are we willing to *sell* to acquire the pearl of great price? It is never easy as we are asked for more and more surrender from God. To bid farewell to what has been most important to us in our life: power, money, renown for our talents, or positions of honor among our friends or in society in general is difficult. Each time we are faced with that surrender, and the resistance arises in us, we have an increasingly difficult choice to make, either to go toward God or away from Him. When we get far along in the spiritual journey toward union with God, and He makes it clear that what He wants from us is total detachment from all that is not Him, especially detachment from ourselves, choosing the Kingdom of God is excruciatingly difficult. We are consoled by the realization that nothing is asked of us without the grace to accomplish it.

In chapter 10 of *The Way of Perfection,* St. Teresa makes one of the most incisive statements contained in all her works, demonstrating her keen understanding of the importance of detachment from the self. She says:

> Oh my sisters, do not feel secure and fall asleep, or you would be like a man who goes to bed quite peacefully, after bolting all his doors for fear of thieves, when the thieves are already in the house.

> And you know there is no worse thief *than the one who lives in the house* (WP 10:1).

St. Teresa then goes on to say that it is to die for Christ that she and her nuns have come to the reformed monastery, not to practice self-indulgence for Christ. It is the abandonment of all things that allows the entry into God's Kingdom: the *selling* of everything to acquire the treasure in the field or the pearl of great price. She emphasizes that abandoning everything for the sake of the Beloved does not mean entering religious life. The abandonment required is interior. It is a detachment, so complete that worry about our circumstances and position in the world ceases, and the will of God becomes the end of all one's actions and desires. When that occurs, one has truly chosen the pearl of great price. What would have been the scene in the gospel if the rich young man had rejected his possessions and position to indifference, and set out to reach the Kingdom of God as Christ instructed? He would not have gone away sad, but rejoicing.

We must here distinguish between the detached soul who chooses his detachment, and the one who is without possessions, power or fame through circumstances in his life that leave him without these things. While the latter is impoverished, perhaps much more than the former, it is not by his choice. Rather, he may long for riches, possessions power and fame, but cannot acquire them because he lacks the means to do so. He has not chosen his condition, and would choose the opposite if he could. This man has not disposed himself to receive the Kingdom of God. It is likely that this is the furthest thing from his mind, as he goes about trying to acquire the goods of this world by honest or even dishonest means. On the other hand, the former may have an abundance of this world's goods, both tangible and intangible, but has wished to dispose himself by his detachment to receive the grace to enter into the Kingdom of God. He would easily give up all his successes if required to do so that he might retain God's predominance in his life. The Kingdom of God is possible for him because he has chosen it interiorly. St. Teresa examines this in chapter 12 of *The Way of Perfection:*

> I do not mean by "leaving everything" entering religious life, for there may be obstacles to this, and the soul that is perfect can be detached and humble anywhere. It will find detachment harder in the

world, however, for worldly trappings will be a great impediment to it (WP 12:5).

If one renounces all his goods and possessions of this world, we should be able to conclude that he has *sold* all to acquire the Kingdom of God through his own choice. But there is one thing more: the seeker after God's Kingdom must renounce and surrender his very self, his will, and his life. Imagine the person who, like St. Francis of Assisi, disposes of all that he owns and concludes that he has thereby reached spiritual perfection. This is not so; that is too easy. If he goes about indulging his fancy and willfulness as a poor man, what has he gained? Perhaps he has only escaped from the responsibility of managing his former affairs. Perhaps he is only lazy. The renunciation that allows entry into God's kingdom divests the soul of all willfulness except that aspect of his will that conforms perfectly to the will of God, no matter what His will is. In fact, this soul merges his will with the will of God, and the two wills become one: God's. He wills what God wills. His life belongs to God and he lives his life according to that form. Within his soul is the silence and solitude characteristic of the withdrawn soul: the one who has retained nothing for himself except God. This soul spurns the world and its pleasures and satisfactions in order to remove all obstacles to union with God. He recognizes that those values of the world are incompatible with his desire to enter the Kingdom of God, and actually would, if indulged, prevent him from entering His Kingdom. Life now means only loving and serving God. He has *sold* all else to acquire this treasure. St. Teresa expresses this well:

> I repeat that this consists mainly or entirely in our ceasing to care about ourselves and our own pleasures, for the least that anyone who is beginning to serve the Lord truly can offer Him is his life. Once he has surrendered his will to Him, what has he to fear? (WP 12:2)

The soul that succeeds in the degree of surrender and renunciation required in order to enter the Kingdom of God is never lacking for a reward. However, the task is an arduous one requiring perseverance through trials of a rather severe sort. The lifting of a soul from its natural state of sin and imperfection to union with God is an enormous elevation that cannot be accomplished easily or quickly. Grace that is bestowed <u>and accepted</u> usually determines the f time for the journey, along with the degree of imperfection ,oted out. Every step is accompanied by suffering, ever g in intensity as the purgation goes deeper. This suffering comes from the imperfections that are illuminated by the light of God shining on the soul, exposing heretofore unknown failings. The soul recoils from this exposure, and is only sustained by Grace bestowed when needed to bear the humiliation and the painful excising of these failings. This process is a re-making of the soul in the image of Christ. Here we see what it means and how difficult it is to imitate Christ in everything. But the end result, *the pearl of great price*, gives courage and strength to the soul to enable it to persevere to the end.

> To me, then, it seems that, of the many joys to be found in the Kingdom of Heaven we shall have no more to do with the things of earth; for in Heaven we shall have an intrinsic tranquility and glory, a joy in the rejoicing of all, a perpetual peace, and a great interior satisfaction which will come to us when we see that all are hallowing and praising the Lord, and are blessing His name, and that none is offending Him (WP 30).

Since the Kingdom of God must be chosen by each soul, the possibility exists that some souls may choose not to enter that Kingdom. Choice always presents at least two alternatives. In this case, there are only two: to choose to enter God's Kingdom or to choose not to enter that Kingdom. One cannot really be *sort of* in that Kingdom and *sort of* not. However, many say that they will not forsake certain things such as power, money, and the self-indulgence of fame and recognition. They will not leave certain intrinsically sinful relationships that are obstacles to entering the Kingdom of God, or occasions of sin, that will lead to sin inevitably. Here the soul places limits on the power and influence of God in its life. The Kingdom of God is rejected by the elevation of these things and relationships with other people above the easily discovered Will of God. They deceive themselves into thinking they are living a God-centered life by some half-hearted efforts at religion and religious observance, but the fact is they have boarded up the Kingdom of God, and prevented their entry into it. Entry into the Kingdom of God is rendered impossible by this erroneous order of priorities. In the *Way of Perfection*, St. Teresa addresses this problem with regard to the necessity of her nuns placing their relationships with their relatives, whom they have left in order to live the life of contemplation in the monastery, in its proper order of things. We can obtain an insight into the proper ordering of everything in our lives from her words on this subject.

> All the advice which the saints give us about fleeing from the world is, of course, good. Believe me, then, attachment to our relatives is, as I have said, the thing which sticks to us most closely and is hardest to get rid of. Just as we find everything in Him, so for His sake we forget everything (WP 9).

We understand that if we are in the world, we do not eliminate our relationships, but in order to enter the Kingdom of God, we subject them all to the Will of God that is evident in all the circumstances of our life. We can always understand God's Will through the grace that is always given us to do so if we are open to it. The words of St. Teresa to her nuns can be transposed into the circumstances of our own lives in order to understand that the failure to properly order everything is in fact a choice against the Kingdom of God. Remember that Christ instructed the rich young man to sell **all** that he had, and then to come follow Him. If we love God and respond to His Will only when it is easy, then we are like the hard ground on which the seed fell, and was quickly trodden under foot.

Poor in Spirit

Holy detachment

In *The Way of Perfection,* St. Teresa is instructing the nuns in the Monastery of St. Joseph how to advance in holiness and how to become good contemplatives in the reformed Discalced Carmelite Order. However, whatever she teaches her sisters regarding detachment in order to dispose one's soul to union with God applies equally to all souls who are seriously seeking that union. She begins immediately in this work to address the subject of holy detachment. Her words are reminiscent of the following words of Christ's regarding worry about the needs of tomorrow:

> Therefore, do not be anxious, saying, 'What shall we eat?' or 'What shall we drink?' or 'What are we to

put on?' (For after all these things the Gentiles seek); for your Father knows that you need all these things. But seek first the Kingdom of God and His justice, and all these things shall be given to you besides. Therefore, do not be anxious about tomorrow; for tomorrow will have anxieties of its own. Sufficient for the day is its own trouble (Mt. 6:31-34).

In chapter 2 of *The Way of Perfection,* St. Teresa echoes the words of Christ in this manner:

> Worrying about getting money from other people seems to me like thinking about what other people enjoy. However, much you worry, you will not make them change their minds nor will they become desirous of giving you alms. Leave these anxieties to Him Who can move everyone, Who is the Lord of all money and of all who possess money…Let us not fail Him, and let us have no fear that He will fail us; if He should ever do so it will be for our greater good…(WP 2).

St. Teresa does not limit her teaching to exterior detachment from the things of the world and of the flesh. A man can be detached from these things for the reason that, try as he may, he cannot acquire them or through sloth, avoids the effort to take care of his own needs. However, in his heart he longs for riches that he will never obtain because of his own fault or the circumstances of his life. This person frequently does things like purchasing lottery tickets, engages in other forms of gambling, even to the point of addiction; or worse than these, steals the goods of others. This is hardly detachment, but rather it is an extreme form of attachment to what he does not have. St. Teresa points out in chapter 10 of *The Way of Perfection,* that the detachment must be interior.

> It will be a great help towards this (to soar to our Maker) if we keep constantly in our thoughts the vanity of all things and the rapidity with which they pass away, so that we may withdraw our affections from these things which are so trivial and fix them upon what will never come to an end (WP 10).

There are also other souls that manifest an attitude of being poor in spirit, but in truth are not so. They are more proficient in acting than they are in detachment. Opportunities to acquire the goods of this world are not missed, and are even sought. However, the object of their false detachment is to convince those around them that they have achieved poverty of spirit. They appear to be dedicated to the spiritual life and manifest a demeanor of humble poverty in order to elicit praise and admiration. This acting is not unfamiliar to St. Teresa:

> The devil has yet another temptation, which is to make us appear very poor in spirit; we are in the habit of saying that we want nothing and care nothing about anything; but as soon as the chance comes of our being given something, even though we do not in the least need it, all our poverty of spirit disappears (WP 38).

Lastly, in *The Way of Perfection,* St. Teresa addresses the most important detachment: detachment from the self and all that one thinks is best for him. This detachment is the hardest to achieve, and causes the soul the most pain. It is a dying of sorts, and our fallen nature rebels against this dying to self every time we are faced with an event or circumstance that advances this death. However, this death is indispensable to union with God. There is no room in a soul for God that is full of itself.

> ...But it remains for us to become detached from ourselves and oppose ourselves and it is a hard thing to withdraw from ourselves and oppose ourselves, because we are very close to ourselves and love ourselves very dearly (WP 10).

Humility

St. Teresa mentions repeatedly the essential place that humility occupies in the quest for union with God. In this work and in all her other writings, humility is the indispensable virtue. Her simple definition of humility is well known: humility is truth. It is not truth as we would have it, but as it really is. It starts with our understanding of the right relationship to our Creator. That recognition should be enough to render us humble in every area of our lives. This death to self, engendered by humility, is hard to achieve because it lowers the self from the lofty heights it would prefer to inhabit. The concept of self-esteem that we hear so much about today is, if properly understood, not in conflict with true humility. However, that concept is rarely understood properly. To most people it means that I deserve everything I desire and I am worthy to receive it, regardless of whether I have done anything to really merit esteem. Correctly understood, the concept of self-esteem is grounded in God's love, created by Him in an act of love for me. The more I belong to God the greater my self-esteem should be, because I view myself, with all my imperfections, through the eyes of God as an object of His love.

In discussing this virtue, St. Teresa sees it as a sister virtue to detachment. She says that the two virtues are inseparable. Where one is found, the other is always present. This is easy to see, for one cannot have the virtue of detachment, especially from the self, unless humility precipitates true detachment and enables a soul to accomplish the separation from the things of the world and from the self. A proud man cannot perceive the desirability of detachment. He believes he is entitled to all that he wants and pursues these wants with all his efforts.

> It is here that true humility can enter, for this virtue and that of detachment from self, I think, always go together. They are two sisters, who are inseparable…Oh, how sovereign are these virtues, mistresses of all created things, empresses of the world, our deliverers from all the snares and entanglements laid by the devil, so dearly loved by our Teacher, Christ, Who was never for a moment without them (WP 10).

B. St. Teresa of Jesus: The Interior Castle

The very name of this work of St. Teresa elicits the idea of a king who exercises His sovereignty over His domain, in this case, His castle. This castle is interior, and not one of brick and mortar. It is this castle in the spiritual realm into which the soul seeks to enter, and find the deepest center where God dwells. St. Teresa was inspired to elucidate the spiritual life in its fullness by the use of the metaphor of this interior castle that is made up of seven dwelling places, each containing many rooms. In fact, this castle is a reflection of the Kingdom of God which, as Christ tells us, is within us. All the stages and experiences of a soul's spiritual journey toward union with God, toward the Kingdom of God, are treated here in substantial detail. So, if we have a castle, it must be the domain of a sovereign Lord who rules over it.

Sovereignty of God over His Kingdom

The First Three Dwelling Places

St. Teresa begins this work with the *First Dwelling Place* which is the outer wall or the human body. While God reigns here, as he does in all the dwelling places and in all of their rooms, the soul here is unable to submit itself to His sovereignty. There are too many deeply ingrained attachments and evil habits in this soul and they remain in control of the heart and the actions of this soul. However, the first stirrings of love and fear of God are being felt, so that if responded to, will lead the soul to an ever increasing submission to the King. But something begins to happen here: self-knowledge begins to expose the soul to itself with resulting pain at the first dawning of recognition of the true condition of the soul.

> For humility, like the bee making honey in the beehive, is always at work. Without it everything goes wrong...So it is with the soul in the room of self-knowledge; let it believe me and fly sometimes to ponder the grandeur and majesty if its God. Here it will discover its lowliness better than thinking of itself, and be freer from the vermin that enter the first rooms, those of self-knowledge (IC 1:2).

> She is here making the point that it is from the soul's glimpses of the majesty of God that the humility of self- recognition begins to grow. That is, the soul is compelled to lower its view of itself when it begins to see the immensity of God's grandeur in relation to itself. By gazing at His grandeur, we get in touch with our own lowliness; by looking at His purity, we shall see our own filth; by pondering His humility, we shall see how far we are from being humble (IC 1:2).

Entry into God's Kingdom is a gradual process, just as the growth of the mustard seed in our Lord's metaphor grows gradually into the great shrub. Each of the dwelling places used by St. Teresa in this work reflects the slow and arduous task of entering the Kingdom of God. The first dwelling place is the mustard seed, as it is when it enters the ground and begins to germinate. The entry into this dwelling is a slow awakening, submission to, and recognition of, the sovereignty of God. The whole journey is more than mouthing the words. The soul must eventually be exposed, its inner motivations, attachments, and goals excised and replaced with a life heretofore unknown to it. The first part of this project is the beginning of the emptying required. The mustard seed begins to die. As each miniscule change occurs, the soul suffers an ever increasing pain of loss, bewilderment, and insecurity over where it is going, and what has happened to the old self. The whole change, if the soul perseveres, is profound and unimaginable to the soul at the early stages. The soul truly proceeds in blind faith, animated by a love for God that grows with each advance. This is what St. Teresa gives us in *The Interior Castle*: the journey, with all its phases and stops along the road leading to the Kingdom of God. We should continue to examine a few examples of her explanation of this journey in each dwelling place in to order to see how she views the growth of the mustard seed, and the rising of the leaven finally terminating in entry into the Kingdom of God. Each step by the soul, as we shall see, is accompanied by increasing awareness of the sovereignty of God in this Kingdom.

In the second dwelling place, the soul is beginning to practice prayer and an awareness of the futility of the world and all its allurements is beginning to enter the consciousness of this soul. The Lord is beginning to call the soul to come close to Him in His Kingdom. His voice is sweet and has captured the attention of the soul. But the soul is unable to respond to His voice, because as yet it is not spiritually equipped to do so; the natural attachments and affections still dominate its life. This inability causes the soul great suffering. The hearing of God's voice and not being able to respond is a greater trial than not hearing His voice at all. In that case, there were no yearnings and longings resulting from God's voice, and the soul went about its life oblivious to the fact that there was such a thing as the Kingdom of God in this life. Here the soul seeks desperately and in pain for consolations from God. However, St. Teresa says:

> His Majesty knows best what is suitable for us. There's no need for us to be advising Him about what He should give us, for He can rightly tell us that we don't know what we're asking for. The whole aim of any person who is beginning prayer – and don't forget this, because it's very important – should be that he work and prepare himself with determination and every possible effort to bring his will into conformity with God's Will (IC II:1:8).

These are very basic admonitions from St. Teresa. But the soul is beginning to show some movement forward in its journey toward God's Kingdom. It is hearing God's invitation to come closer. But a new danger now appears. The devil becomes very active against this soul as he sees it turning toward God's realm and away from the world. There is confusion in this soul: reason says that the things of the world are worthwhile and to be sought after. Faith however, says something different:

> Faith, however, teaches it about where it will find fulfillment. The memory shows it where all these things end, holding before it the death of those who found great joy in them....Some whom it had known in great prosperity are under the ground, and their graves are walked upon (IC II:1:4).

The great battle is joined over the seeking of God's Kingdom and His sovereignty over the soul. The mustard seed is struggling to begin growing into a shrub. However, in this dwelling place it has barely broken the ground. The object at this stage is not to give up the battle. Falling from grace is not the same as giving up the battle. One can fall as a result of human weakness and again turn to the King for forgiveness, and begin the battle anew. It is hard to imagine that one at this stage would not experience these occasional falls, some serious, some not so serious. But this soul is still on the road to God's Kingdom, albeit in the ditch along the road looking for rescue. It is willing to be pulled out of the ditch by God's forgiveness, and again to proceed along the way. The soul that gives up the quest leaves the road and goes off in some other direction, sadly seeking some other destination, like the rich young man who could not part from his possessions. It is curious why this young man made this choice if it made him sad. Alas, the lure of the material world, with the assistance of the devil, overwhelmed him.

The soul that has resisted the temptation to turn back from its journey to the Kingdom of God, and has advanced to this stage through Grace, will find that God's Kingdom is now becoming recognizable. It can see, even though only slightly, what the Kingdom of God means for it personally, as well as for other souls. Since we acknowledge that God's Kingdom is within us, this interior castle of St Teresa's imaginative creation is an excellent metaphor for our purpose here. We see in her writings an exposition of the gradual conversion of the interior of the soul, from one cluttered with the world, the flesh, and the devil into a suitable habitat for God, and also a soul that is gradually becoming capable of entering into the Kingdom of God. The conversion of the soul requires the tearing down and rooting out of sin and the attachments to the things of the world which are peculiar to each individual soul. Then the soul can make room for the things that pertain to God and union with Him. A soul tied to any attachment, to the things of this world in an inordinate way, is held by that attachment, and cannot achieve the union with God in its fullness. This whole exposition by St. Teresa of the willing soul's journey through gradual spiritual growth manifests the soul's increasing recognition and willingness to accept the absolute sovereignty of God. This willingness must permeate the soul entirely and always, if the soul is to be brought into full union with God. This dwelling place represents a significant advancement toward that goal as St. Teresa says:

> They long not to offend His Majesty, even guarding themselves against venial sins; they are fond of doing penance and setting aside periods for recollection; they spend their time well, practicing works of charity toward their neighbors; and are very balanced in their use of speech and dress and in the governing of their households – those that have them. Certainly, this is a state to be desired (IC III: 1).

At this stage what is needed more than anything else, along with determination to continue the journey, is humility. One must never assume that he deserves to gain entry into God's Kingdom. We must always see the grace to continue as God's unearned gift gratuitously given by a loving King. There is frequently a temptation to see ourselves as deserving of God's gift of certain graces, and that we have somehow earned them, and that God is bound by justice to bestow upon us the graces that we want and when we want them. What a denial of God's sovereignty such an attitude is. We place ourselves in charge of God, and demand that He conform to our will. We believe that we know what is best for us spiritually and insist upon it being given. This of course is foolishness. What we consider best for us is frequently the very worst thing for our souls. In our natural state, we yearn for ease, consolations, and rest, when for our advancement the opposite of these things is what is needed. Remember, the requirement to enter into God's Kingdom is to sell _all_, and secondly to "take up your cross daily and come follow me." This lack of humility, if not corrected, is an insurmountable obstacle to union with God, and acceptance of His sovereignty.

> With humility present, this stage is a most excellent one. If humility is lacking, we will remain here our whole life – and with a thousand afflictions and miseries. For since we will not have abandoned ourselves, this state will be very laborious and burdensome...If there is some lack in humility, they will feel an inner distaste for which they will find no reason. For perfection as well as its reward does not consist in spiritual delights but in greater love and in deeds done with greater justice and truth (IC III:2:9).

Poor in Spirit

The First Three Dwelling Places

Holy detachment

St. Teresa begins immediately to address the issue of detachment in her description of the first dwelling place. This early dwelling place deals with the soul at the beginning of its journey toward spiritual perfection and union with God. This soul is dealing with very basic problems of spiritual immaturity and confronting many obstacles to the desired relationship with God. This soul remains very enamored of the things of this world even though it is beginning to stir interiorly toward seeking God.

> Even though it may not be in a bad state, it is so involved in worldly things and so absorbed with its possessions, honor, or business affairs, as I have said, that even though as a matter of fact it would want to see and enjoy its beauty, (the rooms of this dwelling), these things do not allow it to; nor does it seem that it can slip free from so many impediments. If a person is to enter the second dwelling places, it is important that he strive to give up unnecessary things and business affairs (IC I:2:14).

Throughout *The Interior Castle,* St. Teresa repeatedly raises the specter of self- knowledge. This knowledge is the principal source of interior pain and affliction in the soul. Here the deceptions, once so easily practiced by the soul, begin to be uncovered and shown for what they are. After the uncovering, the truth leaps up in front of the eyes of the soul and figuratively smacks it in the face. Discouragement at this point may become a problem. The need for detachment from the self, but reluctance to do so is most keenly felt here. This experience of the need to deny the self begins to become prominent in the third dwelling place. In the third dwelling place, the soul has accomplished a great deal in matters pertaining to the natural development of the spiritual life. This accomplishment is essentially a removal of obstacles to going forward in spiritual development that are within the control of the willing soul and the overcoming of inertia that tends to make a soul want to stay where it is. We know that staying in one place spiritually is unlikely, because a soul that seeks to stop will inevitably fall back and begin to give up the rough road and the narrow way. Detachment and humility remain the necessary ingredients for progress.

> A person has plenty to eat and even a surplus; the opportunity presents itself for him to acquire more wealth; all right, let him do so if it is offered to him. But if he strives for wealth and after possessing it strives for more and more, however good the intentions may be (for he should have a good intention because, as I have said, these are virtuous persons of prayer), he need have no fear of ascending to the dwelling places closest to the King (IC III:2:4).

Humility

The virtue of humility dominates the spiritual thought of St. Teresa. We see it emphasized in everything she has written and in her own approach to the multiplicity of supernatural favors granted to her. Using her simple definition of humility as truth, she teaches us the sometimes hard to accept truth of our existence. We are weak creatures capable of very little in either the natural or supernatural realm. However, some never tire of trying to convince themselves of their power to rule their own lives and to do so without any assistance from God. Not only is this obvious in the world and the society around us, but it is also present in our spiritual life. It is a powerful obstacle to spiritual growth, both when striving on the natural level for spiritual growth and when being moved by God on the supernatural level. Teresa's solution, constantly repeated, is self-knowledge. If the knowledge of self is true, humility must follow. The further a soul advances the deeper the self-knowledge penetrates the soul and illuminates each soul's imperfections that have never before been seen. Along with this illumination comes the realization that the removal of these imperfections and sinfulness cannot be accomplished by ourselves. They are too deeply ingrained within us, and in fact, constitute our share in fallen human nature. If humility is lacking, the soul <u>cannot</u> advance. Pride will block all attempts at growth and progress. Soon the prideful soul will find itself falling back or choosing other goals instead of growing in the spiritual emptying necessary, and if humility is not restored, all could be lost spiritually. St. Teresa attaches great importance to this virtue from the very beginning of her treatise on the spiritual journey.

> In my opinion we shall never completely know ourselves if we don't strive to know God. By gazing at His grandeur, we get in touch with our own lowliness; by looking at His purity, we shall see our own filth; by pondering His humility, we shall see how far we are from being humble (IC I:2:9).

In the second and third dwelling places, St. Teresa focuses on the struggle of the soul to keep from abandoning the desire to advance toward God. A great effort is required of the soul to avoid pitfalls and obstacles placed in its way by either the devil or the soul itself. This soul is already experiencing dryness and anxiety over its perception of its failure to please God. There is a transition that is taking place that will change everything in the soul's spiritual life. God is preparing it for the afflictions and sufferings ahead that will be necessary to achieve union with Him. These afflictions are inescapable because they result from the process of extraction of imperfections that have been in the soul from the beginning, and have taken deep root over time. When the light of God shines on these imperfections and illuminates them for the first time, the soul suffers great sorrow over what it now sees, and suffers from the expected pain of removing these imperfections. In this sorrow and suffering, the soul accurately perceives the rough road and narrow way ahead. It cannot understand why so much has changed and the consolations of yesterday are over, and only hardship and labor lie before it. Can such a soul endure this affliction without humility? Can this soul advance to the supernatural phase of its development that begins in the fourth dwelling place?

> Oh, humility, humility! I don't know what kind of temptation I'm undergoing in this matter that I cannot help but think that anyone who makes such an issue of this dryness is a little lacking in humility (IC III:1:7).

> With humility present, this stage is a most excellent one. If humility is lacking, we will remain here our whole life – and with a thousand afflictions and miseries. For since we will not have abandoned ourselves, this state will be very laborious and burdensome (IC III:2:9).

The Last Four Dwelling Places

Holy detachment

The soul enters God's Kingdom slowly. We also know that the soul does not take the Kingdom of God by force. Rather, grace is given to the soul to follow the path, arranged by God from all eternity. We know that the road is rough and the path is narrow that leads to His Kingdom. One cannot try to follow someone else's path because it is more appealing and expect to arrive where God wants that soul to be. Usually, the reason for desiring to search for another path to God's Kingdom is prompted by some spiritual weakness. We think the other path will be more visible to those around us, and we will be well thought of. The other path holds the promise of much consolation, we believe. The other path will result in less suffering, less rejection, less defense of our Lord and His Church. Our path appears to us as obscurity, rejection, and suffering. Can we really choose the way for ourselves, and avoid or ignore the obvious movements of Grace to proceed in one way rather than another? Don't say that I cannot discern what God wants. He is not stumped by our intransigence. He will make the way clear, but perhaps it will appear undesirable because of our weakness and tendency to recoil from the rough road and the narrow way.

In the fourth dwelling place, St. Teresa describes the divine touches which are now given to the soul by God. She calls them *spiritual delights* and confirms that they are supernatural experiences. She says that consolations originate in our own nature, and are usually the result of virtuous acts. However, spiritual delights are of a higher kind. They originate in God. They are the result of an exercise of His sovereignty over the soul.

> For the Lord gives when He desires, as He desires, and to whom He desires. Since these blessings belong to Him, He does no injustice to anyone (IC IV:1:2).

These supernatural experiences are not characteristic of the earlier stages of the spiritual life of a soul, although they are sometimes given to chosen souls earlier in their lives. St. Teresa clarifies how a soul progresses in the spiritual life by one of her best known metaphors: that of the two troughs of water. The first trough is filled by water carried by aqueducts and represents efforts by the soul to advance. This trough represents the first three dwelling places. This process is very laborious. The second however, is filled by a spring and requires no effort to transport the water. This is God's work which is the exclusive active agent from the fourth dwelling place through the seventh dwelling place. The first trough consists of consolations on the natural level and the second trough of the spiritual delights supplied by God, as and when He pleases.

> With this other fount, the water comes from its own source, which is God. And since His majesty desires to do so – when He is pleased to grant some supernatural favor – H produces this delight with the

> greatest peace and quiet and sweetness in the very interior part of ourselves (IC IV:2:4).

The important words used by St. Teresa in this quote are, "His majesty desires to do so," and, "He produces this delight..." God has now taken complete charge of this soul's path to His Kingdom, and will bring the journey to a wonderful conclusion if the soul will surrender to His sovereignty over it. The soul now must only surrender in humility, and avoid setting up obstacles to God's work. The mustard seed must be allowed to grow.

In the fourth dwelling place, St. Teresa describes a soul that is beginning to receive true divine favors which she calls spiritual delights. She emphasizes that these favors are not received through the souls own efforts, but are a pure and gratuitous gift of God. This soul must have reached a high degree of detachment from the things of this world in order to be prepared to receive these gifts from God. However, there are examples of very worldly and even sinful persons receiving a profound spiritual experience of God, totally unexpected, but these are rare exceptions, and are usually aimed at effecting an immediate conversion of the receiving soul. Recall the experience of St. Paul on the road to Damascus as an example of a soul at the level of the fourth dwelling place that has indeed traveled far in grace. Now the work of God directly in the soul is necessary to move it beyond the natural to the supernatural state of spirituality. Not only must this soul become detached from the things of the world and creatures, but it must also give up its attachment to its own spiritual preferences. This is so that its incompetence to enter deeper into the King's realm can be replaced by God's incomparable competence to bring the soul there.

> This spiritual delight (the warmth and fragrant fumes spread throughout the soul) is not something that can be imagined, because however diligent our efforts we cannot acquire it. The very experience of it makes us realize that it is not of the same metal as we ourselves but fashioned from the purest gold of the divine wisdom. Here, in my opinion, the faculties are not united but absorbed and looking as though in wonder at what they see (IC IV:2:6).

In the fifth dwelling place, St. Teresa introduces us to the prayer of union; a connection with God so sublime that it could only be brought about by God. All the faculties of the soul, intellect, will, and imagination are as she says, *asleep* in this state, *asleep* to the world, and to its own self. This state involves the whole soul, not just part of it. The prayer is temporary, rarely lasting more than a half- hour. The soul is increasingly not in control of these favors. God is truly exercising His sovereignty over this soul. He is elevating it to Himself. The mustard seed is becoming a substantial shrub because the soul has *sold* all to acquire this treasure. This is what the rich young man who went away sad has given up. The pearl of great price is now within the grasp of this soul.

> But reflect, daughters, that He doesn't want you to hold on to anything, so that you will be able to enjoy the favors we are speaking of. Whether you have little or much, He wants everything for Himself...thus the soul is left with such wonderful blessings, because God works within it without anyone disturbing Him, not even ourselves (IC V:1:3).

The great change in the spiritual journey that has occurred in this dwelling place and in the previous one is the dominance of God as the acting agent. We must remember that the union here is between our human nature and the divinity of God. In order to establish this union, deeply within the Kingdom of God, supernatural power is required. The soul that desires to go forward must be completely submissive to the Will of God in this process that is necessary in order to achieve union. God must reign supreme in His Kingdom.

In the fifth dwelling place, the soul has advanced in spiritual growth and awareness to the point, that not only could it not have reached this dwelling place without a great deal of holy detachment, but also it will not long remain in such an advanced state unless that detachment is preserved. The devil can enter the soul through the smallest crack in its armor. Vigilance is required because the devil sees that this soul is escaping his grasp, and the escape will be permanent unless he can stop it from going forward. Revival of old attachments to the world, and even to old sins is his surest chance of success, and he will strive constantly to win the soul back to his domain. Constant prayer and great grace in the face of this onslaught is necessary to persevere in the pursuit of union with God.

> From the very unhappiness caused by worldly things arises the ever so painful desire to leave this world. Any relief the soul has comes from the thought that God wants it to be living in this exile; yet even this is not enough, because in spite of all these benefits it is not entirely surrendered to God's will...although it does not fail to conform itself. But it conforms with a great feeling that it can do no more because no more has been given it, and with many tears. Every time it is in prayer this regret is its pain (IC V:2:10).

St. Teresa introduces us to a new aspect of the Kingdom of God in the sixth dwelling place, into which this soul has entered deeply. In this part of God's Kingdom, far from the world and its allurements the soul encounters profound interior suffering. This is a part of the *selling* of all one possesses. Here the soul is passively having extracted, like a dentist pulling a tooth, all attachments to anything that is not God. One cannot enter fully into the Kingdom of God in a state of imperfection, no matter how small and insignificant the imperfection is. This state of soul is not easy to arrive at. The trials, both interior and exterior, necessary to reach this state are very great. They are absolutely essential in order to enter completely into God's Kingdom, because by these trials the roots of imperfection are removed. The mustard bush must be pruned and then fed and watered in order to become the great shrub God intended it to be. The pruning are the trials and the feeding and the watering are the sublime graces, not only of consolations and divine touches, but also of suffering and tribulations, given as gifts by God to the soul that has advanced this far. The consolations, when given, are sublime beyond description. It is a strange mixture of suffering and joy. "O sweet cautery," as St. John of the Cross calls them; a burning wound, but one that is sweet to the soul. St. Teresa describes it as a delightful pain that the soul actually desires. This soul is so far into the Kingdom of God and away from the world and creatures that it is hard to imagine such a soul turning back having come so far in its quest for the pearl of great price.

> You may wonder why greater security is present in this favor than in other things. In my opinion, these are the reasons: first, the devil never gives delightful pain like this. He can give the savor and delight that seem to be spiritual, but he doesn't have the power to join pain-and so much of it-to the spiritual quiet and delight of the soul. For all his powers are on the outside and the pains he causes are never, in my opinion, delightful or peaceful but disturbing and contentious. Second, this delightful tempest comes from a region other than those regions of which he can be lord. Third, the favor brings wonderful benefits to the soul, the more customary of which are the determination to suffer for God, the desire to have many trials, and the determination to withdraw from earthly satisfactions and conversations and other similar things (IC VI:2:6).

At this time, the soul has come so close to God that intimate contact with Him in the interior of the soul is not uncommon. Although the nature of these contacts is beyond the scope of this book, we can identify them as various forms of locutions and flights of the spirit that are treated at length by St. Teresa and St. John. Here also, the soul suffers greatly from the memory of its sins, although it knows with certainty that God has forgiven them all. Its greatest fear is that it will withdraw from God and offend Him again. If the soul departs from the Kingdom of God where shall it go, now that it is penniless, having sold all to acquire the field with the treasure? The answer is the same as Peter's answer to Christ's question: "Will you also leave me?" To which Peter answers, "To whom shall we go Master? You alone have the words of everlasting life." (Jn 6:68).

The seventh dwelling place represents the furthest development of a soul's spiritual growth possible in this life. St. Teresa says several things about the characteristics of this dwelling place. She says that the summit of perfection possible in this life is complete conformity of our will with the Will of God so that there is only one will – God's. She says that the unity with the Holy Trinity is constant, although sometimes more intensely experienced than at other times. But most interestingly, she says that here the sacred humanity of Christ and of His Holy Mother must be preserved in the soul's consciousness. We must not assume that all thought of corporeal reality must now be discarded, since that is a trait of angelic spirits. Christ, His Mother, and the saints are our models throughout life. Compare this idea with the observation of Pope Benedict XVI, in his book *Jesus of Nazareth*, that the Kingdom of God under one theory is in fact Christ Himself. If we look back to the sixth dwelling place, we see this illustrated well:

> How much more is it necessary not to withdraw through one's own efforts from all our good and help which is the most sacred humanity of our Lord Jesus Christ...For if they lose the guide who is the good Jesus, they will not hit upon the right road...The lord Himself says that He is the way; the Lord says that He is the light and that no one can go to the Father but through Him, and "anyone who sees me sees the Father" (IC VI:7).

In her discussion of the seventh dwelling place, St. Teresa enumerates the effects on the soul of the life it has now found: life in the Kingdom of God as it is lived in this world by the perfected soul. The first effect is a forgetfulness of self. The soul sees that what it can now do by its own efforts amounts to nothing. The second effect is that the soul has a great desire to suffer: a great interior joy when it is persecuted. There is great detachment from everything and a desire for solitude. The only thing that willingly arouses the soul from its solitude is to be engaged in something that will help some other soul. How dismayed it is to be drawn by circumstances back to the mundane necessities of life in the physical world. This soul is now encapsulated in the Kingdom of God, peacefully resting in the bosom of Abraham. It is now completely animated by God.

> For just as a great gush of water could not reach us if it didn't have a source, as I have said, so it is understood clearly that there is Someone in the interior depths who shoots these arrows and gives life to this life, and that there is a Sun in the interior of the soul from which a brilliant light proceeds and is sent to the faculties. The soul , as I have said, does not move from that center nor is its peace lost; for the very One who gave peace to the apostles

when they were together can give it to the soul (IC VII:2:6).

It is one of the peculiarities of the spiritual life that the further one advances the more the soul encounters affliction and spiritual suffering. However, there does come a time when the afflictions diminish, and in fact disappear. St. Teresa discusses the gradual elimination of afflictions in the sixth and seventh dwelling places. The favors that have been granted to the soul that has reached these dwelling places and the sufferings that have been endured results in a purified soul. Any attachment to things of the world and to the self, have been purged out of this soul and the life of the soul is now entirely bound up in God within its very substance.

> You may wonder why greater security is present in this favor (the action of God's love that causes the soul to dissolve in desire to suffer the pain of longing for union with God) than in other things. In my opinion, these are the reasons; first, the devil never gives delightful pain like this. He can give the savor and delight that seem to be spiritual, but he doesn't have the power to join pain – and so much of it–to the spiritual quiet and delight of the soul…Second, this delightful tempest comes from a region other than those regions of which he can be lord. Third, the favor brings wonderful benefits to the soul, the more customary of which are the determination to suffer for God, the desire to have many trials, and the determination to withdraw from earthly satisfactions and conversations and other similar things (IC VI:2:6).

And so the battle for holy detachment is won in this dwelling place. This soul rejoices in its rejection of the things of this world and the satisfactions of its own ego, for it has found its true home in poverty of spirit: the Kingdom of God. All things are now in their proper order of importance, and peace and joy have become the norm in this soul.

Humility

If poverty of spirit in the form of humility is necessary in these dwelling places already examined, this virtue is indispensable to the last two dwelling places. In fact, the supernatural nature of the last dwelling places and the experiences of the soul in them engender a degree of humility that the soul acquires without a special effort to do so and that would have been impossible earlier. Holy detachment must be far advanced in order to enter these dwelling places. The degree of detachment required to enter the sixth and seventh dwelling places cannot be acquired without an equal degree of humility, or without poverty of spirit. The favors that will be granted to a soul in these dwelling places include a deep understanding of the grandeur of God and an intense and sublimely painful love and yearning for union with the Bridegroom of the soul. These favors do not and cannot co-exist with attachments to anything that is not God or of God, or without perfect humility in the interior of the soul. This soul truly belongs to God and has acquired the poverty of spirit desired by Christ in this *Beatitude*.

> After you have done what should be done by those in the previous dwelling places: humility, humility! By this means the Lord allows Himself to be conquered with regard to anything we want from Him. The first sign for seeing whether or not you have humility is that you do not think you deserve these favors and spiritual delights from the Lord or that you will receive them in your lifetime (IC IV:3:9).

> It seems that our Lord wishes all to understand that the soul is now His, that no one should touch it. Well and good if its body, or honor, or possessions are touched for this soul draws honor for His Majesty out of everything. But that one touch the soul-absolutely not: for if the soul does not withdraw from its Spouse through a very culpable boldness, He will protect it from the whole world and even from hell (IC VI:4:16).

> What I said seems to me very beneficial to help you understand how pleased our Lord is to know that we

know ourselves and strive to reflect again and again on our poverty and misery and on how we posses nothing that we have not received (IC VI:5:6).

And if souls aren't determined about becoming His slaves, let them be convinced that they are not making much progress, for this whole building, as I have said, has humility as its foundation. If humility is not genuinely present, for your own sake the Lord will not construct a high building lest the building fall to the ground (IC VII:4:8).

C. St. John of the Cross: The Ascent of Mt. Carmel

In this work of St. John, we shall endeavor to find a relationship between his spiritual doctrine and this *Beatitude*. We will examine the spiritual doctrine of St. John to find the manner in which he treats the concept of the Kingdom of God. In particular, we want to see how the descriptions given by our Lord of His Kingdom relate to the doctrine of St. John of the Cross and then we will look for his meaning of the words *poor in spirit*.

Sovereignty of God over His Kingdom

This book of St John is the exposition of the beginnings of the spiritual life. We recall that St. John's spiritual doctrine divides the stages of the spiritual life into two main divisions: the active nights and the passive nights. Each of these stages is further subdivided into two sub- nights: the night of sense and the night of the spirit. The soul moves through the active nights of sense and spirit first; and then if so willed by God, through the passive nights of sense and spirit. This sequence must be followed in every case because one night prepares the soul for the next. One cannot start in the middle or near the end. Each night has characteristics that prepare the soul for the next night. Each progression is a step forward toward union with God, and each is more difficult than the one that went before it. A detailed description of each night and its characteristics is beyond the scope of this book. It is sufficient for our purposes if we keep in mind the sequence of nights and relate that sequence to our subject. The sovereignty of God in the works of St. John describes sovereignty not only over the end goal of His Kingdom, but also of the means to reach that goal. As each step is reached, the sovereignty of God increases until at long last the soul is completely dependent on the work of God in order for it to advance.

In *The Ascent of Mt. Carmel* St. John gives us an explanation of the first two stanzas of his poetry to describe the beginnings of the soul's quest for God. For our purpose, it is useful to read those two stanzas:

> 1. One dark night,
> Fired with love's urgent longings
> -Ah, the sheer grace –
> I went out unseen,
> My house being now all stilled;

> 2. In darkness, and secure,
> By the secret ladder, disguised,
> -Ah, the sheer Grace!-
> In darkness and concealment
> My house being now all stilled;

Let us focus on the words, "I went out unseen." We see here the beginning of the *selling* of every possession. There is something being put in motion from within the soul. Change is imminent. When St. John says, "Went out," we well might ask, went out from where? He immediately answers this question:

> The soul sings in this first stanza of its good luck
> and the grace it had in departing from its inordinate
> sensory appetites and imperfections (AS I:1:1).

The soul that is going out from its inordinate appetites and imperfections is indeed looking for the Kingdom of God that lies ahead. There can be no such going out from inordinate appetites and imperfections in a soul that remains self-willed and self-centered. This beginning step is what the rich young man in the gospel could not make because he was unwilling to relinquish his attachments to his possessions. He would keep the commandments as long as it cost him only a little. And what is it that begins this movement? It is *love's urgent longings*. This is how God draws a soul slowly into His Kingdom; gradually, slowly by the increase of love like the gradual growth of the mustard seed. We see now that God's sovereignty is a sovereignty of love not of domination. It is an invitation like that extended to the rich young man, not an exercise of force.

It is also a *sheer grace* to go out unseen. By this phrase, St. John means that the departure for the Kingdom of God, leaving behind the kingdom of the world, is a beginning that is not obstructed by the natural appetites. The departure is unseen. The natural appetites have in a sense been by-passed, and are not the cause of the movement of the soul toward God's Kingdom. It is supernatural grace that prods the soul to begin its journey. The end will be the sovereignty of God over the soul, rather than the sovereignty of the natural appetites.

> All the sovereignty and freedom of the world compared with the freedom and sovereignty of the Spirit of God is utter slavery, anguish, and captivity (AS I:4:6).

> All the delights and satisfactions of the will in the things of the world in contrast to all the delight that is God are intense suffering, torment and bitterness (AS I:7).

In these few lines, St. John clearly expresses the incomparable value of the treasure in the field, and the wisdom of giving up everything to gain it. Why feed on the scraps on the floor when the table is full of sweet meats and candies?

The last verse of each of these first two stanzas is, "my house being now all stilled." What are described as stilled are the inordinate natural appetites. This is the reason the rich young man could not part with his possessions *because he had many*. When the soul has sold all it has in order to acquire the Kingdom of God and His sovereignty, it has stilled its house and quieted its natural appetites. Now the mustard seed is ready to grow.

In Book III of *The Ascent of Mt. Carmel*, St. John of the Cross approaches the subject of the annihilation of the objects of both the memory and the will as a prerequisite to union with God. The memory is of no help in union with God because its objects are all natural and incapable of sustaining the union that the soul seeks. Objects stored in the memory are stirred by the passions and inordinate appetites. They become a source of temptation. Falsehoods are also stored there and lead the soul off in the wrong direction away from God rather than toward Him. Knowledge involving creatures which are stored in the memory should only be recalled if they lead to love for God.

Likewise, the passions of the will; joy, hope, sorrow and fear must be purified of all inordinate feelings or thoughts directed to their natural objects in order to preserve all of one's self for the love of God. If one of these passions reigns inordinately in the soul, the entire soul is held captive and in chains by the tyranny of that passion. When these passions are regulated reasonably by the will, God can occupy the center of the consciousness of that soul, rather than some lesser natural object of the will in the natural realm. All must be *sold* or the union with God will never be achieved. From this, it is easy to see that Christ meant what he said in the parable of the pearl of great price and the field containing the treasure. To acquire the Kingdom of God, nothing less than all will suffice to acquire that pearl or that field. One must truly be detached from all that the heart clings to that is less than God.

St. John sets forth a guiding principle for the faculties of memory and will which will enable the soul to reach the Kingdom of God. The first for the memory and the second for the will are set forth as follows:

> Our aim is union with God in the memory; the object of hope is something unpossessed; the less other objects are possessed, the more capacity and ability there is to hope for this one object, and consequently so much less of hope; accordingly in the measure that a person dispossesses his memory of forms and objects which are not God, he will fix it upon God and preserve it empty, in the hope that God will fill it. That which a person must do in order to live in perfect and pure hope in God is this: as often as distinct ideas , forms and images occur to him, he should immediately, without resting in them, turn to God with loving affection, in emptiness of everything rememberable…(SG AS: Unit 25: p. 55). The will should rejoice only in what is for the honor and glory of God, and the greatest honor we can give

Him is to serve Him according to evangelical perfection; anything unincluded in such service is without value to man (SG AS: Unit 26: p. 56).

In these two quotes, St. John echoes the words of our Lord in the parables of the pearl of great price and the treasure in the field, that the soul who wishes to acquire these valuables must be prepared to abandon all that does not lead directly to that goal. We see that the conversion must be interior and not just a superficial attempt at religion for a purpose other than union with God in His Kingdom. The sovereignty of God over the soul must be total.

We now turn to *The Ascent of Mt. Carmel* of St. John of the Cross to examine his views on the importance of poverty of spirit that will result in a soul gaining the Kingdom of God. We can easily translate this *Beatitude* into the language of St. John of the Cross. Poverty of spirit is the result that occurs in the soul that traverses the dark nights of the spiritual doctrine of this saint. The core of St. John's teaching concerns the dying of the soul to all the attachments it has to the world and its attractions, the devil and his wiles, and most of all to the self defined as the center of the soul's consciousness and the object of its activities. As the soul progresses through each of the dark nights, of sense and spirit, active and passive, poverty of spirit increases. Each of these nights requires an increasingly painful separation from an attachment to creatures that is deeply imbedded in the soul. Later in its journey, the soul will be required by God to detach itself from spiritual satisfactions and delights that are in fact obstacles to union with God. They are obstacles because they are treated as ends in themselves, rather than means to the true end: union with God.

These attachments are barriers to poverty of spirit because they bind the soul to practices and methods of approaching God that are contaminated with self–interest, and seek as their object something that is less than God. In this way, the soul tends to retain something for itself and its own delight, and therefore poverty of spirit is limited until these spiritual attachments are also surrendered and abandoned and no longer treated as ends. It would be possible to write an entire book on this subject alone. However, with a little discipline we will limit the following analysis of St. John's doctrine to this *Beatitude* and attempt a succinct explanation of how the concept of poverty of spirit is at the center of his major works on the spiritual and mystical life.

Poor in Spirit

Holy detachment

The overall scheme of the spiritual doctrine of St. John is that the senses are purified and mortified first, followed by the purification of the spirit accompanied by the accommodation of the senses to the spirit. In this way, a soul presents a unified and purified self to the Lord, in which the union can occur. The first efforts of the soul must be directed toward mortification of the voluntary appetites. St. John defines these voluntary appetites as those in which inordinate attachments to creatures or things in the natural realm are retained in the soul. Like road-blocks, they must be removed in order to proceed ahead along the rough road and the narrow way. This is the bare beginning of poverty of spirit: the first dark night:

> This dark night is a privation and purgation of all sensible appetites for the external things of the world, the delights of the flesh, and the gratifications of the will…One is not freed from the sufferings and anguish of the appetites until they are tempered and put to sleep (AS I:1:4).

We recall the words of Christ regarding two masters, "One cannot serve both God and mammon (Mt. 6:24)." Poverty of spirit requires that God be the master of the soul. The natural things of this world and the flesh are the masters that must be set aside in order that room is made in the soul for the mastery of God. One cannot have one foot in the world and the other foot reaching out for God. Such a division will always lead to the defeat of the purification of the soul that is necessary to advance toward union with God. Such a divided soul will inevitably fall further and further away from any real union with God. If one has two glasses, one filled with water, and the other with wine and wishes to put the wine into the glass filled with water, the water must first be removed.

> Any inordinate act of the appetite causes both this privative and positive harm. To begin with, it is

> clear in speaking of the privative harm, that a person by mere attachment to a created thing is less capable of God, according to the degree of the entity of that appetite. For two contraries cannot coexist in the same subject...Since love of God and attachment to creatures, are contraries, they cannot coexist in the same will (AS I:6:1).

If a soul succeeds in mortifying its inordinate appetites for the objects of the senses, it has begun well on its path to union with God. Remembering that the words of our Lord were, *poor in spirit*, we ask the question: Does St. John claim that the purification of the spirit is the final goal of the soul's purgation of its appetites? The answer is in the affirmative. He states quite clearly that the purification of the senses conform the sensory part of the soul to the spirit before the purification of the spirit begins. When that occurs, the soul is a unity of sense and spirit, so that the purification of the spirit, when completed, will also complete the purification of the sensory aspect of the soul. The two parts are joined and now journey together.

St. John then introduces a new concept into his spiritual doctrine of purgation and purification of all imperfections in the soul. The spirit now proceeds in its purification by faith. The soul is now to be brought beyond its own capabilities by the supernatural virtue of faith. The night becomes darker and all understanding will be suspended so that the deep purgation of the spirit can proceed. Poverty of spirit is the indispensable disposition of the soul. The work in the spirit will be accomplished in the darkness of faith, unseen in many instances by the soul being purified. Faith and understanding cannot exist in the same subject at the same time because they are contradictories: where understanding exists, faith is unnecessary. Where faith is required, understanding cannot reach the object being considered.

> Such is faith to the soul-it informs us of matters we have never seen or known, either in themselves or in themselves or in their likeness; in fact nothing like them exists. The light of natural knowledge does not show us the object of faith, since this object is unproportioned to any of the senses (AS II:3:3).

> Similarly, if the soul in traveling this road leans upon any elements of its own knowledge or experience of God, it will easily go astray or be detained for not having desired to abide in complete blindness, in faith which is its guide...A man, then, is decidedly hindered from the attachment of this high state of union with God when he is attached to any understanding, feeling, imagining, opinion, desire, or way of his own, or to any other of his works or affairs, and knows not how to detach and denude himself of these impediments (AS II:4:3-4).

No soul comes before God in eternal life with imperfections remaining within it. The poverty of spirit spoken of by Christ in this *Beatitude* goes beyond the soul's own power to fully achieve. What is required of the soul is to be open to the work of God in the soul, and to stay the course as He purifies the soul with purgations and afflictions that are frequently painful to the soul. The final state will be extreme: emptiness of the soul of all that is not God. This desirable end comes about gradually, just as the mustard seed grows gradually into the great shrub.

Humility

Poverty of spirit is as foreign to the thinking of the world and those attached to the world, as it is possible to be. Worldly people always approach life with a selfish objective, and a desire to demonstrate superiority over others. More so in our own time than ever before, the formula for living is to get as much for one's self as possible, and never allow the impression among others that one has been bested by another in any endeavor. Deception and disguise are the means frequently used to get what is desired, or to engender a belief about us in others that is not a true one. A soul in this frame of mind cannot even begin a journey toward God until changes begin to happen. One as proud and self-centered as this description provides no good ground for the seed of truth to take root. St. John of the Cross points out the need to turn away from our confidence in our own power and ability to advance unaided in our quest for union with God. He makes it clear that such an approach in response to the urgings of Grace will result in failure. This lack of humility that the world admires is foolishness to God.

> A man who is in darkness does not comprehend the light, so neither will a person attached to creatures be able to comprehend God. Until a man is purged of his attachments he will not be equipped to possess God, neither here below through the pure transformation of love, nor in heaven through the beatific vision (AS I:4:3).

> Anyone, therefore, who values his knowledge and ability as a means of reaching union with the wisdom of God is highly ignorant in God's sight and will be left behind, far away from this wisdom…Only those who set aside their own knowledge and walk in God's service like unlearned children receive wisdom from God (AS I:4:5).

If sufficient humility will enable a soul to abandon its own powers and faculties as the means to strive for union with God, then what is the means that the soul must use in order to acquire this virtue and accomplish this sublime result? The first thing a soul must do is to accept the fact that the journey to God is beyond the capacity of its faculties. Our faculties must be stilled and darkened so that they do not become obstacles to progress. Next, we must have the humility to accept these limitations, and have the confidence that God will become our guide along the rough road and the narrow way.

> I should like to persuade spiritual persons that the road leading to God does not entail a multiplicity of considerations, methods, manners, and experiences- though in their own way these may be a requirement for beginners- but demands only one thing necessary: true self-denial, exterior and interior, through surrender of self both to suffering for Christ and to annihilation in all things (AS II:7:8).

We must have the willingness to give up our own capacities as the means to reach our goal of union, and instead surrender to faith and grace in order to proceed along this narrow way in the correct manner which can only come from God. Poverty of spirit is not only the absence of cravings for the things of the world and the flesh, but must also include separation from the things of this world, from ourselves and our desire for *self-esteem*. This disposition of soul is not possible without the virtue of humility.

D. St. John of the Cross: The Dark Night

In *The Dark Night,* St. John describes for us the pain that must be endured to obtain the treasure of union with God. He puts in bold relief what the rich young man foresaw in the necessity to sell all his possessions to obtain the Kingdom of God, and which he could not do. In this book, St. John treats of what he calls the passive nights: the passive night of sense and the passive night of spirit. The principal characteristic of these passive nights is that the primary, and in many cases the only agent and cause of growth is God. In the active nights, the principal agent, supported by grace was the soul itself. The difference between these two nights is very significant to the soul seeking union with God. We will attempt to see that difference as it relates to our subject.

Sovereignty of God over His Kingdom

Most souls enter upon a spiritual journey in great darkness regarding what lies ahead. If the soul does not undergo the fundamental change required at each step along the way, progress stops and the soul will usually fall back. It is quite rare that a soul who stops along the way remains where it stopped. Grace constantly prods the soul to go forward, and the only way to escape the *hound of Heaven* is to run from Him. The soul must remember that God truly has sovereignty over His Kingdom and all that is in it. The choice to continue to seek His Kingdom is an act of the will supported by grace, just as the decision to stop and retreat is an act of the will.

St. John of the Cross, in *The Dark Night*, describes the passive night of the senses and the passive night of the spirit as stages of ever increasing painful experiences. It is much more difficult to purge the spirit than it is to purge the senses. St. John says that many enter the passive night of the senses, but only a few enter the passive night of the spirit. To some extent, the choice is God's, but many times the offer to enter the passive night of the spirit is made by God and refused by the soul. When the soul perceives the movement of Grace to enter each of these nights, it also senses the cost that will be paid in order to advance. When one is stripped of all attachments to creatures in the night of sense, we see an exercise of sovereignty by God over this soul. There can be no other kings in God's Kingdom. St. John gives the following explanation of the beginning of this night.

> As I said, when God sees that they have grown a little, He weans them from the sweet breast so that they might be strengthened, lays aside their swaddling bands, and puts them down from His arms that they may grow accustomed to walking by themselves. This change is a surprise to them because everything seems to be functioning in reverse (DN I:8:3).

We must see this act of putting the soul down from His arms as a gentle urging of the soul by God to truly begin to sell all to acquire His Kingdom. A soul that has entered into a quest for the Kingdom of God for any reason other than union with God is now at a cross roads: is it worth what is being asked of me? Shall I go away sad as the rich young man did? Shall I submit to God's sovereignty over me?

These questions take on a much more dire meaning to the soul that is being invited into the passive night of the spirit. We see again that Christ meant what he said about *selling all* to enter His Kingdom. This night digs deep into the heart of the soul to eradicate the roots of imperfections and attachments to the things of this world. Sovereignty takes on a new meaning and the choice becomes more difficult. However, the commitment of the soul gained thus far to enter completely into the Kingdom of God renders the soul nearly helpless to refuse God's invitation. While the road indeed has become rough and the way narrow, the soul's yearning for God is also greatly increased. Nothing else appears to be worthwhile. It now is approaching the point at which it cannot live without the actual awareness of God's love and its own response to that love. This is very fortunate for the soul, because this road of the passive night of the spirit is the final sale of all to acquire the pearl of great price.

> God divests the faculties, affections, and senses, both spiritual and sensory, interior and exterior. He leaves the intellect in darkness, the will in aridity,

the memory in emptiness and the affections in supreme affliction, bitterness, and anguish, by depriving the soul of the feeling and satisfaction it previously obtained from spiritual blessings (DN II:3:3).

As fire consumes the tarnish and rust of metal, this (dark) contemplation annihilates, empties, and consumes all the affections and imperfect habits the soul contracted throughout its life (DN II:6:5).

Happy is the soul that can bear the gentle touch of God's hand in these nights. So much suffering of the soul cannot be in vain. We will begin to see that reward in the next section, St. John's *The Spiritual Canticle*.

In this most famous work of St. John of the Cross, he gives us an exposition of the next stage of the spiritual life of a soul: the passive nights of sense and spirit. These nights are called passive because through the intervention of grace, the soul is withdrawn from its own faculties and powers in order to advance its spiritual life. Instead, God now takes control of the soul's advancement, and introduces it to greater purging of its imperfections. This depth of purgation cannot be carried out by the soul because the roots of its imperfections are beyond the soul's reach or even awareness. The suffering during this stage of purgation is of such a magnitude that the soul would not choose it. It must be imposed by God on the soul that truly desires to love Him. God alone can see the imperfection and choose the affliction to purge it from the soul. We can say that this time of suffering of this soul cannot be tolerated without a high degree of poverty of spirit, the disposition that surrenders in trust to the work of God in the soul.

Poor in Spirit

Holy detachment

A soul that has surrendered to God's Providence regarding its spiritual life, will find itself engaged in interior battles against aridity, desolation of spirit, and the afflictions that accompany the purgation of imperfections. The exposure of the depths of the soul to the dark contemplation of this night is wont to overwhelm it with grief.

> The first and chief benefit of this dry and dark night of contemplation is the knowledge of self and of one's own misery. Besides the fact that all the favors God imparts to the soul are ordinarily enwrapped in this knowledge, the aridities and voids of the faculties in relation to the abundance previously experienced, and the difficulty encountered in the practice of virtue make the soul recognize its own lowliness and misery, which were not apparent in the time of its prosperity (DN II:12:2).

All of this suffering brings significant benefits to the soul. We said that the work in the soul now being carried out by God's intervention is impossible for the soul to do unaided. Also, the results of God's work require divine illumination to first identify the causes and roots of imperfections that have become a part of a soul through its life. These are different for each soul and divine grace is necessary to extricate them from the soul. An absence here of poverty of spirit would ruin the entire endeavor and prevent it from ever getting started.

> These aridities, then, make a person walk with purity in the love of God. For he is no longer moved to act by the delight and satisfaction he finds in a work, as he was perhaps when he derived this from his deeds, but by a desire of pleasing God. He is neither presumptuous nor self-satisfied, as was his custom in the time of his prosperity, but fearful and disquieted about himself and lacking in self-satisfaction (DN I:13:12).

When the soul moves from the first passive night of sense into the passive night of spirit, the poverty of spirit gained in the former will help the soul to endure the torments in the latter. There is now nothing to cling to except the blind trust that God is moving the soul in accordance with His Will. The torments of soul in this night of dark contemplation are truly horrible and hard to bear. No relief or consolation from these afflictions can be found anywhere.

The former attachments, imperfections, and affections of the soul are immersed and annihilated in the divine illumination cast upon the soul.

> That the soul with its faculties be divinely tempered and prepared for the divine union of love, it must first be engulfed in this divine and dark spiritual light of contemplation, and thereby be withdrawn from all creature affections and apprehensions. The duration of this absorption is proportionate to the intensity of the contemplation (DN II:8:2).

Humility

St. John of the Cross begins his treatise on the passive night of sense in *The Dark Night* with a discussion of the problems of beginners. These defects in the spiritual life of the soul coincide with the seven capital sins. The most intractable of these obstacles to poverty of spirit are spiritual gluttony, spiritual avarice, and spiritual pride. St. John explains how the sufferings of this night purge the soul of these defects through self-knowledge, resulting in the suffering that always accompanies the revelations to the soul of its own imperfections. Further, these imperfections are so firmly entrenched in the substance of the soul that only divine assistance will be able to remove them. As we have seen, God is the acting Agent of change in this night, and the soul must remain passively receptive to the graces bestowed on it by God that purge these defects. Spiritual gluttony and spiritual avarice, the desire for more spirituality than God is willing to give at this stage, are purged by the afflictions associated with aridity experienced more often and more severely in this night. Spiritual pride is purged by the self-knowledge so painfully experienced as a result of the illumination of the soul's faults by the light of God.

> In the dryness and emptiness of this night of the appetite, a person also procures humility, that virtue opposed to the first capital vice, spiritual pride. Through this humility acquired by means of self-knowledge, a person is purged of all those imperfections of the vice of pride into which he fell at the time of his prosperity. Aware of his own dryness and wretchedness, the thought of his being

> more advanced than others does not even occur in its first movements, as it did before; on the contrary, he realizes that others are better (DN I:12:7).

The soul that began its spiritual journey full of enthusiasm and consolation fell into the errors of spiritual gluttony, avarice, and pride. It was sure that it had climbed to a very high state of spiritual perfection that exceeded the perfection of all others around it. Any recognition of holiness in any one else filled it with envy because its own holiness was not being lauded. But then *the axe fell* upon it as the saying goes. God introduced aridity, affliction, and self-knowledge into the soul, and desolation descended upon it. Suffering terribly, it could not see what was happening to it. The first conclusion of the soul about this new experience, that God had rejected it and left it to its own devices, was erroneous. In fact, what was happening was immensely valuable to the soul. God was removing from the soul, like a skilled surgeon, the vices the soul could not eliminate by itself. The result would be a deep humility and poverty of spirit.

> Yet when this spiritual light finds an object on which to shine, that is, when something is to be understood spiritually concerning perfection or imperfection, no matter how slight, or about a judgment on the truth or falsity of some matter, a man will understand more clearly than he did before he was in this darkness. And easily recognizing the imperfection which presents itself, a man grows conscious of the spiritual light he possesses...(DN II:8:4).

E. St. John of the Cross: The Spiritual Canticle

The concept of sale includes a transfer of ownership and some recompense for what has been sold. If the soul agrees with Christ's invitation to sell all and follow Him, the recompense is entry into God's Kingdom. If a soul strives to accomplish this entry, and in fact begins to succeed by undergoing the torments of the dark nights described above, the transformation will surely occur. Since God is a loving God, we are justified in expecting that His sovereignty over His Kingdom will include His benevolence toward the soul that has sold all or one that is in the process of selling all, in order to enter His Kingdom. In this work, St. John of the Cross is not lacking in a superb treatment of this aspect of God's disposition toward the soul that loves Him.

Sovereignty of God over His Kingdom

This work of St John retraces some of the ground already covered in *The Ascent of Mt. Carmel* and *The Dark Night* with regard to the soul's searching and longing for union with God, the Beloved. However, the main thrust of *The Spiritual Canticle* is to treat of the spiritual betrothal and the spiritual marriage. These are both very high states of spiritual development. The soul at this point has in fact completed its *sale* of all, and is in the act of acquiring the pearl of great price. St. John, in this work, gives many descriptions of the rewards the soul reaps from its willingness to sell all in exchange for the Kingdom of God. These rewards are unobtainable except from the sovereign King. They are a promise of the joys that only He can give to the soul that has traveled this far.

> Nothing can reach or molest her now that she has withdrawn from all things and entered into her God where she enjoys peace, tastes all sweetness,, and delights in all delight insofar as this earthly state allows (SC 21:15).

The important thing to notice here is that the soul, having been divested of all inordinate attachments to the things of the world, has submitted itself to the sovereignty of God completely, and has thereby gained entry into God's Kingdom. The completeness of the surrender is indispensable. One cannot stand with one foot in God's Kingdom and one foot in the kingdom of the world. We see how loyalty and commitment are divided in that case. The two masters will not have equal importance to this soul. The soul that has surrendered all in order to enter God's Kingdom will not be found wanting for rewards. This soul is now entirely God's possession and God surrenders completely to the soul, and He is its reward.

> ...It should be known that the soul is conscious at this time that the torrent of God's spirit is besieging and taking possession of her so forcibly that all the rivers of the world seem to have flooded in upon her and to be assailing her.

The second property the soul experiences at this time is that of the divine water filling the low places of her humility and the voids of her appetites.

The third property she experiences in these resounding rivers of her Beloved is a spiritual clamor and outcry, louder than any other sound or call (SC 14:9).

This quietude and tranquility in God is not entirely obscure to the soul as in the dark night; but it is a tranquility and quietude in divine light, in the new knowledge of God, in which the spirit elevated to the divine light is in quiet (SC 15:23).

This spiritual marriage is incomparably greater than the spiritual espousal, for it is a total transformation in the Beloved in which each surrenders the entire possession of self to the other with a certain consummation of the union of love. The soul thereby becomes divine, becomes God by participation, insofar as possible in this life (SC 22:3).

The word *all* in the parable of the pearl of great price takes on new meaning and importance when we reflect on the words of St. John of the Cross. In God's Kingdom, the Ruler becomes the servant of the subject in the realm of divine love. The pearl of great price and the treasure in the field are the divine love which is given to the soul by which it loves God. This entire phenomenon is on the supernatural level of reality. The world of creatures can have no participation here. The sale of all is now known to have been well worth the detachment, suffering, and privation necessary to enter here.

This magnificent work of St. John was written for the most part while he was a prisoner of the Calced Carmelites in their monastery in Toledo, Spain. While redacted later, the substance of the work as composed in prison remained the same and more stanzas were added later. In this work is described a soul longing for union with God. The soul sets out to find its Beloved who has remained hidden. Gradually the soul finds Him, and this canticle tells of the ecstatic joy that grows in the soul at each new discovery about the Beloved. Eventually the spiritual betrothal begins, and the soul rests in its closeness to the Bridegroom. Finally, the spiritual marriage is consummated, and thereafter the soul longs for the Beatific Vision when the actual union with God will never end. This highest state of spiritual perfection possible in this world, the spiritual marriage, could not have happened without poverty of spirit brought about in the sufferings endured in the nights that preceded the spiritual marriage.

Poor in Spirit

Holy detachment

The soul that is approaching the spiritual betrothal is being saturated with supernatural insight and love. As the union grows closer and deeper, the soul receives supernatural graces capable of absorbing the soul completely into divine union. The substance of the soul is transformed from the ordinary to the profound. Every other consideration or interest of this soul is subordinated to the divine love that now flows into it like a great river.

> The reason is that the drink of highest wisdom makes her forget all worldly things. And it seems that her previous knowledge and even all the knowledge of the world, in comparison with this knowledge is pure ignorance.

> Hence, the wise men of God and the wise men of the world are foolish in the eyes of each other, for the one group finds the wisdom and knowledge of God imperceptible and the other finds the same of the knowledge of the world. Wherefore, the knowledge of the world is ignorance to the knowledge of God, and the knowledge of God is ignorance to the knowledge of the world (SC 26:13).

St. John makes it clear that while the soul turns away from natural knowledge in this state of spiritual espousal, it does not lose its acquired knowledge of the natural world. Rather this knowledge is perfected by supernatural knowledge.

> When a faint light is mingled with a bright one, the bright light prevails and is that which illumines. Yet, the faint light is not lost, but rather perfected, even though it is not the light which illumines principally (SC 26:16).

Poverty of spirit is a spiritual disposition of mind and soul, not feigned ignorance. All aspects of the natural faculties are informed by the supernatural infused love and wisdom granted to these souls by God in the spiritual marriage. But, the natural faculties remain able to function according to their nature.

When the soul reaches the spiritual marriage, all the natural appetites are sublimated to this state. One of the things that have happened in this soul that has been brought to this elevated state is the loss of the dominance of these natural appetites.

> It should be known that however spiritual a soul may be there always remains, until she reaches this state of perfection, some little herd of appetites, satisfactions, and other imperfections, natural or spiritual after which she follows, In an effort to pasture and satisfy it (SC 26:18).

> Some have more and others less of this herd, and they follow until, having entered the interior wine cellar to drink all transformed in love, they lose it entirely. In this wine cellar, these herds of imperfections are more easily consumed than the rust and tarnish of metal is consumed by fire. Thus the soul now feels free of all the childish likes and trifles which she pursued, and can say: "And lost the herd which I was following" (SC 26:19).

Humility

The essence of humility is recognition of the immeasurable gap between God and His creation, especially our human soul. Within this recognition, we must come to the realization that our elevation to union with God is only possible by the grace of God to affect that union. The elimination of the appetites and attachments to the things of this world involves some participation on the part of our wills. However, the elimination of the obstacles to union that remain deeply in the substance of the spirit is solely God's work. Submission to the afflictions necessary to move us toward union with God requires trust and a high degree of humility. The soul seeking union must be willing to accept, in poverty of spirit, the fact that there will be no understanding of God as He is, except as He reveals himself, as union is approached. Understanding is a function of the natural faculties, and these faculties are incapable of bringing about this union. Faith in the spirit is the proximate means of receiving the union that the soul so earnestly desires.

> You do very well, O soul, to seek Him ever as one hidden, for you exalt God immensely and approach very near Him when you consider Him higher and deeper than anything you can reach. Hence, pay no attention, neither partially or entirely, to anything which your faculties can grasp. I mean that you should never desire satisfaction in what you understand about God, but in what you do not understand about Him.

> Do not be like the many foolish ones who, in their lowly understanding of God, think that when they do not understand, taste, or experience Him, He is far away and utterly concealed. The contrary belief would be truer...Thus in drawing near Him, you will experience darkness because of the weakness of your eye (SC 1:12).

F. St. John of the Cross: The Living Flame of Love

This work of St. John does not describe a new level of spiritual advancement, but rather looks into the spiritual marriage to describe the properties of that state and the experiences of the fortunate soul that has entered this intimate embrace with its loving God.

Sovereignty of God in His Kingdom

What we find of great interest in *The Living Flame of Love* is that the King has exercised His sovereignty by surrendering Himself to His subject in love beyond telling. This is something God is always willing to do for a soul that is prepared to receive Him, but much purification and purgation must occur first in the soul in order for it to be disposed and able to engage God in this way. How different is this Kingdom from those of the world. It is now apparent beyond contradiction, that entry into God's Kingdom truly requires the shedding of all attachments to creatures except insofar as they are valued solely in God. This union with God in the spiritual espousal and the spiritual marriage, possible only after much suffering and affliction is impossible to over-value or to hold in too much esteem. It is in fact the <u>sole</u> reason for our creation in love by God. The intermediate goals of our life in the natural world must be oriented to this end or they are without value. This soul is now all God's and He is all to it.

> It is in the soul in which less of its own appetites and pleasures dwell where he dwells more alone, more pleased, and more as though in His own house, ruling and governing it. And He dwells more in secret, the more He dwells alone. Thus in this soul in which neither appetite nor other images or forms, nor any affections for created things, dwell, the Beloved dwells secretly with an embrace so much the closer, more intimate, and interior, the purer and more alone the soul is to everything other than God (LF 4:14).

The soul that has entered the spiritual marriage has indeed detached itself from all the attractions and allurements of the world. Otherwise, it could never have arrived at this lofty state. A soul full of God is necessarily empty of all that is not God. Having endured the nights of sense and spirit, humility is firmly established in the consciousness of this soul. It is impossible to exaggerate the separation from the mundane and worldly that has occurred in this soul. The degree of poverty of spirit that has resulted allows this soul to enter substantially into God in this life. The only veil remaining to be torn is that of natural death.

We are accustomed to say, in reference to the Kingdom of God, that it is something that we strive to enter. While in one sense that is true when we say that we have abandoned the kingdom of the prince of this world so that we can enter the Kingdom of God, it is also accurate to say that the Kingdom of God enters into us. St. John of the Cross speaks of the Kingdom of God in this latter sense when he describes the soul's experience of divine love and intimacy in the spiritual marriage. He emphasizes the active role of God and the passive role of the soul in this state of spiritual marriage. In all that has been said by St. John from the beginning of the passive nights until the soul reaches the spiritual marriage, we conclude that throughout this entire period the soul is engaged in a dynamic that is beyond its own power to effect. St. John therefore, sees the Kingdom of God coming into the soul, in addition to the soul entering that Kingdom.

> Thus in this state the soul cannot make acts because the Holy Spirit makes them all and moves it toward them. As a result, all the acts of the soul are divine, since the movement toward these acts and their execution stems from God (LF 1:4).

Holy detachment

It is superfluous to say that a soul in the spiritual marriage is detached from the things of the world and of the flesh, and most importantly from the self. A soul with the least attachment to any of these would never be able to enter the spiritual marriage. We recall St. John's well-known metaphor of the tethered bird. It doesn't matter whether a bird is tethered by a thin thread or a rope; in either case, it cannot fly freely.

> The first two veils (the temporal and the natural) must necessarily be torn in order to obtain this union with God in which all the things of the world are renounced, all the natural appetites and affections mortified, and the natural operations of the soul divinized (LF 1:29).

The soul that has entered the spiritual marriage has also entered the Kingdom of God to an exemplary degree. The unity with God is so great that natural death is a movement within the Kingdom of God, rather than a movement into that Kingdom. Natural death is the perfecting of the union by the removal of the final veil. The death of such a one as this is different from the death of all others. There is nothing of this world for this soul to cling to because the detachment from all that is not God is complete. We hear from time to time of persons who die filled with joy that is inexpressible. Having already entered God's Kingdom, they are anticipating the perfection of their participation in God.

> The death of such persons is very gentle and very sweet, sweeter and more gentle than was their whole spiritual life on earth. For they die with the most sublime impulses and delightful encounters of love resembling the swan whose song is much sweeter at the moment of death (LF 1:30).

Humility

Poverty of spirit, which cannot exist in a soul that has not developed the virtue of humility to a high degree, is possessed by the soul that has entered the spiritual marriage. Pride is the greatest obstacle to growth in the spiritual life. One who is proud believes his progress in the spiritual life to be his own doing. We know that there comes a point in every soul's spiritual journey when it hits a wall that it cannot penetrate. St. John describes this period of aridity and inability to pray as before as the interval between the active nights and the passive nights. The principal distinction between these two nights is that when the active nights are completely finished, the soul that has been an active participant in its spiritual development can go no further through its own efforts. In the passive nights, God must conduct the soul forward, and the soul becomes a receiver of the gifts offered it by God for its spiritual advancement. Without great humility, a soul could never accept this passive role, and would constantly make efforts to retain control of its spiritual life, thus spoiling the whole enterprise. On the other hand, a humble soul that accepts God's sovereignty over it in spiritual matters will advance at a fast pace.

> Spiritual acts are produced instantaneously in the soul, because God infuses them. But those the soul makes of itself can better be referred to as dispositive acts by means of successive desires and affections, which never become perfect acts of love or contemplation, unless, as I say, when God sometimes forms and perfects them very quickly in the spirit (LF 1:33).

I say this in order to make it clear that he who would go to God relying on natural ability and reasoning will not be very spiritual. There are some who think that by pure force and the activity of the senses, which of itself is lowly and no more than natural, they can reach the strength and height of the supernatural spirit. One does not attain to this peak without suppressing and leaving aside the activity of the senses (LF 2:14).

I will close this chapter on the first *Beatitude* with the following quote of St. John of the Cross from *The Living Flame of Love*.

There is nothing else to say about the soul's enjoyment here except that it realizes how appropriately the kingdom of heaven was compared in the Gospel to the grain of mustard seed which, by reason of its intense heat, grows into a large tree, despite its being so small. For the soul is converted, into the immense fire of love which emanates from that enkindled point, at the heart of the spirit.

CHAPTER 2

BLESSED ARE THE MEEK, FOR THEY SHALL POSSES THE EARTH

Meekness is considered weakness by the people of worldly minds. It is frequently looked upon as an inability to muster the courage to resist injustice. Toughness and aggressiveness are celebrated by our society in sports, business and even in driving a car on the roads of the world. In the great false religion of Islam, the lack of meekness reaches deadly proportions. The penalty for having a bible in one's possession in Saudi Arabia is death by decapitation. The means of settling disputes or perceived injustice in the Islamic world is the suicide bomber. On the other hand, in contrast to this mind set, we have Christ before the high Priest standing silent and submissive to the horrors that awaited Him. As a result, all of Christianity, in imitation of Christ, is characterized by the humble, meek submission to injustice. In the eyes of the worldly man, this attitude spells the defeat of the meek. But, in the eyes of Christ, meekness has a much different result: the possession of the earth. What does He mean by possession of the earth?

In the *New Illustrated Edition of Haydock's, Catholic Family Bible, Very Reverend Dr. Husenbeth's Edition, Douay Bible and Rheims Testament*, the note by the commentator Menochius about Mt V: 4, defining the words "possess the earth," states the following about the word earth: "The land of the living, or the kingdom of heaven."[1] In our discussion of the meaning of the second part of this *Beatitude*, we will adopt this concept of the meaning of the words "possess the earth."

We speak of the triumph of the Cross in liturgy and in music. How is it, that such an ignominious scene can be considered a triumph? The answer is easy: by its effects. Our Savior conquered death and redeemed the entire human race by this act of self-giving. Can any greater triumph be imagined? From this triumph, all of Christianity draws its inspiration to imitate the Master. The servant

---

[1] The evangelist prefers calling it the land of the living in this place, to show that the meek, the humble, and the oppressed, who are spoiled of the possession of this earth by the powerful and the proud, shall obtain the inheritance of a better land.

is not greater than the master. The faithful Christian will rise above those who attempt to destroy the meek follower of Christ. This ultimate victory will come about by removing the would-be rulers of this world. However, the triumph is, like His, a spiritual one with eternal consequences. As already seen in the previous chapter, the pearl of great price is obtained by the passive soul that relinquishes all the goods and values of the world in exchange for the ultimate triumph of meekness: the spiritual marriage.

A. St. Teresa of Jesus: The Way of Perfection

Blessed are the meek

In the spiritual doctrine of St. Teresa, humility and meekness are used interchangeably. One of these virtues begets the other, and vice-versa. In each case, these virtues are indispensable for growth in the spiritual life. To be truly humble, one must be meek; and to be truly meek, one must be humble. It is meekness that enables us to bear injustice without complaint or retaliation. It is of our nature to rise up in anger and indignation when we perceive ourselves as being wronged or otherwise treated unjustly. However, St. Teresa counsels against giving into this instinctive response.

> I never seem unable to find a reason for thinking I am being virtuous when I make excuses for myself. There are times when this is lawful, and when not to do it would be wrong, but I have not the discretion (or, better, the humility) to do it only when fitting. For, indeed, it takes great humility to find one-self unjustly condemned and be silent, and to do this is to imitate the Lord Who set us free from all our sins...The truly humble person will have a genuine desire to be thought little of, and persecuted, and condemned unjustly, even in serious matters
> (WP 15).

When the Will of God manifests itself in bringing us hardship and affliction, the meek soul receives the trial willingly, and prepares to endure it for as long as God wishes it to last. The soul lacking the meekness that imitates Christ rises up in rebellion against what God sends to it. Frequently, the hardship becomes the justification for turning one's back on God in anger, failing to glimpse the grace hidden in the event. This soul will then believe it has gotten even with God by leaving Him and resolving never to return. It is alarming how many people succeed in going to their grave in this frame of mind. I am sure that, sadly, each of us knows at least a few people who are on this track to destruction. These souls inherit nothing but eternal sorrow and despair. On the other hand, the soul that receives the Will of God with meekness and acceptance reaps a great reward of holiness and joy, even when in the most miserable of trials. This is the soul that will possess the earth, when in glory all things are made new.

> I repeat that this (never indulging our own will and desire) consists mainly or entirely in our ceasing to care about ourselves and our own pleasures, for the least that anyone who is beginning to serve the Lord truly can offer Him is his life. Once he has surrendered his will to Him, what has he to fear (WP 12)?

> When, on the other hand, some offense is done to us (and we do not feel it an offence to us that it should be so described), I do not see what we can find to complain of. Either we are the bride(s) of this great King or we are not. If we are, what wife is there with a sense of honor who does not accept her share in any dishonour done to her spouse, even though she may do so against her will (WP 13)?

If we are to be where Christ is, we must meekly submit to the abuse that is only too readily at hand for His faithful disciples. If there is any opposition that should be offered, what form it should take will be given to us by the Holy Spirit. The object is not to prevail in victory over our adversaries, but to adhere to the truth no matter what the cost or loss will be. We must be patient and await the inheritance that is promised in this *Beatitude* to the meek.

For they shall possess the earth

Remembering our working definition of the words *possess the earth*, we recall that the land of the living is equated with the kingdom of heaven. The nature of that kingdom has been dealt with extensively in the preceding chapter. However, we can reiterate some of the qualities of that better land from the doctrine of St. Teresa on this subject. The meek are deprived unjustly of what should be theirs by right in the experience of many, and even though so deprived, they do not rise up aggressively and demand justice from their oppressors. Is there any pay-off for this mild behavior, which imitates Christ before the High Priest and before Pilate? There is a reward for this behavior and we must see the reward in spiritual terms. The ultimate good for any soul is not only justice in its many forms, but even more, there is the receiving of the gifts of God given to souls from His mercy.

> The aim of all my advice to you in this book is that we should surrender ourselves wholly to the Creator, place our will in his hands, and detach ourselves from the creatures. As you will already have understood how important this is, I will say no more about it, but I will tell you why our good Master puts these words here. He knows how much we shall gain by rendering this service to His Eternal Father. We are preparing ourselves for the time, which will come very soon, when we will find ourselves at the end of our journey and shall be drinking of living water from the fountain I have described (WP 32).

We cannot say that the masters of this world who have oppressed the meek and deprived them of justice will share the same end as the souls described by St. Teresa in the above quote (Unless, of course, a true repentance and conversion occurs in those souls). In chapter 32 of *The Way of Perfection,* St. Teresa discusses the words from *The Lord's Prayer*, "Thy Will be done." All movements of a soul toward perfection reflect these words of our Lord. These words are the total summary of the spiritual life at all of its various stages. St. Teresa treats those words in exactly that way.

> The *more resolute* we *are in soul and the more* we show Him by our actions that the words we use to Him are not words of mere politeness, the more and more does our Lord draw us to Himself and raise us above all *petty* earthly things, and above ourselves, in order to prepare us to receive great favors from Him, for His rewards for our service will not end with this life (emphasis in the original) (WP 33).

B. St. Teresa of Jesus: The Interior Castle

Blessed are the meek

The Gospels contain several statements by our Lord admonishing his disciples to become like little children. He thanks His Father for revealing to *little ones* the mysteries of His Kingdom. The common attribute of children and little ones is meekness. They are the opposite of the rich, the powerful, and the learned. These little ones are not of sufficient importance that they could affect the course of any worldly or historical event. They are pushed or pulled by those in power in the direction that best suits the ambitions of those in control. But in this *Beatitude,* Christ announces that all of this will be reversed. The meek and child-like will inherit the earth. They will be the rulers over those who will fall from power and over the very earth itself. But their power will be a very different manner of ruling. They will rule with the power of divine love in perfect conformity to the Will of God.

The quality or virtue of meekness should translate into submission to the Will of God. All acts or even thoughts of rebellion against what He desires for us will disappear with the correct degree of meekness. Love of God prompted by this attitude of meekness is not an emotion of passivity, but is a willingness to accept from God what He wishes to send us.

> ...the important thing is not to think much but to love much; and so do that which best stirs you to love. Perhaps we don't know what love is. I wouldn't be very surprised, because it doesn't consist in great delight but in desiring with strong determination to please God in everything, in striving, insofar as possible, not to offend Him, and in asking Him for the advancement of the honor and glory of His Son and the increase of the Catholic Church (IC IV:1:7).

We frequently find disappointment in our spiritual life if the things we earnestly pray for are not granted, or not soon enough to satisfy us. We are tempted to conclude that God does not pay attention to our prayer, or is indifferent to our needs. The temptation to stop praying is very great. "What's the use," we say, "God cares little for me if He will not grant my prayers, even the ones I raise to Him for spiritual things, or for the strength to overcome a persistent sin or fault." This spiritual attitude evidences an absence of a needed element in the soul: meekness, understood as a failure to bow to the Will of God.

> Provided that we don't give up, the Lord will guide everything for our benefit, even though we may not find someone to teach us. There is no other remedy for this evil of giving up prayer than to begin again; otherwise the soul will gradually lose more each day – and please God that it will understand this fact (IC II:1:10).

The soul that perseveres regardless of its perception of indifference on the part of God to its petitions and its afflictions will, in every case, be rewarded in God's good time. The reward will primarily be what it most earnestly seeks: greater union with God and with His Will. This result, to be valued above all other things, cannot be obtained by a prideful demand for certain results or for divine favors or consolations, but only by the willing acceptance of what God wishes to send us. The union desired will belong only to the meek and humble who follow our Lord's admonition: "learn from me, for I am meek and humble of heart" (Mt 11:29).

> The soul must wait until the Lord desires to give this favor, (great consolation after a great spiritual trial) just as there is no way to resist it or remove it when it comes. The soul is left with greater contempt of the world than before because it sees that nothing in the world was any help to it in that torment, and it is much more detached from creatures because it now sees that only the Creator can console and satisfy it (IC VI:11:10).

For they shall possess the earth

The comments of Menochius to Mt V:4 calls the inheritance to be received by the meek a better land. That, of course, would have to be the Kingdom of God. St. Teresa treats the qualities that a soul has acquired that has entered the Seventh Dwelling place. I could place here the entire treatise on the Seventh Dwelling place in order to present a complete picture of these qualities that she enumerates. They are all characteristics of a better land, so to speak, in which the soul now dwells. However, the soul's dwelling place is now interior and it rejects exterior and physical benefits in order to preserve this new interior dwelling place. In Chapter VII: 3, she nicely summarizes some of the more outstanding qualities of this new and better land.

> Now then, we are saying that this little butterfly has already died, with supreme happiness for having found repose and because Christ lives in it. Let us see what life it lives, or how this life differs from the life it was living. For from the effects, we shall see if what was said is true. By what I can understand, these effects are the following:
>
> The first effect is a forgetfulness of self, for truly the soul, seemingly, no longer is, as was said. Everything is such that this soul doesn't know or recall that there will be heaven, life, or honor for it, because it employs all it has in procuring the honor of God.
>
> The second effect is that the soul has a great desire to suffer, but not the kind of desire that disturbs it as previously.
>
> These souls also have a deep interior joy when they are persecuted, with much more peace than that mentioned, and without any hostile feelings toward those who do, or desire to do, them evil.
>
> There is a great detachment from everything and a desire to be always either alone or occupied in something that will benefit some soul. There are no interior trials or feelings of dryness, but the soul lives with a remembrance and tender love of our Lord (IC VII:3:1, 2, 4, 5 & 8).

We could not imagine a better land than this.

C. St. John of the Cross: The Ascent of Mt. Carmel

Blessed are the meek

The early steps in the spiritual journey described by St. John in *The Ascent of Mt. Carmel* are accompanied by the barest beginnings of an attitude of surrender: surrender of our willfulness and self-centeredness. He says that the soul "went out unseen, my house being now all stilled." This soul is *unseen* because its movement toward God is not hindered by natural appetites and basic imperfections, especially pride, although the roots of these imperfections remain imbedded deeply in the soul, and must await greater growth in order to be eliminated. However, the soul is now changed by grace and the change allows it to begin its movement toward God. The greatest obstacle to true union with God is pride, both natural and supernatural. Pride is the root cause of self-centeredness and the principal obstacle to the acceptance of grace. The opposite virtue to pride is humility a close cousin of meekness. Both partake of the correct understanding of the soul's position in relation to God. The sufficiently humble soul is necessarily meek in its demeanor because its desire for personal gain is diminished to the point of indifference toward recognition and reward in this world. St. John instructs the soul beginning its journey to God to strive for a disposition that will enable it to advance:

> First, try to act with contempt for yourself and desire that all others do likewise.
>
> Second, endeavor to speak in contempt of yourself and desire all others to do so.
>
> Third, try to think lowly and contemptuously of yourself and desire that all others do the same (AS I:13:9).

Reflection on these thoughts of St. John will readily lead us to conclude that the virtue of meekness will be the inevitable result of the effort to acquire these dispositions, which flow from the humility engendered from the attitudes described above.

If one were to undertake a spiritual journey intending to end at union with God, and believe that he could attain to that end by the use of his own abilities, he would fail. Such a soul thinks that if he eliminates obvious sin from his life and adopts a regimen of prayer and fasting, the desired end would be achieved without anything more to be added to these things. This is a soul immersed in pride, and completely lacking in the meekness that comes from the imitation of Christ. Christ did not endeavor to control His fate. Rather, He humbly surrendered to the Will of His Father, and went meekly and silently to His death. The element missing from the soul described above is not only faith, the only proximate means of achieving union with God, but also the surrender of his will to God's desire for his life. Faith perfects and replaces understanding, and charity perfects and replaces natural love. Both of these Theological Virtues are gifts from God, and without them union with God cannot be achieved. The soul that believes it can reach God through its own abilities is lacking in both humility and meekness. In such a soul, the gift of the Theological Virtues will not find acceptance.

> Such is faith to the soul – it informs us of matters we have never seen or known, either in themselves or in their likenesses; in fact nothing like them exists. The light of natural knowledge does not show us the object of faith, since this object is un-proportioned to any of the senses...Faith manifestly, is a dark night for man, but in this very way it gives him light (AS II:3:3).

> The entire matter of reaching union with God consists in purging the will of its appetites and feelings, so that from a human and lowly will it may be changed into the divine will, made identical with the will of God (AS III:16:3).

Notice that when St. John speaks of transforming the will into the divine will, he uses terms of passivity: "may be changed into." Without the meekness that imitates Christ, the necessary passivity to be receptive to God's work in the soul will be missing. As a result, the soul will not experience the transformation described. The first efforts of the soul should be the development of the attitude of passive meekness and receptiveness to the workings of God in the soul.

For they shall possess the earth

Returning to our examination of the words *inherit the earth*, we recall the comments of Menochius on these words to the effect that the true meaning of them is that the inheritance will be of the kingdom of heaven, and not of a natural place on the earth. St. John makes the same point quite clearly regarding the instances of misunderstanding the word of God in scripture.

> It is impossible for someone unspiritual to judge and understand the things of God correctly; and one is not spiritual if one judges them literally. And thus even though they are clothed in that literal meaning, they are not understood (AS II:19:11).

Added to this, St. John of the Cross explains further how some souls misunderstand the meaning intended by God in His words to us by their applying a literal meaning to words heard in the soul, read in scripture, or in rare cases communicated by God to the soul audibly. This error leads to much consternation in souls who expect God's words to come to a literal conclusion for them or for others, as they understand these words. What God promises His creatures are always fulfilled, but not always understood. To illustrate this phenomenon let us look at two examples that St. John uses:

> Suppose God says to a saintly man who is deeply afflicted because of persecution by his enemies: "I will free you from your enemies." This prophecy could be very true; nonetheless, it will happen that his enemies prevail and kill him. Anyone who had given these words a temporal interpretation would have been deceived, because God had been speaking of the true and principal freedom and victory-salvation, in which the soul is free and victorious over its enemies much more truly and loftily than if liberated from them here below (AS II:19:12).
>
> Here is another example: A soul has intense desires to be a martyr. God answers, "You shall be a martyr"; and He bestows deep interior consolation and confidence in the truth of this promise. Regardless of the promise, this person in the end

does not die a martyr; yet the promise will have been true. Why, then, was there no literal fulfillment? Because the promise will be fulfilled in its chief, essential meaning: the bestowal of the essential love and reward of a martyr. God truly grants the soul the essence of both its desire and His promise, because the formal desire of the soul was not a manner of death, but the service of God through martyrdom and the exercise of a martyr's love for him (AS II:19:13).

These two examples of St. John clarify for us that Christ did not mean that meek souls will eventually become powerful in this world, but will receive their inheritance in the life to come. This leads to the conclusion that the *earth* to be inherited is the *new earth* spoken of in the book of Revelation that will descend from heaven. "And I saw a new heaven and a new earth. For the first heaven and the first earth passed away, and the sea is no more" (Rev 21:1). The literal meaning of inheriting the earth by the meek would be scant reward indeed.

D. St. John of the Cross: The Dark Night

Blessed are the meek

In this work, St. John examines the affliction and suffering each soul must endure if it is to advance along the road to union with God. He treats here of the passive nights of sense and spirit; those nights in which all the transforming work in the soul is accomplished by God. The soul at this point is in an attitude of receptive passivity to this work of God. What is required in these nights in order to advance toward union with God is beyond the capacity of the soul to do. The imperfections of the soul are so deeply rooted as a result of original sin that the human soul cannot reach those roots in order to excise them from its self. First, the sensory part of the soul must be conformed to the spirit, and then the spirit must be purged of all imperfection. The reality of this condition cannot be grasped by the soul lacking in the meekness of Christ that allows it to accept the afflictions that come to it and that are essential to the transformation required for divine union. The idea of some kind of achievement through its own efforts in the spiritual life must be eliminated from the thinking of this soul. This soul should recall Christ's admonition: "learn from me for I am meek and humble of heart," and how that attitude was lived out in His own life. These attitudes are the absolute absence of worldly achievement by Him, the apparent failure of His life, which ended on the cross, and the manner with which He went to His end, meek and silent. All of which illustrates the disposition of soul required to receive the Graces to be given by God in these passive nights. Great trust in God is indispensable to such a passive attitude, as is a willingness to receive what God gives, be it sweet or painful. Abundant joy is very likely to fill such a soul, even when it is afflicted with suffering.

> They must be content simply with a loving and peaceful attentiveness to God, and live without the concern, without the effort, and without the desire to taste or feel Him. All these desires disquiet the soul and distract it from the peaceful quiet and sweet idleness of the contemplation which is being communicated to it (DN I:10:4).

In the passive night of the spirit, the soul experiences acute pain caused by its awareness of its inability to perfect itself. If such a soul was not of a meek disposition before, this night and its afflictions will bring it to the meekness that imitates Christ. The first cousins of humility and meekness are imposed on the soul from the sufferings of this night. Whatever was lacking of these two virtues before entering this night of dark contemplation will be supplied here.

For they shall possess the earth

The fruits of a perfected soul that unites its will with God and abandons all self-seeking are now harvested for the benefit of the soul itself and for the benefit of others with whom it comes into contact. If this soul perseveres in the passivity of humility and meekness before God's will, its soul and its growth will resemble the famous metaphor of the burning log employed by St. John in this work.

> For the sake of further clarity in this matter, we ought to note that this purgative and loving knowledge or divine light we are speaking of, has the same effect on a soul that fire has on a log of

wood. The soul is purged and prepared for union with the divine light just as the wood is prepared for transformation into the fire. Fire, when applied to wood, first dehumidifies it; dispelling all moisture and making it give off any water it contains. Then it gradually turns the wood black, makes it dark and ugly, and even causes it to emit a bad odor. By drying out the wood, the fire brings to light and expels all those ugly and dark accidents which are contrary to fire. Finally, by heating and enkindling it from without, the fire transforms the wood into itself and makes it as beautiful as it is itself. Once transformed, the wood no longer has any activity or passivity of its own, except for its weight and its quantity which is denser than the fire. For it possesses the properties and performs the actions of fire: it is dry and it dries; it is hot and it gives off heat; it is brilliant and it illumines; and it is also light, much lighter than before. It is the fire that produces all these properties in the wood (DN II:10:1).

E. St. John of the Cross: The Spiritual Canticle

Blessed are the meek

This most poetic and charming of all the works of St. John of the Cross follows a soul along the road to spiritual espousal and ultimately to spiritual marriage. The painful longing and searching for the Beloved is described in the early stanzas with expressions of impatience and disappointment on the part of the soul over being deprived of union with its Beloved. These stanzas tell of the searching and the questioning of created things regarding the whereabouts of the object of the soul's love. As the soul progresses along its way, it gradually comes into contact with the Bridegroom through His creation, and through His desire to unite with the soul. Then at last, both the soul and its Bridegroom unite in a mutual surrender to each other. More than anything else, by His surrender of Himself to a created soul, the meekness of the Bridegroom is manifested. The great and all-powerful Creator condescending to a lowly and powerless creature is almost impossible to grasp and accept. But nevertheless, it is true beyond dispute. The same meekness and surrender is true of the soul that has learned meekness from its Beloved along the way of affliction and mortification that it has traveled.

> Because this grace exalts, honors, and beautifies her in His sight, God loves her ineffably. If before she had grace, He loved her only on account of Himself, now that she is in grace He loves her not only on account of Himself but also on account of herself (SC 33:7).

For they shall possess the earth

Such an expression of God's love, and what it accomplishes, in the willing and meek soul, leaves one speechless. This soul that has reached such a sublime union with God and possesses Him so completely has surely inherited all that properly belongs to God. The Beloved has held back nothing from such a fortunate soul. And in return, the soul has meekly and oh so willingly surrendered its entire self to the Bridegroom, and desires none but Him. All that made this soul unsightly and blemished with imperfections has been wiped away by the love of God manifested by the profound graces extended to it over the course of its journey to Him.

The soul that has advanced so far in spiritual perfection has done so, not its own extraordinary efforts, but because of the work of God in this soul. Its willingness to accept the favors extended to it by God is the total of its participation in the growth in spirituality it has experienced. What has really happened to this soul is that it has begun to resemble God Himself in its perfection, and therefore God loves the soul in the same manner He loves Himself. No soul could possibly bring this transformation about through its own efforts alone.

> With God, to love the soul is to put her somehow in Himself and make her His equal. Thus, He loves the soul within Himself, with Himself, that is, with the very love by which He loves Himself (SC 32:6).

In stanza 34, St. John expresses the gentleness and love with which God is disposed toward this soul. He puts into the mouth of the Bridegroom the description of the soul as a *small white dove*.

This description comes from the Song of Solomon in the Old Testament (Ct 2:14) from which St. John frequently draws, in order to set forth his concepts of God's gentle love for His creatures. The dove is unsurpassed as an example of meekness and sweetness both in poetry and in reality. It always appears in pairs as a demonstration of endearing love for another of its species, and has no aggressiveness toward any other creature. The use of the word *white* indicates the purity of the soul that has reached the spiritual marriage.

> He calls the soul a "white dove" because of the whiteness and purity imparted by the grace she has found in God. And He calls her "dove" because this is the name He gives her in the Canticle (Ct. 2:10) to denote both the simplicity and meekness of her character and her loving contemplation. For the dove is not only simple and meek, without gall, but also has bright and loving eyes (SC 34:3).

F. St. John of the Cross: The Living Flame of Love

Blessed are the meek

The soul that St. John of the Cross describes in this work is one that has gone as far as a soul can advance in spirituality in this life. Unity with God has been realized and is described with particularity in *The Spiritual Canticle*. The latter verses of that work concern the spiritual marriage and the manner in which it has been achieved in the soul by God. This spiritual marriage is the high water mark of spirituality possible in this life. Among the many attitudes required of the soul along the way to spiritual marriage, meekness and humility are among the most important. So we can say that one who has arrived at the spiritual marriage has developed the virtue of meekness to a high degree. In *The Living Flame of Love,* St. John of the Cross looks into the spiritual marriage to examine the quality of the union of love between God and the soul. There is no further need to discuss or analyze progress in the virtue of meekness at this point because this soul has acquired meekness in a highly perfected form, along with many other virtues and spiritual qualities.

> It should be understood that the soul now speaking has reached this enkindled degree, and is so inwardly transformed in the fire of love and has received such quality from it that it is not merely united to this fire but produces within it a living flame. The soul feels this and speaks of it thus in these stanzas with intimate and delicate sweetness of love, burning in love's flame, and stressing in these stanzas some of its effects (LF Prologue:4).

For they shall possess the earth

In this work, St. John describes the depth and the exaltation of the soul that has abandoned all that is not God, and has entered the spiritual marriage with its Beloved. Since this work is concerned with the results of the generous bestowing by God of Himself upon a soul, the discussion centers on the profound new life the soul has entered because of the marriage. This new life is its inheritance received from its Father. It's all is God and it has in effect left behind all creatures, except as they exist from God and in God. To this soul, all of creation has no value other than the extent to which it exists in God. In itself and separate from God creation and particularly the world and its interests and pursuits are without value. A soul completely absorbed into God, as it is in the spiritual marriage, looks nowhere else for its life. It has in effect inherited everything: its spiritual legacy and all that belongs to God including *the earth* in the sense set forth in this *Beatitude*.

> It is in the soul in which less of its own appetites and pleasures dwell where He dwells more alone, more pleased, and more as though in His own house, ruling and governing it. And He dwells more in secret, the more He dwells alone. Thus in this soul in which neither any appetite nor other images or forms, nor any affections for created things, dwell, the Beloved dwells secretly with an embrace so much the closer, more intimate and interior, the purer and more alone the soul is to everything other than God (LF 4:14).

CHAPTER 3

BLESSED ARE THEY WHO MOURN, FOR THEY SHALL BE COMFORTED

There are many causes of mourning. We mourn for losses of all kinds: death of a loved one, loss of a valued object, loss of employment, failure at an important task or the failure, illness or adversity of a dear friend or family member. These are all natural causes of mourning. There are also supernatural causes for mourning among which is the dismal condition of the society in which we live, namely the absence of obedience to the commands of God clearly enumerated in the Ten Commandments. In addition, there is the refusal to accept and put into the proper perspective in our lives, the teaching of Christ, the Logos and of His Church. Christ, the revelation of all truth regarding God and His creation, is not only ignored by this world, but He is also aggressively attacked in order to destroy His presence and influence in the world. All of these things are cause for mourning, and in some cases for great mourning. It is for these causes of mourning that comfort is promised by Christ, but not only for these causes. There is another kind of mourning that more closely parallels the subject matter of this book. It is this mourning and its causes that we will focus on in this chapter. Many of the other causes for mourning will be touched on tangentially, but they will be related to our main cause for mourning in a secondary way. This principal mourning that we shall discuss, along with its causes, is the dreadful trials and affliction of the soul that is traveling the rough road and the narrow way to union with God. This is the core of Carmelite spirituality: the hoped for goal of union with God, and the privation, purgation and suffering that must be endured to reach that goal. The cause for mourning and the comfort that is given by God to the mourning soul is the principal theme of the writings and spiritual doctrine of our two Carmelite Doctors of the Church. Because of the clear dichotomy between mourning and comforting, I will first address a particular cause for mourning found in the works of our two saints, and then find the comforting that either accompanies that mourning or soon follows it. We will see that it is possible that eventually all cause for mourning ceases, and only the comfort of union with God remains at the end of the spiritual journey.

A. St. Teresa of Jesus: The Way of Perfection

The mourning and the comfort

When a soul, by the movements of Grace, begins its trek along the road that leads to union with God, it finds that there are many things in its life, both exterior and interior imperfections that should be the cause of mourning. However, the level of awareness of these imperfections is nearly non - existent at this time, and so the typical soul at the beginning of its journey does not mourn over what will later cause it great anguish. In this work, St. Teresa addresses some matters that are of great concern to her regarding the attitudes and dispositions of heart of her sisters that constitute obstacles to the way of perfection, matters that equally apply to those in the lay state. She first laments the attachment to money and with it, an attachment to the honor money usually brings to its possessor, as well as the anxiety that the lack of money usually causes in one who is without it. She cautions us to not mourn the absence of wealth or the goods of the world, and instead to look only to the riches bestowed by the Lord:

> For the love of the Lord, let us not forget this: you have forgone a regular income; forgo worry about food as well, or you will lose everything. Worrying about getting money from other people seems to me like thinking about what other people enjoy...Leave these anxieties to Him who can move everyone, who is the Lord of all money and of all who possess money...seldom or *never* is a poor man honoured by the world; however worthy of honour he may be, he is apt rather to be despised by it (WP 2).

We know from experience that those who are in poverty are disdained by the world. They are shunned by the well-to-do and frequently even by those who are of modest means. We conclude that they *are not one of us* or *in our class* and we should avoid it whenever possible. The poor of the world mourn not only over their dire need, but also over the response the world gives to their poverty: the shunning and disdain manifested toward them. They receive no comfort in the form of assistance, understanding, or sympathy from these people of the world. But there is another source of comfort for them from One who values their poverty.

While St. Teresa is addressing her sisters in the convents of the Reform in *The Way of Perfection*, what she says applies equally to all regardless of their state in life. So it is with this question of poverty. Both the mourning it causes, and the comfort that is available to the soul, applies to everyone:

> It is when I possess least that I have the fewest worries and the Lord knows that, as far as I can tell, I am more afflicted when there is excess of anything than when there is lack of it...Keep your eyes fixed upon your Spouse: it is for Him to sustain you; and if He is pleased with you, even those who like you least will give you food, if unwillingly, as you have found by experience...Let us to some extent resemble our King, Who had no house save the porch in Bethlehem where He was born and the Cross on which He died (WP 20).

The greatest cause for mourning expressed in the writings of St. Teresa is the lack of virtue and spirituality that draws the soul toward union with God. There are two subjects in *The Way of Perfection* that she attaches great importance to and which cause her great sorrow when they are lacking - love and prayer.

Love of creatures and the things of this world, when they completely occupy the attention of a soul, present a very large obstacle to the love of God that St. Teresa seeks for all the readers of her writings. If a soul has limited its affections to these other loves, it is a great cause for mourning. This kind of love of creatures and the things of the world is frequently self-seeking and oriented inwardly toward the benefit of the one who loves. On the other hand, what St. Teresa seeks for us is a love outwardly directed to God primarily and to His creatures secondarily, but only as they are in Him, and not only for themselves. If this love is lacking, it is cause for great mourning by such a soul or for this soul by others.

> Now it seems to me that, when God has brought someone to a clear knowledge of the world, and of its nature, and of the fact that another world (or let us say, another kingdom) exists, and that there is a great difference between the one and the other, the one being eternal and the other only a dream; and of

> what it is to love the Creator and what to love the creature (this must be discovered by experience, for it is a very different matter from merely thinking about it and believing it); when one understands by sight and experience what can be gained by the one practice and lost by the other, and what the Creator is and what the creature, and many other things which the Lord teaches to those who are willing to devote themselves to being taught by Him in prayer, or whom His Majesty wishes to teach – then one loves very differently from those of us who have not advanced thus far (WP 6).

The soul that advances to the true love of God is blessed indeed. It is only from this love that real consolation comes to the soul uncluttered by concerns for the things of this world. This love seeks only union with the Beloved. There is no thought of personal gain for the soul that loves this way. Even in the face of great affliction, joy and consolation are present in this love. It is unlike any other love experienced by man, because it resides entirely in the spirit. In this love, comfort is bestowed on the soul beyond all measure.

> I repeat once more that this love is a similitude and copy of that which was borne for us by the good Lover, Jesus. It is for that reason that it brings us such immense benefits, for it makes us embrace every kind of suffering, so that others, without having to endure the suffering, may gain its advantages (WP 7).

In the beginning, many souls experience problems in their approach to prayer. St. Teresa discusses these problems in great detail. These imperfections will cause the soul trouble in its advancement in prayer and should alert the soul to the possibility of being misled by its own nature, or in some cases by the devil, resulting in a loss of the benefits that should flow from prayer. These imperfections are cause for mourning as the soul struggles to advance in purification of its prayer, and to remove self seeking from its search for God.

The first imperfection in prayer discussed by St. Teresa is distraction during meditation. She observes that a soul ruminating about the end of all things may find itself concentrating on the attractiveness of the things that will be lost. She distinguishes between meditation brought on by the soul itself and the contemplation given by God. In the former, distraction is very common and very disturbing to the soul when it realizes that it has been taken from its prayer to matters that focus on the self and the things of the world. In contemplation, God so dominates the soul and suspends its natural faculties that it is without distraction regardless of the circumstances surrounding these moments of prayer.

In a more serious discussion of imperfection in prayer, St. Teresa raises a caution to the soul that has an excess of fervor in prayer. The consolations are so sweet that they are sought constantly. She suspects that in some cases, this is the work of the devil, and prudence in prayer should always be exercised.

> I advise anyone who attains to an experience of this fierce thirst to watch herself carefully, for I think she will have to contend with this temptation (indiscretion). She may not die of her thirst, but her health will be ruined, and she will involuntarily give her feelings outward expression, which ought at all costs to be avoided…Whenever we are assailed by these strong impulses stimulating the increase in our desire, let us take great care not to add to them ourselves but to check them gently by thinking of something else (WP 19).

The soul that sets out to reach a relationship with God that transcends the power of the human faculties, and one who is receptive to the outstretched hand of God, will always find its reward in the response He desires to give. His touches of the soul will lift the soul above itself and bring it to the point of a real loving exchange with its Creator. While the rewards of consolation will not always be present to a soul pursuing God in prayer, He will give the soul all it needs to encourage it to proceed forward toward Him.

> I now repeat this: His Majesty, being Who He is and understanding our weakness, has provided for

us. But He did not say: "Some must come by this way and others by that." His mercy is so great that He has forbidden none to strive to come and drink of this fountain of life. Blessed be He forever (WP 20).

B. St. Teresa of Jesus: The Interior Castle

This masterpiece of the spiritual life by St. Teresa is in fact a study of growth in prayer. In the course of analyzing the various levels of prayer, she examines the state of the soul at each level of spiritual advancement and she equates that advancement with growth in prayer. The beginnings of the soul's spiritual journey are meager indeed. Very little growth is experienced until the soul reaches the third mansion of the castle, at which time the soul has become somewhat proficient in the spiritual life. This soul is not in such constant danger of giving up and falling back as it was in the earlier mansions. However, in the third mansion the soul has not yet entered into the deep spiritual transformation of the later mansions that will raise it to union with God.

The First Three Dwelling Places

The mourning

In the first mansion of the interior castle, the soul is not occupied with the things of God. Its movement forward in matters spiritual is very tenuous and constantly threatened with abandonment and failure. The weakness of the soul causes it to fall from Grace while a small interest in moving toward God flickers in its heart, but never really ignites into even a small flame. Its affections are truly, very divided. This soul is not yet aware of how to respond to God's grace, and frequently runs from it when it is presented to it.

> Thus, there are some souls so ill and so accustomed to being involved with external matters that there is no remedy, nor does it seem they can enter within themselves. They are now so used to dealing always with the insects and vermin that are in the wall surrounding the castle that they become almost like them (IC I:1:6).

> Sometimes they do put all these things aside, and the self-knowledge and awareness that they are not proceeding correctly in order to get to the door is important. Finally, they enter the first, lower rooms. But so many reptiles get in with them that they are prevented from seeing the beauty of the castle and from calming down…(IC I:1:8).

As the soul moves into the second mansion, a conflict between faith and the soul's undeveloped reason occurs. Reason insists that the things of the world should not be disdained and rejected, but valued for themselves. Faith, on the other hand points out that all of these natural attractions will end, and that those who devoted their lives to them are in their graves without the things they loved. Faith must triumph in this contest or the soul will be unable to advance.

> But, oh my Lord and my God, how the whole world's habit of getting involved in vanities vitiates everything! Our faith is so dead that we desire what we see more than what faith tells us. And, indeed, we see only a lot of misfortune in those who go after these visible vanities (IC II:1:5).

The conflict in the soul between the natural things of the world, and those matters pertaining to faith intensifies in the third mansion. However, this soul is now more able to resist any inclination to fall back from its pursuit of God, and rather searches harder for the union it now so desires. This soul is still very much functioning on the natural level of its being, although moments of supernatural contact are occasionally given by God to encourage the soul to endure the obstacles to its advancement: its own weakness and the onslaughts of the devil and the world. At this time perseverance is the most needed virtue, along with humility that prevents discouragement from becoming so dominant that it leads to giving up the task of going on toward union with God. The backward impetus becomes quite insistent at times, and we will never be able to succeed in our quest without the grace of perseverance.

> This renunciation (of all worldly things and possessions) is a good enough preparation if one

perseveres in it and doesn't turn back and become involved with the vermin in the first rooms, even if it is only in desire. But this perseverance includes the condition – and note that I am advising you of this – that you consider yourselves useless servants, as St. Paul or Christ, says and believe that you have not put our Lord under any obligation to grant these kind of favors (IC III:2:8).

The comfort

The soul is striving through these first three mansions to *keep alive* in the spiritual life. So many circumstances and people seem to be pulling and tugging at the coat tails of the soul to pull it back from its task. It is in great need of comfort and consolation from God which has the effect of strengthening the soul, and He will not be found wanting in this regard.

> Just as it doesn't do us any harm to reflect upon the things there are in heaven and what the blessed enjoy – it doesn't do us any harm to see that it is possible in this exile for so great a God to commune with foul-smelling worms; and, upon seeing this come to love a goodness so perfect and a mercy so immeasurable (IC I:1:3).

> For just as all the streams that flow from a crystal-clear fount are also clear, the works of a soul in grace, because they proceed from this fount of life, in which the soul is planted like a tree, are most pleasing in the eyes of both God and man (IC I:2:2).

> Yet this Lord desires intensely that we love Him and seek His company, so much so that from time to time He calls us to draw near Him. And His voice is so sweet the poor soul dissolves at not doing immediately what He commands (IC II:1:2).

We should not make the mistake that because we are so actively involved in our own advancement in spiritual perfection in the first three mansions, that God is only an interested observer and by-stander. On the contrary, we would never even begin to look toward Him if it had not originated in His gratuitous movement of the soul, by His Grace, to seek Him. And as we proceed along our spiritual journey, He remains constant in his watchful solicitude of us and of our progress in making our way to Him.

It is not uncommon for a soul that has reached the third mansion to have periods of discouragement. This discouragement takes two forms. First, one is discouraged over some event or the person's perception of something that has happened. Perhaps it is a failure to respond well to a situation that presents itself, either a natural everyday human thing or something pertaining to the spiritual life and practices of this soul. This causes the soul regret and sorrow. Second, one becomes discouraged over one's inability to remain tranquil and trusting toward God as they go through the matter that is afflicting them. They believe that their spiritual development and growth is further along than it really is, and therefore they should not be troubled as they are over these events that disturb their peace. This discouragement demonstrates a lack of humility. If the soul passes out of the third mansion to the higher mansions, this discouragement should diminish and eventually disappear. However, while the soul is struggling with this matter, it stands in great need of God's comfort, strength, and assistance. Even when God allows the soul to suffer these kinds of afflictions, and sometimes for a long time, He usually brings the soul comfort and consolation.

> We shall be walking while weighed down with this mud of our human misery, which is not so with those who ascend to the remaining rooms. But in these rooms of which we are speaking, the Lord, as one who is just or even merciful, does not fail to pay; for He always gives much more than we deserve by giving us consolations far greater than those we find in the comforts and distractions of life (IC III:2:9).

The Last Four Dwelling Places

The mourning

One might think that after the soul moves ahead from the third mansion into the fourth mansion and the subsequent mansions that all mourning is turned to comfort. This is certainly not the case. The causes of sorrow that the soul endures after the third mansion are of a different kind, and not just a difference in degree. It is here that the soul enters the realm of the supernatural. God is more active in these later mansions in bringing the soul forward, and this movement is accompanied by a new kind of suffering. It is now God who afflicts the soul rather than the natural events and relationships of the individual's life. Great weaknesses that were always in the soul unseen remain. These weaknesses cause trouble by inclining the soul to seek what it does not deserve from God, rather than wait for His mercy to give what He desires and what the soul needs. When it fails to receive these favors, the soul very often allows discouragement to invade its tranquility. Discouragement is one of the devil's most powerful weapons against a soul that is earnestly seeking a close relationship with God. With discouragement goes a loss of trust in God and His mercy, and no progress is possible if that happens. Such an unfortunate soul remains motionless until its trust returns.

> We go about here below like foolish little shepherds, for while it seems that we are getting some knowledge of You it must amount to no more than nothing; for even in our own selves there are great secrets that we don't understand (IC IV:2:5).

> I advise them so strongly not to place themselves in the occasion of sin because the devil tries much harder for a soul of this kind than for very many to who (sic) the Lord does not grant these favors. And even though the devil may have no other reason than to see who it is to whom His Majesty shows particular love, that's sufficient for him to wear himself out trying to lead the soul to perdition (IC IV:3:10).

As the soul moves into the fifth mansion, an old problem begins to intensify: that of deception by the devil. He sees this soul growing so greatly in its relationship with God that he realizes that this soul will soon escape his grasp unless he acts quickly and decisively. His avenue of entrance into the soul is the imagination. The soul's will is firmly fixed on God's Will at this stage (this unity of wills will increase in the later mansions), and so the devil must seek the only entryway available to him – the imagination. In this period, the soul experiences many favors in prayer that are of a supernatural origin, but it is still afflicted with trials.

> Briefly, in one way or another, there must be a cross while we live. And with respect to anyone who says that after he arrived here he always enjoyed rest and delight I would say that he never arrived but that perhaps he had experienced some spiritual delight – if he had entered into the previous dwelling place – and his experience had been helped along by natural weakness or perhaps even by the devil who gives him peace so as afterward to wage much greater war against him. (IC V:2:9).

We see from this quote that the devil enters through the natural faculties. The manner by which God enters the soul to make His abode there is the domain of God alone, from which the devil is forever excluded.

As one progresses to the sixth mansion, a severe increase in trials is presented to the soul. What God is prepared to bestow on this soul must come at a price commensurate with the immense gifts He wishes to grant. And so this strengthened soul is afflicted with trials that it could not bear earlier in its journey to union with God. These trials are of a different nature than its earlier trials that came from conflicts engendered by its own will refusing to surrender completely to God's Will, and from deep imperfections that remained unpurged and unpurified. These trials stem from its painful longing for complete union with God in the spiritual marriage that still remains beyond the soul's reach.

> Oh, God help me, what interior and exterior trials the soul suffers before entering the seventh dwelling place!

> Indeed, sometimes I reflect and fear that if a soul knew beforehand, its natural weakness would find it most difficult to have the determination to suffer and pass through these trials, no matter what blessings were represented to it – unless it had arrived at the seventh dwelling place (IC VI:1:1-2).

The experiences of great spiritual pain mixed with moments of ecstatic love for God are so varied and frequent in the soul in the sixth mansion, that a complete analysis of these phenomena would extend this book to nearly twice its planned length. We will have to be satisfied with a summary explanation of this remarkable co-existence of seemingly opposite experiences in the soul at the same time: one of great joy and one of exquisite pain. This soul that has moved very close to God enjoys its increasing love for Him; while at the same time its sorrow over its sins and failures to love God as He deserves, intensifies to an unbearable degree. This soul would not be able to bear this pain unless God strengthened it with His grace, and gave it the courage to bear the pain. When its love for God was much less it was not so disturbed by its sins, and the injustice of treating God with mediocrity. But now, in this mansion, the soul's faculties have been opened and enlightened, and touched by God in a more intimate way, and its grief over its failures is in truth unbearable. Consequently, as it is enraptured by God's many favors, its suffering increases greatly.

> Even though they feel secure and cannot believe that the favor when granted by His Majesty, is from any other spirit than from God, the torment returns immediately since the favor is something that passes quickly, and the remembrance of sins is always present, and the soul sees faults in itself, which are never lacking (IC VI:1:8).

> In this respect, too, great courage is necessary, for this favor (raptures) is something frightening. If our Lord were not to give such courage, the soul would always go about deeply distressed. For it reflects on what His Majesty does for it and turns back to look at itself, at how little it serves in comparison with its obligation, and at how the tiny bit it does is full of faults, failures and weaknesses (IC VI:5).

> You will think, Sisters, that these souls to whom the Lord communicates Himself in this unusual way will already be so sure of enjoying Him forever that they will have nothing to fear nor sins to weep over. Those especially who have not attained these favors from God will think this, for if they had enjoyed

> them, they would know what I'm going to say. But to think the above would be a great mistake because suffering over one's sins increases the more one receives from our God. And, for my part, I hold that until we are there where nothing can cause pain this suffering will not be taken away (IC VI:7:1).

The principal lesson to be taken from the above quoted passages is that, in this stage of spiritual growth represented by St. Teresa's description of the soul in the sixth mansion, the work in the soul is being carried out by God. The favors granted and the painful self-knowledge are both beyond the power of the unaided soul to produce in itself. The insights into both God and the soul that come with the divine touches are so deep and so uncomfortable and conflicting, that we cannot imagine a soul inflicting this torment upon itself, even if it could. The only thing that allows the soul to go forward is its determination to unite with God, a gift that is given by God throughout this journey.

The cause for mourning in the Seventh Dwelling place is different from all the trials encountered in the previous dwelling places. The pain experienced here comes mainly from the soul's sense of being unable to adequately adore and serve God. However, this trial never disturbs the soul's peace. In this dwelling place, the soul experiences the spiritual betrothal and spiritual marriage. God has entered the deepest center of the soul, and remains there to the great content and tranquility of the soul. Even the trials, while causing a suffering unique to this dwelling place, do not alter the serenity of this fortunate soul.

> But it (the soul) goes about with much greater fear than before, guarding itself from any small offense against God and with the strongest desires to serve Him, as will be said later on, and with habitual pain and confusion at seeing the little it can do and the great deal to which it is obliged. This pain is no small cross but a very great penance. For when this soul does penance, the delight will be greater in the measure the penance is greater. The true penance comes when God takes away the soul's health and strength for doing penance (IC VII:2:9).

> I tell you, Sisters, that the cross is not wanting but it doesn't disquiet or make them lose peace. For the storms, like a wave, pass quickly (IC VII:3:15).

The comfort

In the Fourth Dwelling place, St. Teresa begins to discuss the difference between consolations and spiritual delights. It is here that supernatural experiences begin. In the course of what has been said already, I have pointed out some of the joyful comforts that accompany the afflictions of the soul suffered in these last mansions. What I want to do here is to describe and distinguish the comforts given to the soul by God as it moves through the last mansions toward perfect union with God. These different comforts are well known to Carmelites from their own study of these writings of St. Teresa.

<u>Consolations</u>: This favor from God originates in the natural faculties of the human soul. When it is experienced, it is frequently the result of a period of time spent in meditative prayer or the performance of an act of charity. It is God's reward to a soul that has responded to His Will which is known by all, even those with a passing and superficial awareness of Christ and His teachings.

> ...the term "consolations" I think, can be given to those experiences we ourselves acquire through our own meditation and petitions to the Lord, those that proceed from our own nature-although God in the end does have a hand in them; for it must be understood, in whatever I say, that without Him we can do nothing (IC IV:1:4).

<u>Prayer of Recollection:</u> This favor is a gentle drawing inward away from the world around us. It is a desire for solitude and silence. It is a favor granted initially by God in His desire to close the soul off from all that is not God, but the soul must respond to this urging, and not flee from it. It requires a certain degree of letting go of all the turmoil of the moment in our lives, and allowing us to be drawn into interior silence.

> In the case of this recollection, it doesn't come when we want it but when God wants to grant us this

> favor...So I believe that if we desire to make room for His Majesty, He will give not only this but more, and give it to those whom he begins to call to advance further (IC IV:3:3).

Spiritual delights: This comfort originates with God and ends in ourselves. St. Teresa also calls this the prayer of quiet. Those who reach the point of not thinking much, but loving much and who love God without self interest, but more for Himself alone are likely to experience this supernatural favor. St. Teresa, in attempting to explain this favor uses the well-known metaphor of the two troughs of water. The first is fed by an aqueduct and requires a great deal of effort to transport the water to the trough. The second trough is fed by a spring, and no effort is required to acquire the water. The latter describes the spiritual delights. They are given by God. The trough is our soul that is filled from the spring of God's love.

> The spiritual delights begin in God, but human nature feels and enjoys them as much as it does those I mentioned-and much more (IC IV:1:4).

> This spiritual delight is not something that can be imagined, because however diligent our efforts we cannot acquire it. The very experience of it makes us realize that it is not of the same metal as we ourselves but fashioned from the purest gold of the Divine Wisdom (IC IV:2:6).

Prayer of Union: St. Teresa uses her finest metaphor here: the life cycle of the silk worm resulting in the butterfly to explain this favor from God. This prayer is a transforming supernatural form of prayer different from all other forms and experiences of prayer. She begins this metaphor by describing the first stages of life of the silk worm as it develops from a seed to a rather ugly worm. Thereafter, the worm dies, but when it does, a beautiful butterfly emerges as the final stage of life of this little creature. The soul that has advanced far enough in the spiritual life where the prayer of union occurs will experience the pinnacle of prayer. In this prayer, the faculties of the soul are suspended for the short duration of this union, and there is no awareness of what goes on around this soul while the prayer of union lasts. This soul has learned that the world holds no interest or attraction for it. It is now weaving the house (the cocoon) in which it will die.

> ... you now see that God has made this soul a fool with regard to all so as better to impress upon it true wisdom. For during the time of this union it neither sees, nor hears, nor understands, because the union is always short and seems to the soul even much shorter than it probably is. God so places Himself in the interior of that soul that when it returns to itself it can in no way doubt that it was in God and God was in it (IC V:1:9).

> Oh, greatness of God! How transformed the soul is when it comes out of this prayer after having been placed within the greatness of God and so closely joined with Him for a little while – in my opinion the union never lasts for as much as a half hour (IC V:2:7).

> In it (the prayer of union), there no longer takes place the exchanging of gifts, but the soul sees secretly who this Spouse is that she is going to accept. Through the work of the senses and the faculties she couldn't in any way or in a thousand years understand what she understands here in the shortest time (IC V:4:4).

<u>Spiritual Betrothal:</u> As the soul passes into the last two mansions, a new phenomena occurs beginning with the spiritual betrothal. We noted earlier that the soul in the sixth mansion experiences intense trials: trials from its friends from praise, and from its enemies' condemnation; and trials from itself in its interior insight into its own imperfections. But in this mansion, something else happens. Unity with God is becoming very intense and very imperturbable, even in the midst of the trials typical of this mansion. These trials contain an unexplainable sweetness that makes the soul sad to have them removed.

> It (the soul) feels that it is wounded in the most exquisite way, but it doesn't learn how or by whom it was wounded. It knows clearly that the wound is

> something precious, and it would never want to be cured (IC VI:2:2).

In this mansion, St. Teresa discusses, with great caution and, I think, with some reluctance, the very special favors that come to some souls. They are gifts from God to His betrothed spouse. She calls them locutions and raptures. Locutions are a great favor that carries with it great danger of demonic deception. If it is authentic, it is a great comfort to the laboring soul. They are words that come either from the interior of the soul, the exterior of the soul, are sometimes heard, or come from the superior part of the soul. Fortunately, St. Teresa gives us a means to discern the origin of such favors.

> The surest sign that they are from God that can be had, in my opinion, are these: the first and truest is the power and authority they bear, for locutions from God effect what they say (IC VI:3:5).

> The second sign is the great quiet left in the soul, the devout and peaceful recollection (IC VI:3:6).

> The third sign is that these words remain in the memory for a very long time, and some are never forgotten, as are those we listen to here on earth – I mean those we hear from men (IC VI:3:7).

Raptures bring the soul into the spiritual betrothal. These are profoundly supernatural favors for the very few, who have utterly surrendered to the loving Will of God completely. Great courage is required to endure this favor because the soul is removed from its sensible life and is momentarily in a divinely suspended existence of indescribable joy and peace.

> Our nature is very timid and lowly when it comes to something so great, and I am certain that if God were not to give the courage, no matter how much you might see that the favor is good for us, it would be impossible for you to receive that favor. And thus you will see what His Majesty does to conclude this betrothal, which I understand comes about when

> He gives the soul raptures that draw it out of its senses (IC VI:4:2).

Spiritual Marriage: In the seventh mansion St. Teresa describes the soul that has entered into the Spiritual Marriage, a new and exalted relationship with God. This relationship is characterized by an enlightenment of the mind regarding the great mysteries that surround the Blessed Trinity and the Incarnation. Peace in the soul is now habitual, and the soul concerns itself with finding ways to serve God, through prayer and acts of charity toward others. The presence of God is now not intermittent, but constant: not exalting, but tranquil. However, the embers of the love for God which smolder uninterruptedly are frequently fanned into flares of flame which sustain the soul in its efforts to serve God.

> Between the spiritual betrothal and the spiritual marriage the difference is as great as that which exists between two who are betrothed and two who can no longer be separated (IC VII:2:2).

> But that which comes to pass in the union of the spiritual marriage is very different. The Lord appears in this center of the soul, not in an imaginative vision but in an intellectual one, although more delicate than those mentioned, as He appeared to the Apostles without entering through the door when He said to them *pax vobis* (IC VII:2:3).

Certain effects manifest this state that the soul has been brought to by the mercy of God. St. Teresa describes the three principal effects as follows: First, the soul is brought to a forgetfulness of self since now all its efforts are expended for the glory of God. Second, the soul has a great desire to suffer, but not as it felt this before. Now the Will of God solely motivates it regardless of the effect His Will has on them. Third, these souls have a deep interior joy when they are persecuted following which they have a greater identification with the suffering Christ.

> All its (the soul) concern is taken up with how to please Him more and how or where it will show Him the love it bears Him. This is the reason for

prayer, my daughters, the purpose of this spiritual marriage: the birth always of good works, good works (IC VII:4:6).

C. St. John of the Cross: The Ascent of Mt. Carmel

In the previous section that examined the writings of St. Teresa as they incorporate the third *Beatitude*, we have treated the subject of the mourning at great length. The writings of St. John of the Cross regarding this *Beatitude* will be treated at somewhat shorter length. He in many respects confirms what we have already seen from St. Teresa.

The mourning

In *The Ascent of Mt. Carmel,* St. John presents the two active nights: the active night of sense and the active night of spirit. Each of these nights is an affliction to the soul that is enduring them. In these nights, the voluntary appetites that have bound the soul to the world, the flesh, and the devil are mortified and purged of these attachments. In the night of sense, the soul suffers the loss of these attractions and satisfactions that have bound it to a slavery of the senses; a servitude that obstructs any relationship with God except a superficial one that leaves the soul weak and vulnerable to temptation.

> But any one of the voluntary appetites, even if trifling, is sufficient to impede the union, as I have said, if it is not mortified. I am referring here to habitual appetites, because certain scattered acts of different desires are not such a hindrance to union, since they are not a determined habit (AS I:11:3).

The appetites are contrary to the love of God that leads to union. Contraries cannot exist in the same subject at the same time. Therefore, until the appetites about which St. John is speaking, the voluntary appetites, are completely mortified, union with God is impossible. There is always suffering experienced in connection with the rooting out of imperfections and habitual sins. The soul must surrender its desire to retain these appetites in an act of self-denial that is never easy, especially in the beginning. Otherwise, it will retain the harm caused to it by these attachments.

> For the sake of a clearer and fuller understanding of our assertions, it will be beneficial to explain here how these appetites cause two main areas of harm within the person in whom they dwell: they deprive him of God's spirit; and they weary, torment, darken, defile and weaken him (AS I:6:1).

There are two distinct reasons for mourning when appetites remain in the soul as an obstacle to union with God. First, these harms that are caused in the soul are habitual to the extent the appetites are habitual. These appetites are a continuous obstacle preventing the soul from moving toward God. Second, what the soul is depriving itself of in not advancing toward union with God is indeed a reason for great mourning.

> It makes little difference whether a bird is tied by a thin thread or by a cord. For even if tied by a thread, the bird will be prevented from taking off just as surely as if it were tied by a cord – that is, it will be impeded from flight as long as it does not break the thread…This is the lot of the man who is attached to something; no matter how much virtue he has he will not reach the freedom of the divine union (AS I:11:4).

The active night of the spirit introduces the soul to a different set of tasks. This night requires the purification of the spirit from what resides there that will prevent the divine union. The interior faculties of the soul, the intellect, the will, and the memory are not the proximate means to union with God. The chasm that exists between our human nature and the divine nature of God cannot be bridged by any power natural to man. It can only be crossed by gifts given to the soul: the Theological Virtues of Faith, Hope, and Charity, (Charity here understood as love for God). Faith perfects the intellect because no human understanding is sufficient to arrive at knowledge of God. Hope perfects the memory because it begets an emptiness of possessions, both material and spiritual, in the memory. Charity perfects the will because it causes a void in the will of all things that are not God, and causes us to love God above all else.

> We can apply then, what Christ says about the narrow gate to the sensitive portion of man, and

> what He says about the straight way to the spiritual and rational part of the soul. Since He proclaims that few find it, we ought to note the cause: Few there are with the knowledge and desire for entering upon this supreme nakedness and emptiness of spirit (AS II:7:3).

> For they still feed and clothe their natural selves with spiritual feelings and consolations instead of divesting and denying themselves of these for God's sake. They think a denial of self in worldly matters is sufficient without an annihilation and purification of spiritual possessions (AS II:7:5).

In Book III of *The Ascent of Mt. Carmel,* St. John warns us of the dangers of seeking extraordinary favors from God. The purgation and purification of the memory, intellect and will result in the soul not pursuing these favors, and if they are granted by God, the soul will make nothing of these supernatural apprehensions. The soul that pursues and relishes supernatural favors of any kind opens the door to the deceptions of the devil who will try to counterfeit favors that come from God. Attachment to these favors or visions will delay the soul on its way to union with God because they become an end in themselves rather than a means. The soul that values these experiences will be delayed and detoured from the right path to union with God, which is complete denudation of all its faculties and senses of all that is not God, so that He becomes the one end of all the soul's efforts and desires. In addition to this, the soul that seeks and values divine favors will be exposed to pride, believing that God esteems it more than other souls.

> The spiritual person exposes himself to five types of harm if he prizes and reflects upon the ideas and forms impressed within him through supernatural apprehensions (AS III:8:1).

> The first is that he will often be deluded in mistaking the natural for the supernatural. Second, he puts himself in the occasion of falling into presumption and vanity. Third, the devil finds ample power to deceive him through these apprehensions. Fourth, so doing would be an impediment to union with God

in hope. Fifth, his judgment of God for the most part will be base (AS III:8:2).

The comfort

The soul that successfully traverses the night of the senses and purges its appetites that obscure and prevent its movement toward union with God has indeed received a great grace. The very impulse to begin the process of purging these appetites of the senses of their objects, the *urgent longings* of St. John, is a profound grace to be valued very highly. The completion of the task with its arduous self-denial can only be sustained by grace. This grace provides a sufficient love for God to enable the soul to persevere through the inevitable difficulties in moving forward to its goal. Thus, St. John calls this a *sheer grace* because it is not earned and is gratuitous; but it is indispensable to any progress being made in the spiritual life.

> The soul, through original sin, is a captive in the mortal body, subject to passions and natural appetites; when liberated from this bondage and submission, it considers its escape, which is unnoticed, unimpeded, and unapprehended by its passions and appetites, a sheer grace (AS I:15:1).

In Book II of *The Ascent of Mt. Carmel,* St. John reiterates the very great grace that is extended by God to the soul that is able, through pure faith, to pacify and purify the spiritual faculties of the soul. Faith produces a complete darkness in the soul. This darkness is necessary in order to accomplish the desired purification of the spirit, and to conceal the soul from the devil as the soul proceeds along the path on which God has placed it. Achievement of this task is an enormous benefit to the soul. When completed, there remain no obstacles to entering the passive nights that follow. In those nights, God will complete the work that is beyond the soul's power, ending in the union of love that the soul yearns for.

> But all that is required for a complete pacification of the spiritual house is the negation through pure faith of all the spiritual faculties and gratifications and appetites. This achieved, the soul will be joined

> with the Beloved in a union of simplicity and purity and love and likeness (AS II:1:2).

Any soul that succeeds in making this much progress in its spiritual life will be amply rewarded by a generous God. Such a soul has removed the obstacles that keep so many from seeking God. The rich young man in the Gospel could not purge himself of his attachment to the objects of his appetites, and therefore, went away sad. On the other hand, the soul that has endured the active nights goes away rejoicing at the goodness of God that brought him to such a happy state.

> There is nothing worthy of a man's joy save the service of God and the procurement of His honor and glory in all things. His use of things should be directed to this and turned away from vanity, and exclude concern for his own satisfaction and consolation (AS III:20:3).

> There is another exceptional and principal benefit of detachment from joy in creatures which is a preparatory condition for all the favors God will grant to the soul and without which He does not bestow them; it is freedom of the heart for God. The favors are such that for each joy the soul renounces out of love of God and evangelical perfection, it will receive a hundredfold in this life, as promised in the Gospel (Mt 19:29, Mk 10:30) (AS III:20:4).

D. St. John of the Cross: The Dark Night

When a soul has traversed the active nights described in *The Ascent of Mt. Carmel*, it encounters an interval of peace and gains satisfaction from its spiritual exercises, and an enthusiasm for the spiritual life. It rests now as it recognizes the graces and favors it has received while purging its appetites in these active nights. It rests in the confident belief that God is pleased with what it has done, and that He is its constant companion in its prayer and good works; and so He is. However, this soul remains a beginner, even though a somewhat proficient beginner.

The mourning

Unseen by this soul are the roots of many imperfections remaining deeply buried in the soul. These imperfections cannot be purged through the efforts of the soul, but can only be purified and purged by God's intervention. So without effort on the part of the soul, God draws the soul into the passive nights in which He alone performs the task of purgation and purification of the soul. These imperfections are all elements of the seven deadly sins: pride, lust, anger, envy, sloth, gluttony, and avarice, all with a spiritual application contained in the nature of the vices. This soul is far from where it wants to be in its relationship with God, but it is barely aware of that fact.

> Since their motivation in their spiritual works and exercises is the consolation and satisfaction they experience in them, and since they have not been conditioned by the arduous struggle of practicing virtue, they possess many faults and imperfections in the discharge of their spiritual activities. For assuredly, everyone's actions are in direct conformity to the habit of perfection he has acquired, and since these persons have not had time to acquire those firm habits, their work must of necessity be feeble, like that of weak children (DN I:1:3).

After a period of time during which the soul enjoys its spiritual life and its spiritual exercises, signs of a great change begin to appear which cause the soul intense suffering. Aridity and disinterest in spiritual matters begins to grow in this soul, much to its alarm. The entry into the passive night of sense is marked by confusion and darkness because the interior faculties are being engulfed in this night. The soul now experiences no satisfaction in the things of God, even though the memory turns solicitously to God, even while it is unable to meditate on God and His service. The spiritual child is now being weaned from the spiritual breast. The soul suffers greatly as the pure light of God shines upon it because it sees clearly its unworthiness and the impurity of its soul.

> The afflictions and straits of the will are also immense. Sometimes these afflictions pierce the

> soul when it suddenly remembers the evils in which it sees itself immersed, and it becomes uncertain of any remedy. To this pain is added the remembrance of past prosperity, because usually persons who enter this night have previously had many consolations in God and rendered Him many services. They are now sorrowful in knowing that they are far from such good and can no longer enjoy it (DN II:7:1).

It is here in this context that St. John of the Cross employs his brilliant metaphor of the burning log. He demonstrates the steps of the spiritual perfecting of the soul by comparing it to a burning log that gradually gains the purity of fire as it is consumed by the fire. The first stages of this purification are indeed cause for mourning.

> The soul is purged and prepared for union with the divine light just as the wood is purged and prepared for transformation into the fire. Fire, when applied to wood, first dehumidifies it, dispelling all moisture, and making it give off any water it contains. Then it gradually turns the wood black, makes it dark and ugly, and even causes it to emit a bad odor. By drying out the wood, the fire brings to light and expels all those ugly and dark accidents which are contrary to fire…(DN II:10:1).

This passive night is truly dark. The soul is helpless now to remove its suffering resulting from the complete darkness in which it is moving. There is nowhere to look for satisfaction or consolation because all the sources of these rewards have been dried up by the purging fire that is now afflicting the soul. God has refused the soul the tranquility it previously enjoyed from its natural faculties because He is now introducing the soul to supernatural things that do not come from the natural faculties of the soul. These natural faculties must now be extinguished so that they cease to be an obstacle to union with God which is wholly a supernatural relationship. There is no other way by which the union of love with God can be attained.

> One cannot reach this union without remarkable purity, and this purity is unattainable without vigorous mortification and nakedness regarding all

creatures. Taking off the bride's veil and wounding her at night in her search and desire for her Spouse, signifies this denudation and mortification, for she could not put on the new bridal veil without the removal first of her other one. Whoever refuses to go out at night in search of the Beloved and to divest and mortify his will, but rather seeks the Beloved in his own bed and comfort, as did the bride (Ct 3:1), will not succeed in finding Him; as this soul declares, it found Him when it departed in darkness and longings of love (DN II:24:4).

The comfort

One of the peculiarities of the spiritual life is that the worse things seem, the better they really are. When a soul is in great suffering and affliction, the best results are occurring unseen beneath the blanket of aridity and pain. The soul is being scrubbed clean of its attachments and imperfections that obstruct its journey toward union with God; and soon the soul's progress, if it perseveres, will accelerate in proportion to the purification and purging taking place along the rough road and narrow way that leads to union with God. Unfortunately, there is no other way to purge and purify the soul of its faults and imperfection except by a process, conducted by God that is at times very painful. So much so, that the soul is incapable of entering this crucible unaided without the direct intervention of God. The soul is limited in this effort, in part, because it is not even aware of what the faults are, or once it does know, how to rid itself of them. The main reason for comfort and joy in this night is the sure knowledge that the soul is growing in holiness and purity because of the secret work by God in it.

> The first and chief benefit that this dry and dark night of contemplation causes is the knowledge of self and of one's own misery. Besides the fact that all the favors that God imparts to the soul are ordinarily enwrapped in this knowledge, the aridities and voids of the faculties in relation to the abundance previously experienced, and the difficulty encountered in the practice of virtue make the soul recognize its own lowliness and misery, which was

not apparent in the time of its prosperity (DN I:12:2).

This self-knowledge is both a cause for mourning and for comfort. Obviously, it is uncomfortable and even painful to see our imperfections and acknowledge their presence in our souls. However, since no progress can be made until these imperfections are seen, and no purification can occur until they are recognized; this dark night is a cause of great supernatural comfort. Such a soul is on the right and only road to union with God; a matter of great joy and comfort. All of the problems of beginners discussed by St. John of the Cross at the beginning of *The Dark Night* are purged by this method. Spiritual avarice and gluttony are tempered; spiritual pride and envy are exposed when the soul realizes that others are more advanced than it; spiritual lust and sloth are extinguished as the appetite for these imperfections are purged; and as a result of the humility gained from this self-knowledge, the soul is no longer angry at its own faults or those of others.

> Insofar as the soul is buffeted and purged through the war of the dark night in a twofold way (in the sensory and spiritual parts with their senses, faculties, and passions), it also attains a twofold peace and rest, in the faculties and appetites of both the sensory and spiritual parts (DN II:24:2).

> The soul obtains habitually and perfectly (insofar as the condition of this life allows) the rest and quietude of the spiritual house by means of the acts of substantial touches of divine union which, in concealment and hiding from the disturbance of the devil and of the senses and passions, are received from the divinity (DN II:24:3).

When the spiritual life is understood, and its dynamics known, the suffering necessary for advancement will be seen as a cause for joy and comfort. Without this affliction, no progress can be made. That is why the saints prayed for trials. They understood the gold and silver hidden beneath the outer appearance of darkness and affliction.

E. St. John of the Cross: The Spiritual Canticle

The mourning

In this work, we find a new reason for mourning. The early stanzas describe a soul in great distress searching for its hidden Beloved. It is the obscurity of God to the soul that causes such intense mourning in the soul that truly does love God. This obscurity causes continual moaning in the soul. God has wounded the soul with a wound of love. The torment is extreme, not because God has wounded the soul, but because He has wounded it with the wound of love, and yet remains obscure and hidden from it. There is no consummation of the love in unity because the soul is not yet properly prepared for it. There are still many distractions and attachments that serve as obstacles to the union of love.

> Some call the Bridegroom beloved, whereas He is not really their beloved because their heart is not wholly set on Him. As a result, their petition is not of much value in His sight. They do not obtain their request until through perseverance in prayer, they keep their spirit more continually with God, and their heart with its affectionate love more entirely set on Him. Nothing is obtained from God except by love (SC 1:13).

In this state of frustration, the soul sets out to find where God is hidden and to go there. It will employ the virtues, mortifications, penances, and spiritual exercises in its quest. The soul resolves to overcome all the obstacles presented by the world and the devil in order to be where God is to be found. She asks God not to merely reveal Himself in His creation, but in His essence. Natural life in the body conflicts with its intense desire for spiritual life in the unity of the spirit with God. It is a torment to the soul. This soul, so wounded by divine touches of love laments with great mourning that God has wounded it without bringing it to unity with Him.

> And if it (the soul) does not possess completely what it loves, it cannot help being weary, in proportion to its loss, until it possesses the loved object and is satisfied. Until this possession, the soul is like an

> empty vessel waiting to be filled, or like a hungry man craving for food, or like a sick person moaning for health, or like one suspended in the air with nothing to lean on (SC 9:6).

This soul longs fervently for its hidden Beloved, eventually has no interest in anything apart from Him, and all its dealings with others are a burden to it. It begs God to remove the darkness before its eyes regarding the essence of God, and the veils that hide him so that it may unite its essence to the essence of the Beloved. For this to happen, the soul must abandon the bodily senses and the interior faculties as the means to this unity. It can only be achieved in the depths of its purified spirit, and only by God's gift of Himself to the soul in unity and surrender.

> This is the reason the soul's suffering for God at this time is so intense; she is drawing nearer to Him, and so she has greater experience within herself of the void of God, of very heavy darkness, and of spiritual fire which dries up and purges her, so that thus purified she may be united with Him. Inasmuch as God does not communicate some supernatural ray of light from Himself, He is intolerable darkness to her when He is spiritually near her, for the supernatural light darkens with its excess the natural light (SC 13:1).

The comfort

The soul's longing and searching for the Beloved has not been in vain. God has seen the soul's efforts to find unity with Him. Its wound of love has caused a similar wound in the Beloved who now seeks the unity with the soul that the soul has so long desired. God alone causes all the movement in the soul toward unity. This movement is in response to the perseverance of the soul in its pursuit of virtue and its religious practices. It is as if God is now sure that this soul is serious about seeking unity with Him, although we know that our lives are a complete present to God in terms of life's continuum. There is no past or future to Him.

> The Bridegroom now acts similarly. Beholding that the bride is wounded with love for Him, He also,

because of her moan, is wounded with love for her. Among lovers, the wound of one is a wound for both, and the two have but one feeling (SC 13:9).

Now God expresses His delight in the soul by granting many graces and touches in a state of contemplation. This is infused contemplation granted by God, rather than acquired contemplation, that involves some activity on the part of the soul. Now the soul is ready for the spiritual betrothal. Its virtues have opened up its spirit to the action of God within it. It is only here in the depths of the spirit that union can occur. The senses, affections, and attachments to what is not God have been quieted and conquered. The way is now clear for God to bring the soul to Himself without obstruction from those things that before have prevented union. The state of the soul described by St. John here is similar to that of a soul that is about to complete the purifications of Purgatory.

After a long time in the state of spiritual espousal, God raises the soul to the spiritual marriage, in which the soul enjoys a limited consummation of the love between itself and God. In the strength of its spirit gained over many trials and length of time, the soul can now endure the intimate divine embrace.

> Consequently, He is for her an enchanting, desirable garden. For her entire aim in all her works is the consummation and perfection of this state. She never rests until reaching it. She finds in this state a greater abundance and fullness of God, a more secure and stable peace and an incomparably more perfect delight than in the spiritual espousal; here it is as though she were placed in the arms of her Bridegroom. As a result, she usually experiences an intimate spiritual embrace, which is a veritable embrace, by means of which she lives the life of God (SC 22:5).

In the spiritual marriage, the soul enjoys many intimate secrets of God disclosed to it in moments of great grace and divine touches. Matters that were completely unknown to it previously are now shown to it in the intimate embrace of the Beloved. Those things which the soul knew previously are presented with new insights. Not only is the degree of its love increased, but also the nature of its love for God is changed. It is completely lacking in self-interest, and love is raised from the natural to the supernatural. This is a gift from God, wholly beyond the capacity of the soul to experience unaided. Its love is solitary, intense, and uncontaminated by any influences beyond its unity with God.

> The tenderness and truth of love by which the immense Father favors and exalts this humble and loving soul reaches such a degree - O wonderful thing, worth of all our awe and admiration-that the Father Himself becomes subject to her for her exaltation, as though He were her servant and her His lord (SC 27:1)

> For she (the soul) must advance with such love and solicitude as not to set the foot of her appetite on the green branch of any delight, or drink the clear water of any worldly honor and glory, nor should she desire the taste of the cool water of any temporal refreshment or comfort, or to settle in the shade of any creature's favor and protection, nor should she desire in any way to rest in anything, or have the company of other affections, but she should always sigh for solitude in all things until she reaches her Bridegroom in complete satisfaction (SC 34:5).

F. St. John of the Cross: The Living Flame of Love

It seems unlikely that a soul that has entered the spiritual marriage would have any reason for mourning. The spiritual gifts bestowed in this state are so abundant and satisfying that one could not hope for more. The sufferings of the spiritual journey are now behind the soul, and it enjoys a profusion of divine love. However, there is mourning here, but of a different kind. This mourning is unique in all of human experience, because it has its roots in the supernatural.

The mourning

In this work, St. John of the Cross constantly refers to the *wound of love*. He calls the purifying divine touches a cautery. In the natural world, a cautery is applied to heal an injury by burning.

The cautery always leaves a wound at the place it is applied. So in the supernatural realm, St. John describes the process of purification resulting from divine touches a wounding by a cautery. The wound however, from a divine touch is a delightful wound. It is a wound because the soul is afflicted with a love so great that it is nearly unbearable. The soul longs for the complete consummation of unity with God, but there remains one thin veil to be torn: the veil of natural death. It is in this state of life that the soul mourns and longs that this veil be torn by natural death. It must be remembered that the soul that has arrived at this high degree of spiritual perfection has only done so through intense suffering in the spirit and in the senses. Unfortunately, there are few who persevere to this profound spiritual perfection and union with God.

> O souls who in spiritual matters desire to walk in security and consolation! If you but knew how much it behooves you to suffer in order to reach this security and consolation, and how, without suffering, you cannot attain to your desire, but rather turn back, in nowise would you look for comfort either from God or from creatures. You would instead carry the cross and, placed upon it, desire to drink the pure gall and vinegar (LF 2:28).

> And here it ought to be pointed out why there are so few who reach this high state of perfect union with God. It should be known that the reason is not because God wishes that there be only a few of these spirits so elevated; He would rather want all to be perfect, but He finds few vessels that will endure so lofty and sublime a work. Since He tries them in little things and finds them so weak that they immediately flee from work, unwilling to be subject to the least discomfort and mortification, it follows that, not finding them strong and faithful in that little (Mt. 25:21, 23), in which He favored them by beginning to hew and polish them, He realizes that they will be much less strong in these greater trials (LF 4:27).

The comfort

In this work of St. John of the Cross, any phrase or paragraph could be taken from it to demonstrate the comfort and joy that has come to this soul. It is after all a description of a soul that has traversed all the afflictions, dangers and sufferings of the entire spiritual journey, and has conquered them all. It is a soul that is now united to God in the transforming union of the spiritual marriage. This fortunate soul is the recipient of the most sublime divine touches from God. It is frequently in a state of inexpressible joy, and always in a state of complete serenity and peace. In solitude, it is alone with God, and nothing can disturb it from the outside, not the world, the flesh, or the devil. All is now comfort.

> Oh, how happy is this soul which ever experiences God resting and reposing within it! Oh how fitting it is for it to withdraw from things, flee from business matters, and live in immense tranquility, so that it may not even with the slightest mote or noise disturb or trouble its heart where the Beloved dwells (LF 4:15).

> But in this awakening of the Bridegroom in the perfect soul, everything that occurs and is caused is perfect, for He is the cause of it all. And in that awakening, which is as though one were to awaken and breathe, the soul feels a strange delight in the breathing of the Holy Spirit in God, in which it is sovereignly glorified and taken with love (LF 4:16).

CHAPTER 4

BLESSED ARE THEY WHO HUNGER AND THIRST FOR JUSTICE, FOR THEY SHALL BE SATISFIED

Justice is the virtue by which everyone is given their due, that is, they are given what in reality belongs to them by nature. Justice, when applied to God, and what is due Him, encompasses everything possible to be rendered to Him. Every creature must surrender all that it is by nature and all its capacities to the Will of God and to Him in Him. Anything less is an injustice to God, which we know as sin, some greater and some lesser, but all injustices. A violation of justice is at the root of every sin. What is primarily due to God is perfect conformity to His Will. Anything less is to some degree a transgression against justice.

In somewhat the same way, every creature of God is due what his or its nature dictates from the nature God has given it. The higher the nature, the greater is the importance of rendering to that creature its due. And the higher the nature, the higher the justice due a creature. To illustrate: If one deliberately breaks a tree branch for no useful purpose, a small harm has been done to that branch and to creation in general. But if one deliberately breaks the arm of his neighbor for no good purpose, he has grievously violated what that person was due, and the virtue of justice. Justice demands that the higher nature of that person and the rights that go with his higher nature forbid inflicting an intentional injury on him. The injustice is so great that it becomes sinful.

The infliction of an injustice upon a person becomes a matter more serious when the harm or injustice is inflicted upon the spirit of a person. The spirit is the part of human nature that is made in the image and likeness of God. It is the highest element of that nature deserving of the most reverence and respect. When an injustice is inflicted upon this aspect of a person, the resulting sin is the greatest possible. This type of injustice is always a distortion of reason and the right order of things. This injustice inflicted on the rational nature of man is a violation and denial of the truth intrinsic to justice. Examples of this kind of injustice could be multiplied a hundredfold. Suffice it for us to consider some of our modern injustices: abortion, unjust war, starvation of populations, refusal to acknowledge God in the public-square and institutions, and genocide by remarkably varied methods.

When we speak of hunger and thirst for justice in this *Beatitude*, we must first hunger and thirst for the just treatment and acknowledgement of God and His proper place in relationship to all things: Creator and sustainer of all being. Therefore, unlimited love and surrender to Him is due from all creatures. Anything less is an injustice of the first magnitude. Next, hunger and thirst for justice must include recognizing and applying what is the justice due all creatures according to their natures. These demands of justice reflect the two great commandments stated in the *Book of Deuteronomy*, love of God and love of neighbor. We can conclude this introduction to the Carmelite reflections on this *Beatitude* by saying that the greatest injustice in the history of mankind was the condemnation of Jesus Christ to death: the greatest sin against the highest Being.

A. St. Teresa of Jesus: The Way of Perfection

Hunger and thirst for justice

We will first examine the concept of hunger and thirst for justice as it applies to our relationship to God. This concept necessarily includes the virtue of justice as it applies to our neighbor. If justice is the giving of what is due to God, then it will also result in the giving of what is due our neighbor; for justice to God requires justice rendered to His creature and His creation that He loves.

In this work of St. Teresa, she emphasizes the utter necessity for one who wishes to serve God to abandon all lesser things and attachments. These things serve only as obstacles to what should be the disposition of every soul towards God: that of complete self-surrender to His Divine Majesty. We would like to say that she cannot mean that for everyone; perhaps it is only meant for the cloistered Carmelite Nuns in her monastery. No, rather, entry into the cloister of the monastery is only one manifestation of the surrender to God required of all creatures. Some creatures do not exercise a choice in submitting to God. The tree manifests its justice toward God by involuntarily growing according to the nature God has impressed upon it. The song-bird sings the song God has placed in its throat, and never considers singing a different song. However, man exercises choices, and out of these choices, he acts either justly or unjustly toward God.

> Now it seems to me that, when God has brought someone to a clear knowledge of the world, and of its nature, and of the fact that another world...exists, and that there is a great difference between the one and the other, the one being eternal and the other only a dream; and of what it is to love the Creator and what to love the creature;...when one understands by sight and experience what can be gained by the one practice and lost by the other, and what the Creator is and what the creature, and many other things which the Lord teaches to those who are willing to devote themselves to being taught by Him in prayer, or whom His Majesty wishes to teach – then one loves very differently from those of us who have not advanced thus far (WP 6).

A common fault of many souls is to approach God in prayer with a divided heart. Our heart is first divided by self-interest, disregarding that we may be seeking something that is either repugnant to God or destructive to our well being. To the extent that we approach God with a demand and without a thought for His Will in the matter, we render Him a great injustice. Who in this case is the Master and who is the servant? Is God to be at our beck and call for the granting of favors?

Our heart is next divided by a severely limited act of adoration and submission, saying to ourselves: "I will be reverent and pious so that I may experience God's favor by receiving an answer to my petition. Then, when my favor is granted, I will return to my indifference to God and my duty to submit to Him and adore Him." This is lukewarm spirituality. Justice demands that my disposition toward God always be one of humble submission to His Will and prayerful gratitude for His mercy. This virtue of justice also requires that I not pass up an opportunity to instruct others regarding this correct attitude toward God. Then He is rendered what is due Him by my actions and dispositions of heart.

> God deliver us from people who wish to serve Him yet who are mindful of their own honour. Reflect

how little they gain from this; for, as I have said, the very act of desiring honour robs us of it, especially in matters of precedence; there is no poison in the world that is so fatal to perfection (WP 12).

They shall be satisfied

When we consider the satisfaction referred to in this *Beatitude*, two possibilities regarding its meaning come to mind. First, the events in life that cause us to experience a sense of outrage because someone else or ourselves are treated with great injustice in a particular matter, will be put right or will cease to occur either in this world or in the next. This is undoubtedly a correct assumption concerning at least part of the meaning intended by the Lord. There is a second and greater possibility to consider concerning the meaning intended by Christ. It should cause a sense of outrage in all right-thinking people over the low place or no-place assigned to God in society. This indifference is an enormous injustice toward God. In everyone that loves God, there must be an intense hunger and thirst that He be accorded the honor and adoration that He is due. When the honor due Him is given, the soul who loves God experiences sublime satisfaction. But, the satisfaction that we hunger and thirst for regarding the honor of God for Himself alone will not be accorded to Him completely until we see it in eternal life. This world remains the devil's playground and his works are everywhere; and likely will continue to be so until the end of time.

> It should be noted here that, when we desire anyone's affection, we always seek it because of some interest, profit, or pleasure of our own. Those who are perfect, however, have trodden all these things beneath their feet-(and have despised) the blessing which may come to them in this world, and its pleasures and delights in such a way that, even if they wanted to, so to say, they could not love anything outside God, or unless it had to do with God (WP 6).

This description of St. Teresa of the love due to God presents a picture of a soul, acting with complete justice toward Him. This love begins with the fear of the Lord, the gift of the Holy Spirit by which we are loath to offend God, more for His sake than for our own. We cling to God by even mere threads of love rather than lose Him by separating ourselves from Him by sin. The least experience of God by infused contemplation is sufficient to create in us a great reluctance to do anything that will deprive us of such a profound love. In this abstention from sin, we are practicing the virtue of justice toward God that leads to the satisfaction referred to by the Lord in this *Beatitude*.

> Oh, what a great thing it is not to have offended the Lord, so that the servants and slaves of hell may be kept under control! In the end, whether willingly or no, we shall serve Him – they by compulsion and we with our whole heart. So that, if we please Him, they will be kept at bay and will do nothing that can harm us, however much they lead us into temptation and lay secret snares for us (WP 41).

B. St. Teresa of Jesus: The Interior Castle

There are far too many souls that value a relationship with God at near zero in importance. These souls occupy themselves with matters of the world and of the flesh. Easy access into these souls is afforded the devil because there are no barriers, and he rarely misses an opportunity to wreak havoc in such a vulnerable soul. These souls will remain outside *the castle* unless they respond to grace when it is given, and begin to enter the outer rooms of this castle of spirituality. If they do not respond, justice remains a virtue that is meaningless to them; and consequently they never experience a hunger and thirst for that virtue.

The First Three Dwelling Places

Hunger and thirst for justice

In *The Interior Castle*, St. Teresa describes those souls who remain outside and who refuse to enter the castle and seek the One who lives in the center-most mansion. To remain in this state of refusal, a soul must resist the grace that comes to all in the form of a call from God. This call is in reality an invitation to seek Him, which the soul is at liberty to refuse. As long as a soul or a society of souls remain in this state of reluctance, a great breach of justice happens because God is not rendered His due by those souls. On the other hand, a faithful soul observes this resistance and denial on the part of some, and hungers and thirsts for the entire world to give to God the justice that is due Him. The faithful souls see clearly the good that God is willing to extend to all; and they long to see all others recognize and respond to that goodness.

> Because we have heard and because faith tells us so, we know we have souls. But we seldom consider the precious things that can be found in this soul, or who dwells within it, or its high value. Consequently, little effort is made to preserve its beauty. All our attention is taken up with the plainness of the diamonds setting or the outer wall of the castle; that is, with these bodies of ours (IC I:1:2).

> Thus, there are souls so ill and so accustomed to being involved in external matters that there is no remedy, nor does it seem they can enter within themselves. They are so used to dealing always with the insects and vermin that are in the wall surrounding the castle that they have become almost like them. And though they have so rich a nature and the power to converse with none other than God, there is no remedy (IC I:1:6).

The gaining of the virtue of justice as it applies to rendering to God His due is a gradual process. The perfection of justice toward God is rarely conceived in its truth by the beginner. One finds this virtue to be something of a moving target, in that every time we think we understand what this virtue requires, we are presented with a new view of it that did not previously occur to us. As the virtue of justice toward God develops and becomes clearer to us, and the soul is more and more inclined to give God His due, the virtue of justice toward our neighbor also grows. Consequently, the violations of justice that we observe in the world cause an ever-growing hunger and thirst for justice to reign in us and in the world both toward God and toward our neighbor. When one begins a spiritual journey, the virtue of justice is minimal both toward God and toward our neighbor. In *The Second Dwelling Place*, St. Teresa examines the less than firm commitment of a soul still ambiguous about acquiring spiritual perfection.

> This stage pertains to those who have already begun to practice prayer and have understood how important it is not to stay in the first dwelling places. But they still don't have the determination to remain in this second stage without turning back, for they don't avoid the occasions of sin (IC II:1:2).

> Someone could think that if turning back is so bad it would be better never to begin but to remain outside the castle. I have already told you at the beginning - and the Lord Himself tells you – that anyone who walks in danger perishes in it and that the door of entry to this castle is prayer (IC II:1:11).

In the *Third Dwelling Place*, St. Teresa discusses the soul that has succeeded in acquiring a well-ordered life of prayer and a healthy fear of the Lord. This soul is loath to offend God, and seeks to glorify Him in its life, taking advantage of opportunities to respond to the love that God has bestowed upon it. While this soul is advanced in virtue, including the virtue of justice, it longs for consolations from its devotion and to feel close to God. It desires sincerely to please God, and to have Him loved by everyone, as is His due. However, this soul is not sufficiently tried in suffering and affliction, and frequently recoils from the trials that God sends to it in order to further perfect it and draw it even closer to Him.

> If, like the young man in the Gospel, we turn our backs and go away sad when the Lord tells us what we must do to be perfect, what do you want His Majesty to do? For He must give the reward in conformity with the love we have for Him. And this love, daughters, must not be fabricated in our imaginations but proved by deeds. And don't think He needs our works; He needs the determination of our wills (IC III:2:7).

What St. Teresa is telling us is that true justice toward God requires the entire commitment of our wills to Him and to His Will. We sometimes enjoy our spiritual lives so much, and the joy that it bestows on us that a real affliction or trial is repulsed, and not seen for what it is: a favor from God to move us to long for His justice and mercy even more than we do. Within the suffering, we will find our crucified Savior to a greater degree than we do in the peace and consolations that are frequently the lot of souls at this stage of their spiritual journey. God knows what is required for us to render perfect justice to Him: the surrender of our complete selves.

> His Majesty will give you through other paths what He keeps from you on this one because of what He knows, for His secrets are very hidden; at least what He does will without any doubt be what is most suitable for us (IC III:2:11).

They shall be satisfied

Rendering to God His due as required by the virtue of justice is impossible without the virtue of humility. Justice requires that we recognize that God is the creator and we are the creatures. We owe our very existence to God. Man could not remain and thrive in this world were it not for the creation by God of all the circumstances necessary to support life here, from the air we breathe to the food and drink that nourishes us. We cannot supply these things that sustain life for ourselves, except to the extent that we are able to employ the laws of nature implanted in creation in order to produce our needs. Therefore, there is really no reason for us to become proud and self-satisfied in matters pertaining to the material world. The same is true in the spiritual realm. What we become spiritually is the result of a gratuitous gift of grace from God. Spiritual growth and development does not originate with the human soul; it results from a proper response to the grace that is offered to it by God. There is no justification for pride in our spiritual gifts and progress, any more than there is justification for pride in the application of the natural law to furnish our material needs. It is from this awareness of material and spiritual reality and our dependence upon God for both that true justice to God results.

> For humility, like the bee making honey in the bee hive, is always at work. Without it, everything goes wrong. But let's remember that the bee doesn't fail to leave the beehive and fly about gathering nectar from the flowers. So it is with the soul in the room of self-knowledge; let it believe me and fly sometimes to ponder the grandeur and majesty of its God. Here it will discover its lowliness better than

by thinking of itself and be freer from the vermin that enter the first rooms, those of self-knowledge (IC I:2:8).

If souls are humble, they will be moved to give thanks. If there is some lack in humility, they will feel an inner distaste for which they will find no reason. For perfection as well as its reward does not consist in spiritual delights but in greater love and in deeds done with greater justice and truth (IC III:2:10).

The Last Four Dwelling Places

Hunger and thirst for justice

As a soul enters The Fourth Dwelling Place supernatural experiences begin in the soul, but they are always mixed with the natural desires of the soul. In the later dwelling places, the supernatural experiences will be more pure in the sense that the natural faculties will not remain engaged as they are in the fourth. The soul begins to experience the prayer of recollection to a greater degree, which leads into the prayer of quiet. The prayer of quiet is given to the soul by God, or as we should say, infused into the soul. The soul cannot enter this prayer by its own powers as it does the prayer of recollection. It is a state of prayer that absorbs the soul in God to a greater degree than any other state previously experienced by the soul.

If the soul intends to seek justice in regard to these supernatural gifts of prayer, it will adopt an attitude of great humility and gratitude. It will recognize that it has done nothing to earn this great favor, and therefore, will not be actively seeking or desiring it to be granted. If a soul does fall into the error of seeking these extraordinary gifts, it will effectively raise an obstacle that will block the gift, even when God desires to grant it.

For the Lord gives when He desires, as He desires, and to whom He desires. Since these blessings belong to Him, He does no injustice to anyone (IC IV:1:2).

> Leave the soul in God's hands, let Him do whatever He wants with it, with the greatest disinterest about your own benefit as is possible and the greatest resignation to the will of God (IC IV:3:6).

The point that St. Teresa makes here is that no one has any claim on these supernatural favors, as if they were entitled to them under some concept of justice, or as a reward for some act of charity or holiness. Strict justice would dictate that no such favors be granted to anyone, for none are worthy of extraordinary gifts from God. God grants them only out of His great mercy and love for the soul. They are His to grant or to withhold as He sees fit.

In the later mansions, St. Teresa laments the great injustices that are done by mankind to God, but at the same time, God grants many souls extraordinary favors out of His very great mercy. It seems that the justice of God is compelled to grant forgiveness and favors to souls, because God knows the weaknesses and tendencies toward evil of His creatures; and therefore His infinite justice cannot deny the granting of mercy to souls. Otherwise, His justice would be lacking to the extent it fails to take into account the misery of His fallen creatures.

> What I said seems to me very beneficial to help you understand how pleased our Lord is that we know ourselves and strive to reflect again and again on our poverty and misery and how we possess nothing that we have not received (IC VI:5:6).

> Once I was pondering why our lord was so fond of this virtue of humility, and as this thought came to me – in my opinion not as a result of reflection but suddenly; It is because God is supreme Truth; and to be humble is to walk in truth, for it is a very deep truth that of ourselves we have nothing good but only misery and nothingness. Whoever does not understand this walks in falsehood (IC VI:11:7).

They shall be satisfied

As was said above, God's mercy flows from His justice, and not in meager ways, but rather in abundance. Union with God is bestowed rather than achieved. When this union is granted, our lowly human souls are lifted far above themselves by the hand of God, and we exist and function on a new plane for as long as the union lasts. We are speaking here of the union of love, and not merely the substantial union. This union of love is the best example of the abundant generosity of God to souls requiring mercy. This generosity does not only involve forgiveness of transgressions; this mercy goes far beyond that in the granting of the union of love. This union of love is in effect a great reward resulting from the soul's willingness to humbly submit to the will of God and to open itself to Him completely (an extraordinary grace itself). Therefore, we can say that the soul that has rendered to God what is His due is satisfied beyond what it could reasonably expect as a reward for this act of justice.

> Thus the soul is left with such wonderful blessings because God works within it without anyone disturbing Him, not even ourselves. What will He not give who is so fond of giving and who can give all that He wants (IC V:1:5)?

> This union is above all earthly joys, above all delights, above all consolations, and still more than that (IC V:1:6).

The greater our love for God, the greater will be our love for our neighbor. One love does not exist without the other. As a result, when we give willingly to God what is His due, we find ourselves doing the same to neighbor. The virtue of justice encompasses both objects: God and our neighbor. We can think of the many evils we encounter in the world and we always find in them some violation of justice. When, however, we pursue justice for all men we find the generosity of God ready to bestow His abundant blessings upon us.

> And be certain that the more advanced you see you are in love for your neighbor the more advanced you will be in the love of God, for the love of His Majesty has for us is so great that to repay us for our love of neighbor He will in a thousand ways increase the love we have for Him. I cannot doubt this (IC V:3:8).

C. St. John of the Cross: The Ascent of Mt. Carmel

To begin with, we can observe that all of the major works of St. John of the Cross, including this one under discussion, *The Ascent of Mt. Carmel,* relate the nature of the journey of a soul that seeks union with God. Those works also explain what must be done on this journey to achieve that union. It is the only goal of human life, the *one thing necessary.* Anything less, any other objective, as an ultimate goal, is an injustice to God. It is an injustice to God in two ways: first, it orders all things wrongly; second, it rejects the goodness of God in His desire for union with the soul.

Hunger and thirst for justice

The first point that St. John makes rather emphatically is that the joys and pleasures of the world when compared to the joys of union with God are worth nothing; and worse than that, they are obstacles to advancing toward union with God. One who decides to remain attached to the things of the world rather than to seek union with God has in fact made a decision against justice. He has elevated the mundane above the sublime, the lesser over the greater. Such a choice denies God what is His due.

> All the delights and satisfactions of the will in the things of the world in contrast to all the delight that is God are intense suffering, torment, and bitterness. He who links his heart to these delights, then, deserves in God's eyes intense suffering, torment, and bitterness. He will not be capable of attaining the delights of the embrace of union with God, since he merits suffering and bitterness (AS I:4:7).

> It is the common knowledge of experience that when the will is attached to an object, it esteems that object higher than any other, even though another, not as pleasing, may deserve higher admiration. And if a man desires pleasure from both objects, he is necessarily offensive to the more deserving, because through his desire for both, he equates the two. Since nothing equals God, a person who loves and is attached to something other than God, or

together with Him, offends God exceedingly (AS I:5:5).

Real justice, as we see from these words of St. John, requires that nothing or anyone be placed ahead of God by the attachment of our wills. The soul that seeks spiritual growth and perfection must begin with this principal constantly before its eyes. This order of the objects of the will also includes spiritual experiences and objects as well as those on the natural level. Objects of the will that are means to an end cannot be made into the end itself. In pursuing union with God, we do not achieve it by pursuing acquisitions of particular religious objects, resting in the regular performance of particular prayers or devotions, or pursuing certain popular claims of religious phenomena. These are all means, and not ends. The soul must forsake all that is not God for His sake and for its own sake if it is to succeed in arriving at union with God ultimately.

> Insofar as he is capable, a person must void himself of all, so that, however many supernatural communications he receives, he will continually live as though denuded of them and in darkness...All these perceptions are a darkness that will lead him astray (AS II:4:2).

> Similarly, if the soul in traveling this road leans upon any elements of its own knowledge or experience of God, it will easily go astray or be detained for not having desired to abide in complete blindness, in faith which is its guide. For, however impressive may be one's knowledge or feeling of God, that knowledge or feeling will have no resemblance to God and amount to very little (AS II:4:3).

When a soul brings all its joys and appetites of its will into subjection and orients all of these toward God, it has complied with the demands of true justice. Anything less, any clinging of its will to creatures and natural things inordinately is always to some degree a violation of the virtue of justice. This disorder of things inverts the hierarchy of importance to the extent that the soul has an attachment to something that supersedes its attachment and submission to God's will. To allow such an attachment to natural things to grow and develop beyond the true intrinsic value of the natural thing, and its value relationship to the true value required to be placed on God's will, leads to the end of spiritual growth. It frequently leads even to falling back in the spiritual life. In this inordinate attachment to natural things, the order of justice has been upset, and chaos in the life of the soul is usually the result.

> The less strongly the will is fixed on God, and the more dependent it is upon creatures, the more these four passions (of the will: joy, hope, sorrow and fear) combat the soul and reign in it. It then very easily finds joy in what deserves no rejoicing, and hope in what brings no profit, and sorrow over what should perhaps cause rejoicing, and fear where there is no reason for fear (AS III:16:4).

> The (fundamental) principle is: The will should rejoice only in what is for the honor and glory of God, and the greatest honor we can give Him is to serve Him according to evangelical perfection; anything unincluded in such service is without value to man (AS III:17:2).

They shall be satisfied

The soul that succeeds in mortifying its natural appetites for the sake of right justice, and places its heart and aspirations on God alone will indeed reap a rich reward. Whatever the trial and suffering incurred in this effort to detach from creatures, the satisfaction that results from the achievement of this separation from natural things will be disproportionately greater than those trials and afflictions. In truth, no satisfaction of soul can be experienced without the right ordering of all things as required by the virtue of justice. St. John of the Cross illustrates this satisfaction that comes from the right ordering of things when he uses the words, "ah, the sheer grace," to explain the nature of the reward that is bestowed by God on the soul that agrees to proceed through the darkness and the nights necessary to arrive at union with Him. It is a sheer grace because it is uncontaminated with any compromise with self-will on the part of the soul. The grace is *sheer* also, because it is unearned by the soul and comes only from the gratuitous mercy of God.

> The soul, through original sin, is a captive in the mortal body, subject to passions and natural appetites; when liberated from this bondage and submission, it considers its escape, which is unnoticed, unimpeded, and unapprehended by its passions and appetites, a sheer grace (AS I:15:1).

> The higher rank and esteem a man gives to all his knowledge, experience and imagining (whether spiritual or not), the more he subtracts from the Supreme Good and the more he delays in his journey toward Him. And the less he esteems what he can possess relative to the Supreme Good – however estimable it may be – the more he values and prizes Him, and, consequently, the closer he comes to Him (AS II:4:6).

If a soul allows lights and images, other than that of union with God, to enter its faculties by any means whatsoever, through either the exterior senses or the interior faculties, the sheer grace being given will diminish. There will be a dilution of God's communication of Himself to the soul, and it will be left with a disorder rather than a right order in the soul. This entry of natural things into the soul in a manner that preserves an attachment places the soul in many dangers, two of which are basic: first, the loss of a perfect union with God when He wishes to bestow it; and secondly, an exposure to occasions of sin because this avenue of the natural faculties is the devil's means of access to the soul. The latter effectively blocks God's wish to bestow His blessing on the soul. This upset of the divine order of things is an injustice to God. On the other hand, the soul that avoids these distractions and diversions from its goal of union with God receives a benefit beyond measure from the hand of God when He communicates Himself to the soul, however slightly or obscurely.

> One should not commingle other more palpable lights of forms, concepts, or figures of meditative discourse, if one wants to receive this divine light in greater simplicity and abundance. For none of these tangible lights are like that serene, limped light. If an individual should desire to consider and understand particular things, however spiritual they

may be, he would hinder the general, limped, and simple light of the spirit; he would be interfering by his cloudy thoughts. When an obstruction is placed in front of a person's eyes, he is impeded from seeing the light and view before him (AS II:15:3).

These obstacles to God's desire to minister to the soul by the granting of these special graces of union are a great injustice to God. They frustrate His will for the soul's benefit, and they penalize the soul by its loss of these gifts of God. The soul that is able to avoid obstructing God's path to the interior of the soul will be satisfied beyond its fondest wishes.

D. St. John of the Cross: The Dark Night

Hunger and thirst for justice

The soul that seeks perfect justice in its relationship and attitudes toward God does not by its desire alone eventually reach the goal of perfect justice toward God. There is a road to be traveled that is often, if not always, arduous and fearful. Our Lord confirms that fact when He points out that the way is narrow and the road is rough that leads to life, and few there are that find it. This description of the path does not only refer to the reluctance and difficulty of the attached soul to give up the things of this world and its own self-will. It also includes the true journey of the willing soul that sincerely seeks union with God. This latter soul embarks upon a task that will include great suffering and self-denial. The raw material of our fallen nature is unsuited to the relationship of union with God desired by this willing soul. This soul must be radically modified and mortified by innumerable trials and afflictions that may not end until its natural life on earth ends. This transformation cannot be accomplished by the soul using its own natural powers. It must be completed by the power of God working in the soul, hammering it into His image by the hammer and chisel of suffering. Therefore, the nights described in this work by St. John are characterized by him as passive nights. This is not suffering for its own sake, but rather the necessary by-product of profound change and elevation of the soul above itself to the union of love with God. This enormous bridging of the gap between the natural and supernatural, between the attachments to the things of the flesh and the world and the extermination of self-will for the sake of God's will is the subject matter of this work of St. John of the Cross. Hence this work's ominous title.

> At the time of the aridities of this sensory night, God makes the exchange we mentioned by withdrawing the soul from the life of the senses and placing it in that night of spirit – that is, He brings it from meditation to contemplation – where the soul no longer has the power to work or meditate with its faculties on the things of God. Spiritual persons suffer considerable affliction in this night, owing not so much to the aridities they undergo as to their fear of having gone astray. Since they do not find any support or satisfaction in good things, they believe there will be no more spiritual blessings for them and that God has abandoned them (DN I:10:1).

This particular suffering of the soul in its grief and fear of not serving God well and according to His will is very pleasing to God. This soul, in its solicitude for pleasing God and becoming closer to Him is really in pursuit of perfect justice. God occupies the principal place in this soul's life even though it does not believe that it is serving Him, as He ought to be served. Its life is dominated now by its desire for God, and there are no other *gods* before Him. This frame of mind is the very definition of perfect justice. The affliction and suffering experienced by this soul is acceptable to it if it will lead to the union with God now so earnestly desired by this soul.

> For it will please and comfort one who treads this path to know that a way seemingly so rough and adverse and contrary to spiritual gratification engenders so many blessings.

> These blessings are attained when the soul departs from all created things, in its affection and operation, by means of this night and marches on toward eternal things. This is a great happiness and grace: first, because of the signal benefit of quenching one's appetite and affection for all things; second, because there are very few who will endure the night and persevere in entering through this small gate and

in treading this narrow road that leads to life, as our Savior says (Mt 7:14) (DN I:11:4).

One must never underestimate the difficulty of these passive nights for the soul that is placed in them by God. This painful aspect of the pursuit of justice, as we have described it here, is a great price to pay for this fortunate soul. The undoing of all that this soul is accustomed to, both in its natural life and in its spiritual experiences, will be total if the soul perseveres along this path. The transformation in this soul desired by God is so extreme that it cannot be accomplished without profound affliction and suffering, because the spiritual contents of this soul are excised by the dark contemplation of these nights. This is accomplished because at one and the same time this soul experiences a sense that God has rejected it and also a sense of its own poverty, so that it believes God is justified in that rejection.

> But what the sorrowing soul feels most is the conviction that God has rejected it, and with an abhorrence of it cast it into darkness…
>
> When this purgative contemplation oppresses a man, he feels very vividly indeed the shadow of death, the sighs of death, and the sorrows of hell, all of which reflect the feeling of God's absence, of being chastised and rejected by Him, and of being unworthy of Him, as well as the object of His anger (DN II:6:2).

The pursuit of perfect justice comes at a great price to the soul, but in reality a small price in comparison to the reward being purchased. The last thing to be said here in describing the soul's pursuit of perfect justice is that the road is alternately rough and difficult, and then smooth and easy. Trials and afflictions are always followed by peace and spiritual joy; which in turn is followed by a return of the trials and afflictions; which in turn is followed by peace and spiritual joy, and so on. St. John of the Cross attributes this to the essential dichotomy of knowing God and knowing the self that occurs more or less at the same period in the life of the soul.

> The reason (for prosperity and trials) is that since the state of perfection, which consists in perfect love of

God and contempt of self, cannot exist without knowledge of God and of self, the soul necessarily must first be exercised in both. It is now given the one, in which it finds satisfaction and exaltation, and now it is made to experience the other and is humbled until the ascent and descent cease through the acquisition of perfect habits, for the soul will then have reached God and united itself with Him (DN II:18:4).

They shall be satisfied

It would be a denial of the goodness of God and also of His justice, to assume that after such an arduous journey seeking union with Him, there is no reward to the faithful soul for its perseverance. What is the satisfaction spoken of by our Lord in this *Beatitude*? St. John of the Cross explains this better than any other spiritual writer. First, we must understand that the soul that is brought into this fearful night of the spirit has received a singular blessing and favor from God. God has chosen not to leave this soul in its primitive and fallen state, but rather has offered to elevate it to its highest potential of union with His very Self. A teacher that ignores a student so that the student will not be burdened with the work necessary to learn has done the student no favor. Rather the teacher has done the student a great disservice. So we must see that affliction that accompanies growth in the spiritual life is itself a great gift stemming from the love of God for the soul so afflicted.

> One ought to have deep compassion for the soul God puts in this tempestuous and frightful night. It may be true that the soul is fortunate because of what is being accomplished within it, for the great blessings will proceed from this night. Job affirms that out of darkness God will raise up in the soul profound blessings and change the shadow of death into light (Jb 12:22).
>
> He will do this in such a way that, as David says, the light will become what the darkness was (Ps 138:12).

> Nevertheless, the soul is deserving of great pity because of the immense tribulation it suffers and its extreme uncertainty about a remedy (DN II:7:3).

Understanding of the benefit of severe affliction imposed on this soul seeking perfect justice, union with God, requires a clear grasp of what is happening in this dark contemplation. Failure to so understand this night will make it appear ludicrous to say that this soul is receiving constant satisfaction in its pursuit of perfect justice. We err when we equate satisfaction with an emotional sense of peace and accomplishment. Many who have not been placed on this road by God have those nice feelings, and they are meaningless to their spiritual welfare. Satisfaction here consists solely in the successful transformation of the soul from a natural orientation to a supernatural orientation. It is only in this context that what St. John teaches in his description of this night will make perfect sense. The satisfactions experienced here by this soul are many and varied. Some are cause for fear and concern, and others are cause for exaltation by the soul.

> Hence, that the soul pass on to these grandeurs (the apprehensions and affections of the perfect spirit) this dark night of contemplation must necessarily annihilate it first and undo it in its lowly ways by putting it in darkness, dryness, conflict, and emptiness. For the light imparted to the soul is a most lofty divine light which transcends all natural light and which does not belong naturally to the intellect (DN II:9:2).

> Moreover, the soul should leave aside all its former peace, because it is prepared by means of this contemplative night to attain inner peace, which is of such a quality and so delightful that, as the Church says, it surpasses all understanding (3rd Sun. of Advent, Epis Phil 4:7) (DN II:9:6).

> Through this inflaming of love we can understand some of the delightful effects this dark night of contemplation now gradually produces in the soul. Sometimes, as we said, it illumines in the midst of these darknesses, and the light shines in the darkness (Jn 1:15), serenely communicating this mystical

> knowledge to the intellect and leaving the will in dryness, that is, without the actual union of love. The serenity is so delicate and delightful to the feeling of the soul that it is ineffable. This experience of God is felt now in one way and now in another (DN II:13:1).

St. John of the Cross teaches us a doctrine of spirituality that is practically unknown in our age, even by Catholics who practice their faith. The failure is upon those who have the duty to teach. Such a treasure lies outside the door to many hearts, seeking entrance, but the door never opens. God stands ready to bestow this gift by an out-flowing of His grace, but He must find a willing soul. Oh, how great is this pearl of great price and how great is the loss of those who refuse it.

> Oh, what a sheer grace it is for the soul to be freed from the house of its senses. This fortune, in my opinion, can only be understood by the man who has savored it. For then a person will become clearly aware of the wretched servitude and the many miseries he suffered when he was subject to the activity of his faculties and appetites. He will understand how the life of the spirit is true freedom and wealth and embodies inestimable goods (DN II:14:3).

E. St. John of the Cross: The Spiritual Canticle

Hunger and thirst for justice

In this work, St. John of the Cross takes us deeper into the pursuit of union with God, which we have described as the expression of perfect justice. It should be understood that there are two kinds of union with God, and only one of those involves our subject here. The first is called the substantial union in which God is present in every creature and sustains its being. St. John calls the other union important to our discussion as the *union of likeness*. This union is not always present and is only found where there is a likeness of love between the soul and God. This union results in a transformation of the soul in God. When the soul has successfully rid itself of everything repugnant to the will of God, it has been transformed in love, and this latter union subsists in the soul. This is perfect justice, since this soul now gives God all that is due Him from this soul. Therefore, by its choice the soul that hungers for this justice also longs to love God and be brought into this union with Him. This longing is perfectly expressed in the first stanza of *The Spiritual Canticle.*

> *Where have you hidden,*
> *Beloved, and left me moaning?*
> *You fled like the stag*
> *After wounding me;*
> *I went out calling You, and You were gone.*

Moaning is the key word here. It is interchangeable with hunger and thirst. In addition, the expression of the soul going out and calling God says the same thing: it hungers and thirsts for this perfect justice that result in the transforming union with God.

> The soul at the beginning of this song has grown aware of her obligations and observed that life is short (Jb 14:5), the path leading to eternal life narrow (Mt 7:14), the just man scarcely saved (1 Pt 4:18), the things of the world vain and deceitful (Eccl 1:2), that all comes to an end and fails like falling water (2 Kgs 14:14), and that the time is uncertain, the accounting strict, perdition very easy, and salvation very difficult. She knows on the other hand of her immense indebtedness to God for having created her solely for Himself, and that for this she owes Him the service of her whole life; and that because He redeemed her solely for Himself she owes Him every response of love (SC 1:Intro:1).

This pursuit of God by the soul is itself a gift of grace. We are describing here a phenomenon that is beyond the capacity of the soul without the movements of grace (sometimes repeatedly given). We notice that God is hidden from this soul seeking Him. St. John tells us in this first stanza that the soul went out calling God, and He was gone. The stanzas following this first one through the twelfth stanza describe the soul's efforts to find the hidden God, the hungering and thirsting of this soul. In its pursuit of this perfect justice, the soul suffers intensely in its efforts and frustration over not being united to its Beloved.

> This is the reason the soul's suffering for God at this time is so intense: she is drawing nearer to Him, and so she has greater experience within herself of the void of God, of very heavy darkness, and of spiritual fire which dries up and purges her, so that thus purified she may be united with Him. Inasmuch as God does not communicate some supernatural ray of light from Himself, He is intolerable darkness to her when He is spiritually near her, for the supernatural light darkens with its excess the natural light (SC 13:Intro:1).

It is one thing to hunger and thirst for justice, and quite another to realize justice. Similarly, the soul that longs for the union of love with God, the transforming union, labors long and arduously for that end. It is not easily achieved, even though God is the moving force. Besides the cooperation of the soul with the graces given toward that end, the soul must be willing to endure the suffering of purgation, purification, and detachment. It must constantly keep its spiritual eye on the goal, and it must desire it enough to persevere over a long period of time, perhaps its entire life in this world.

> It should be known that however spiritual a soul may be there always remains, until she reaches this state of perfection, some little herd of appetites, satisfactions, and other imperfections, natural or spiritual, after which she follows, in an effort to pasture and satisfy it.

> In the intellect, there usually reside some imperfect appetites for knowing things.

> The will is usually allowed to be captivated by some small appetites and gratifications of its own...These (latter) may concern natural things such as eating, drinking, finding more gratification in this than in that, choosing, and desiring the best. Or they may concern spiritual things, such as the desire for

spiritual satisfactions, or other trifles we would never finish listing, characteristic of spiritual persons who are not yet perfect (SC 26:18).

They shall be satisfied

The Spiritual Canticle begins to present the description of the rewards in store for the soul that perseveres in its pursuit of the transforming union with God. The completion of this description of the rewarding gifts of Himself that God gives to the soul is contained in *The Living Flame of Love*; but the content of that work is dependent upon the growth of the soul toward complete union with God contained in *The Spiritual Canticle.* The reason for this interdependency of the two works is that *The Spiritual Canticle* describes the attainment of the soul's goal of the transforming union, sometimes called the spiritual marriage; while *The Living Flame of Love* looks inside the spiritual marriage to see what is being experienced by the soul. So we will first see what descriptions *The Spiritual Canticle* contains regarding the rewarding satisfactions gained by the persevering soul. The poetry itself leads us to an understanding of these satisfactions:

STANZA 26

In the inner wine cellar
I drank of my Beloved, and, when I went abroad
Through all this valley
I no longer knew anything,
And lost the herd which I was following.

STANZA 27

There He gave me His breast;
There He taught me a sweet and living knowledge;
And I gave myself to Him,
Keeping nothing back;
There I promised to be His bride.

This wine cellar (the inner wine cellar) is the last and most intimate degree of love in which the soul can be placed in this life...As a result there are other steps of love, not so interior, by which one ascends to this last (SC 26:3).

> The tenderness and truth of love by which the immense Father favors and exalts this humble and loving soul reaches such a degree – O wonderful thing, worthy of all our awe and admiration – that the Father Himself becomes subject to her for her exaltation, as though He were her servant and she His lord. And He is as solicitous in favoring her, as He would be if He were her slave and she His god. So profound is the humility and sweetness of God (SC 27:Intro).

It is true that God loves His creatures in so far as they resemble His perfection, and goodness. The soul that has treated God justly, and therefore, placed Him above all other creatures and the things of the world receives God's love as an extension of His love for His own perfection.

> He does not love things because of what they are in themselves, but because of what He is in Himself...With God, to love the soul is to put her somehow in Himself and make her His equal. Thus, He loves the soul within Himself, with Himself, that is, with the very love by which He loves Himself (SC 32:6).

Eventually the grace received by the soul to become perfected as far as possible in this life, and to be captured in the spiritual marriage, is now loved differently by God. In addition to being loved by God in Himself, she is now loved by God for herself because of her perfection resulting from grace. Sin and all forms of ugliness having been removed from this soul by grace, God now looks at the soul and loves her for herself. This is sometimes referred to as God's second look at the soul. The first look saw the inferiority of her nature and her weakness from sin. Now that the perfecting light of grace has shown upon this soul, God's second look now results in His loving her for the beauty of her perfection and her union with Him.

> Because this grace exalts, honors, and beautifies her in His sight, God loves her ineffably. If before she had grace, He loved her only on account of Himself, now that she is in grace He loves her not only on account of Himself but also on account of herself (SC 33:7).

In this state of a soul, one in which all other creatures and things have been sublimated and subjected to God, and one in which an intimate union with God in the spiritual marriage has been achieved, perfect justice has been obtained. Nothing else than complete satisfaction on the part of the soul, can follow such a journey of faith and love.

F. St. John of the Cross: The Living Flame of Love

The last of St. John's major works is so interior and spiritual that he delayed in expounding upon the meaning of his verses until he was properly recollected with a proper amount of fervor. This work looks into the spiritual marriage to see what wonders occur in that state between the soul and God. The soul is now inflamed with love for God and makes acts of love toward God that are in fact the work of the Holy Spirit more than that of the soul. All of the work of perfecting and purging the soul of defects and attachments described in the other works of St. John has now reached fruition. There is now no longer the former hungering and thirsting for God and perfect justice, but rather, the soul is now reaping the satisfaction promised by Christ in this *Beatitude*. Therefore, we will not have a separate section regarding the hunger and thirst of the soul for the justice of God, since, as described in this work, it has reached this high level of spiritual and loving union with God. We will only look a little deeper at the satisfactions that have come to the soul as a result of the trials and afflictions already endured which brought this soul to the spiritual marriage. What is said in this work by St. John of the Cross concerns the soul that has traversed the nights of darkness in which it has become perfected by trial and grace.

> This spirit and life is perceived by souls who have ears to hear it, those souls, as I say, that are cleansed and enamored. Those who do not have a sound palate, but seek other tastes, cannot taste the spirit

and life of His words; His words rather are distasteful to them.

Hence the loftier were the words of the Son of God, the more tasteless they were to the impure, as happened when He preached the sovereign and loving doctrine of the Holy Eucharist; for many turned away (Jn 6:60-61, 67) (LF 1:5).

Therefore, it is the more secure, substantial, and delightful the more interior it is, because the more interior it is, the purer it is. And the greater the purity, the more abundantly, frequently, and generously God communicates Himself. Thus the joy and delight and joy of the soul is so much the more intense because God is the doer of all without the soul's doing anything (LF 1:9).

They shall be satisfied

Among the great contributions to the Church and to the spiritual life of Catholics are St. John's vivid descriptions of the rewards of the loving union of the soul with God: the union of likeness, and the exchanges of love between God and the soul. It is in this work that these descriptions are most clearly and fervently set forth. Each line of his poetry announces a new form of God's generosity to the soul that loves Him and has forsaken all other loves in order to subsist in His love alone. Let us examine just a few of St. John's expressions of the satisfactions that come to the soul that has, in perfect justice, relinquished all for its Beloved. Before we proceed to do this, it is essential to look once again at the narrow road and the rough way that must be traversed by the soul desiring to obtain all the satisfactions of union with God. St. John of the Cross makes it clear and unmistakable that this road must be walked before the destination can be reached.

O souls who in spiritual matters desire to walk in security and consolation! If you but knew how much it behooves you to suffer in order to reach this security and consolation, and how, without suffering, you cannot attain to your desire, but rather turn back, in nowise would you look for comfort either from God or from creatures (LF 2:28).

And here it ought to be pointed out why there are so few who reach this high state of perfect union with God. It should be known that the reason is not because God wishes that there be only a few of these spirits so elevated; He would rather want all to be perfect, but He finds few vessels that will endure so lofty and sublime a work (LF 2:27).

STANZA 1

O living flame of love
That tenderly wounds my soul
In its deepest center! Since now You are not oppressive,
Now Consummate! If it be Your will:
Tear through the veil of this sweet encounter!

That tenderly wounds my soul

> That is: O living flame of love that with your ardor tenderly touches me. Since this flame is a flame of divine life, it wounds the soul with the tenderness of God's life, and it wounds and stirs it so deeply as to make it dissolve in love (LF 1:7).
>
> And it should not be held as incredible in a soul now examined, purged, and tried in the fire of tribulations, trials, and many kinds of temptations, and found faithful in love, that the promise of the Son of God be fulfilled, the promise that the Most Blessed Trinity will come and dwell within anyone who loves Him (Jn 14:23) (LF 1:15).

Now consummate! If it be Your will:

> Affliction, then, does not accompany this desire and petition, for the soul is no longer capable of such affliction, but with a gentle and delightful desire it seeks this in the conformity of both spirit and sense to God's will.
>
> Yet the sudden flashes of glory and love which appear vaguely in these touches at the door of entry

into the soul, and which are unable to fit into it because of the narrowness of the earthly house, are so sublime that it would rather be a sign of little love not to try to enter into that perfection and completion of love (LF 1:28).

STANZA 2

O sweet cautery,
O delightful wound!
O gentle hand! O delicate touch
That tastes of eternal life
And pays every debt!
In killing You changed death into life.

O sweet cautery,

This cautery, as we mentioned, is the Holy Spirit...Yet He burns each soul according to its preparation: He will burn one more, another less, and this he does insofar as He desires, and how and when He desires (LF 2:2).

It is a wonderful thing, and worth relating that, since this fire of God is so mighty it would consume a thousand worlds more easily than the fire of this earth would burn up a straw, it does not consume and destroy the soul in which it so burns. And it does not afflict it; rather, commensurate with the strength of the love, it divinizes and delights it, burning gently (LF 2:3).

O delightful wound!

As often as the cautery of love touches the wound of love, it causes a deeper wound of love, and thus the more it wounds, the more it cures and heals. The more wounded the lover, the healthier he is, and the cure love causes is to wound and inflict wound upon wound, to such an extent that the entire soul is dissolved into a wound of love (LF 2:7).

Who can fittingly speak of this intimate point of the wound, which seems to be in the middle of the heart of the spirit, there where the soul experiences the excellence of the delight? The soul feels that that point is like a tiny mustard seed, very much alive and enkindled, sending into its surroundings a living and enkindled fire of love. The fire issuing from the substance and power of that living point which contains the substance and poser of the herb, is felt to be subtly diffused through all the spiritual and substantial veins of the soul in the measure of the soul's power and strength (LF 2:10).

STANZA 3

O lamps of fire!
In whose splendors
The deep caverns of feeling,
Once obscure and blind,
Now give forth, so rarely, so exquisitely,
Both warmth and light to their Beloved.

O lamps of fire!

Since all these lamps of the knowledge of God illumine you in a friendly and loving way, O enriched soul, how much more light and happiness of love will they, that produced that darkness and horror in Abraham, beget in you. How remarkable, how advantageous and how multifaceted will be your delight, for in all and from all you receive fruition and love, since God communicates Himself to your faculties according to His attributes and powers (LF 3:6).

O marvelous thing, that the soul at this time is flooded with divine waters, abounding in them like a plentiful fount overflowing on all sides! Although it is true that this communication under discussion is the light and fire from these lamps of God, yet this fire here is so gentle that, being an immense fire, it is like the waters of life, which satisfy the thirst of the spirit with that impetus the spirit desires (LF 3:8).

Now give forth, so rarely, so exquisitely,
Both warmth and light to their Beloved.

Having been made one with God, the soul is somehow God through participation. Although it is not God as perfectly as it will be in the next life, it is like the shadow of God. Being the shadow of God through this substantial transformation, it performs in this measure in God and through God what He through Himself does in it. For the will of the two is one will, and thus God's operation and the soul's is one (LF 3:78).

This is the soul's deep satisfaction and happiness: to see that it gives to God more than in itself it is worth; and this it does with that very divine light and divine heat and solitude. It does this in heaven by means of the light of glory and in this life by the means of a highly illumined faith (LF 3:80).

STANZA 4

How gently and lovingly
You awake in my heart,
Where in secret you dwell alone;
And in Your sweet breathing,
Filled with good and glory,
How tenderly You swell my heart with love!

How gently and lovingly
You wake in my heart,

How this movement takes place in the soul, since God is immovable, is a wonderful thing, for it seems to the soul that God indeed moves; yet He really does not move. For since it is the soul that is renewed and moved by God so that it might behold this supernatural sight, and since that divine life and the being and harmony of every creature in that life, with its movements in God, is revealed to it with such newness, it seems to the soul that it is God Who moves and that the cause assumes the name of the effect it produces (LF 4:6).

That which a person knows and experiences of God in this awakening is entirely beyond words. Since this awakening is the communication of God's excellence to the substance of the soul, which is its heart, referred to in the verse, an immense, powerful voice sounds in it, the voice of a multitude of excellences , of thousands of virtues in God, infinite in number (LF 4:10).

Where in secret You dwell alone;

It is in the soul in which less of its own appetites and pleasures dwell where He dwells more alone, more pleased , and more as though in His own house, ruling and governing it. And He dwells more in secret, the more He dwells alone (LF 4:14).

But in this awakening of the Bridegroom in the perfect soul, everything that occurs and is caused is perfect, for He is the cause of it all. And in that awakening, which is as though one were to awaken and breathe, the soul feels a strange delight in the breathing of the Holy Spirit in God, in which it is sovereignly glorified and taken with love (LF 4:16).

CHAPTER 5

BLESSED ARE THE MERCIFUL, FOR THEY SHALL OBTAIN MERCY

In the previous chapter, I made the point that God's justice requires the extension of mercy to His creatures for the reason that He recognizes the extreme handicap of weakness under which his rational creatures function. He therefore, does not expect more perfection than we are capable of. God *decided* to send a Redeemer who would earn the grace of mercy for us because of our utter inability to redeem and save ourselves. However, we must not conclude from this statement that there exists on God's part some duty or obligation to extend His mercy to His creatures. It is the perfection of the virtue of justice that subsists in God that results in the extension of mercy to those who seek it through repentance and a firm resolve to reform. This mercy of God manifests itself, not only in His readiness to forgive our transgressions, but also manifests itself in His generosity in extending to us the grace to grow in perfection and become more pleasing to Him. The mercy of God is completely gratuitous. No one can claim that they have earned the right to receive grace and forgiveness of their sins including the greatest of the saints who have reached great heights of perfection and holiness.

God requires that since He has extended His mercy gratuitously to us that we in turn must do likewise to our neighbor. He expresses that principle , not only in this *Beatitude*, but also in the primary prayer Christ taught us; The Lord's Prayer. In fact, He makes His mercy to each one of us dependent on our mercy toward others, forgiving them as we wish God to forgive us, from our hearts. This can be a daunting task when forgiveness is required repeatedly to the same person for the same offenses; which is usually the kind of repetitive forgiveness required by us from God. Christ tells His Apostles that they are to forgive seven times seventy if necessary, which is an ancient expression meaning without limit.

Let us examine the writings of our Carmelite saints in order to discover if this concept, of reciprocal mercy (mercy received to match mercy extended), is found and how it is expressed by them. We must first look at our saint's identification of various forms of mercy extended to others as described in their writings, and then examine in what way they see God's mercy to them and also to us, flowing from this horizontal mercy toward others.

A. St. Teresa of Jesus: The Way of Perfection

Mercy extended to others

St. Teresa approaches the question of extending mercy to others in two places of this work: First, in Chapter 4 in which she discusses the three things necessary for the spiritual life as spelled out in the Constitutions of the Carmelite Order. The first such necessity in the Constitutions is to love each other. The second place in which this matter of extending mercy is discussed is in chapter 36 in which she discusses the words contained in The Lord's Prayer: *Forgive us our trespasses, as* we *forgive those who trespass against us.* Let us examine each of these separately in order to understand how our saint expresses this *Beatitude* in her instruction of her sisters.

St. Teresa first makes a clear distinction between love that is self-seeking and contaminated by affections and passions, and spiritual love that seeks the good of the other. The topic of her writings here is the spiritual love that must exist between her sisters, which is easily applied to all relationships in and out of the cloistered life.

> With regard to the first – namely, love for each other – this is of great importance; for there is nothing, however annoying, that cannot easily be borne by those who love each other, and anything which causes annoyance must be quite exceptional. If this commandment were kept in the world, as it should be, I believe it would take us a long way towards the keeping of the rest; but, what with having too much love for each other or too little, we never manage to keep it perfectly (WP 4).

This spiritual love is a love that has as its object the good of the other, the one loved. This is its distinguishing characteristic. It is a true reflection of the nature of the love God has for His creatures. The primary result that is desired by the one loving another in this way is the salvation of that other soul. This is the desire for the greatest good for that other soul. This love takes no notice of offenses committed against this loving soul, but rushes to forgiveness so that no evil is wished upon the other soul.

> It is strange to see how impassioned this love is; how many tears, penances and prayers it costs; how careful is the loving soul to commend the object of its affection to all who it thinks may prevail with God and to ask them to intercede with Him for it; and how constant is its longing, so that it cannot be happy unless it sees its loved one is making progress...This, as I have said, is love without any degree whatsoever of self – interest; all that this soul wishes and desires is to see the soul (it loves) enriched with blessings from Heaven (WP 7).

The point was made at the beginning of this chapter that God extends His mercy and forgiveness to us because He recognizes our weakness which requires that we receive help from Him. This help comes not only in the form of grace to strengthen us against the assaults of the world, the flesh and the devil, but also in the form of His readiness to mercifully forgive us our transgressions when we repent of them. St. Teresa applies this latter form of God's mercy to those around us who require the same beneficence from us.

> In these matters, then, we must not judge others by ourselves, nor think of ourselves as we have been at some time when, perhaps without any effort on our part, the Lord has made us stronger than they; let us think of what we were like at the times when we have been weakest.

> Note the importance of this advice for those of us who would learn to sympathize with our neighbors' trials, however trivial these may be...They must therefore, try hard to recall what they were like when they were weak, and reflect that, if they are no longer so, it is not due to themselves (WP 7).

In St. Teresa's extensive analysis of the words of The Lord's Prayer, she examines the phrase: *Forgive us our trespasses, as* we *forgive those who trespass against us.* She points out that the soul that follows this command of the Lord to forgive others as it wishes to be forgiven by God has in effect united its will with the will of God. Therefore, the willingness to forgive others in mercy is a manifestation of surrender to the will of God. On the other hand when we follow our own will in matters requiring the forgiveness of others, so influenced and controlled by our emotions, we usually fail to achieve the level of mercy called for by our Lord in this prayer of all prayers.

> Notice sisters that He does not say: "as we shall forgive." We are to understand that anyone who asks for so great a gift as that just mentioned, (God's forgiveness) and has already yielded his own will to the will of God, must have done this already. And so He says, "As we forgive our debtors." Anyone, then, who sincerely repeats this position, Fiat voluntas tua," must at least in intention, have done this already (WP 36).

> This, sisters, is something which we should consider carefully; it is such a serious and important matter that God should pardon us our sins, which have merited eternal fire, that we must pardon all trifling things which have been done to us and which are not wrongs at all, or anything else (WP 36).

St. Teresa takes her cue from Christ in attaching great importance to the necessity of forgiving others the wrongs or presumed wrongs done to us. We recall our Lord's reference to the Old Testament passage: "It is mercy I desire, not sacrifice," instructing those listening to Him to go and learn the meaning of this phrase. Then there are the two subjects under discussion here that further reveal the importance to Christ of forgiveness of our neighbor; this *Beatitude,* and the language we are considering from The Lord's Prayer. She points out the importance to Christ of mutual forgiveness in the following passage:

> The good Jesus might have put everything else before our love for one another, and said, "Forgive us, Lord, because we are doing a great deal of penance, or because we are praying often, and

fasting, and because we have left all for Thy sake and love Thee greatly." But He has never said, "Because we would lose our lives for Thy sake," or any of these (numerous) other things which He might have said. He simply says, "Because we forgive" (WP 36).

They shall obtain mercy

The obtaining of mercy from God, therefore, is conditioned on the extending of mercy to our neighbor. The obtaining of divine mercy is also the reward for doing so. This manner of loving others results in the growth of spiritual perfection that always follows on conformance to the will of God in any respect. This growth in spiritual perfection is itself a built-in mercy from God. We know that we can do nothing without the assistance of divine grace. In this case spiritual perfection increases by our participation in the work of God toward His desired effects from our actions. As a result, we obtain the mercy of increased perfection as a direct reward emanating from our cooperation with the grace of extending mercy to others.

> If all the merit and gain which suffering is capable of producing could be made over to her (the other soul), we should still prefer suffering her trial ourselves to seeing her suffer it, but we are not worried or disquieted.
>
> I repeat once more that this love is a similitude and copy of that which was borne for us by the good lover, Jesus. It is for that reason that it brings us such immense benefits, for it makes us embrace every kind of suffering, so that others, without having to endure the suffering, may gain its advantages (WP 7).

As one grows in holiness and comes closer to union with God and with His will, the awareness of the great mercy of God grows proportionately in such a soul. This awareness comes in part from the self-knowledge that is developing in the advancing soul: a true view of our wretchedness in light of the goodness of God. What promotes mercy toward others more than anything else is a true insight into how much we have been and must be forgiven by God. A soul that has a false and inflated opinion of its own goodness and the source of its goodness, imaginary or real, will find it hard to be forgiving to others who offend it in any way. Therefore, the insight into our own imperfection is in fact the first reception of mercy from God. This is true no matter the distress this insight causes us. Distress is no measure of God's solicitation or absence of solicitation for our welfare. In fact, distress is frequently a sure sign of God's presence in our soul. It is no sign of love and charity that one is spared the suffering necessary for growth in the love of God and the death of the self. The opposite is in fact the case.

> As I have so few, Lord, even of these trifling things, to offer Thee, Thy pardoning of me must be a free gift: there is abundant scope here for Thy mercy. Thy Son must pardon me, for no one has done me any injustice, and so there has been nothing that I can pardon for Thy sake. But take my desire to do so, Lord, for I believe I would forgive any wrong if Thou wouldst forgive me and I might unconditionally do Thy will (WP 36).

> I cannot believe that a soul that has approached so nearly to Mercy Itself and the greatness of God's pardon, will not immediately and readily forgive, and be mollified and remain on good terms with a person who has done it wrong. For such a soul remembers the consolation and grace which He has shown it, in which it has recognized the signs of great love, and it is glad that the occasion presents itself for showing Him some love in return (WP 36).

B. St. Teresa of Jesus: The Interior Castle

The First Three Dwelling Places

Mercy extended to others

The principle that the awakening of mercy toward others in our souls is primarily caused by our knowledge of ourselves and our own multiple imperfections, is examined by St. Teresa in this work. Only one who is completely absorbed in the self and deliberately blind to his own faults and weaknesses could fail to be moved to mercy toward others. This would be true whether our extension of mercy is to forgive a wrong done personally to us, or when it takes the form of great concern and sympathy toward one who cannot or will not find their way to a loving union with God. The soul that is moved to judgment rather than mercy is a soul that has no idea of its own condition. When we observe another involved in error or pride, or some other sin, we can react in one of two ways. We can say interiorly that this poor soul needs prayer and needs to reform its life; and therefore, we shall pray for them. Humility in this case dominates our attitude. We say, "I know this struggle from my own experience, and I am willing to do whatever I can to help this soul overcome its weakness." I imitate Christ who says to the woman taken in adultery, "Neither do I condemn thee. Go, and sin no more." The extension of mercy to others is impossible without humility. Without this basic virtue, our response will deteriorate into a patronizing exercise of pride and self-satisfaction like the Pharisee in the Gospel who thanked God that he was not like other men. The other possible response is to condemn the weak soul that has fallen in some manner, as if we were perfect and without fault or weakness. How hard the fall will be of such a condemning person when it occurs, as it surely will.

> That person I mentioned said she received two blessings from the favor God granted her: the first, an intense fear of offending Him, and so in seeing such terrible dangers she always went about begging Him not to let her fall; the second, a mirror for humility, in which she saw how none of our good deeds has its principle from our selves but from this fount in which the tree, symbolizing our souls, is planted and from this sun that gives warmth to our works (IC I:2:5)

> So it is with the soul in the room of self-knowledge; let it believe me and fly sometimes to ponder the grandeur and majesty of its God. Here it will discover its lowliness better than by thinking of itself, and be freer from the vermin that enter the first rooms, those of self-knowledge (IC I:2:8).

We must recognize the obnoxious factor in the prideful soul that seeks to quickly condemn others for their faults. This soul cannot be an influence for good of others because not only is their attitude repulsive to others, but also others seek to avoid contact with them. They are frequently either abrasive in their manner, or unreachable in their lofty view of themselves. Therefore, they cannot do anything good to or for others, and their advice or counsel is rejected even when it may have some value.

> The soul could lose its peace and even disturb the peace of others by going about looking at trifling things in people that at times are not even imperfections, but since we know little we see these things in the worst light; look how costly this kind of perfection would be (IC I:2:18).

> Well now, it is foolish to think that we will enter heaven without entering into ourselves, coming to know ourselves, reflecting on our misery and what we owe God, and begging Him often for mercy (IC II:1:11).

They shall obtain mercy

The mercy of God takes two principal forms: First, through the sacrament of Penance, the forgiveness of sins committed. This sacrament and all the other sacraments as well, were purchased for us at a terrible cost to Christ. Here is the most fundamental manifestation of mercy from God. These sources of grace were given to us while we were (are) still sinners. The availability of the sacraments of forgiveness and mercy (Penance and the Holy Eucharist) repetitiously confirm God's constancy in bestowing His mercy. It is not a one-time thing, or something that has limits. We remember that God's patience is directed toward salvation. His mercy is always available to the truly repentant sinner.

The second form that God's mercy takes is the availability of grace that leads a soul to gradual perfection by the purgation of faults, which ultimately can lead to intimate union with God. These graces are purely gratuitous and are not earned by any individual, no matter his heroic degree of sanctity. They were earned for all by Christ alone in His life, death, and resurrection. While we can gain supernatural merit by our acts of holiness performed, while in the state of grace, which is itself a response to grace, the availability of this actual grace is a pure gift, from the mercy of God.

> Yet this Lord desires intensely that we love Him and seek His company, so much so that from time to time He calls us to draw near Him...
>
> I don't mean that these appeals and calls are like the ones I shall speak of later on. But, they come through words spoken by other good people, or through sermons, or through what is read in books, or through the many things that are heard and by which God calls, or through illness and trials, or also through a truth that He teaches during the brief moments we spend in prayer; however lukewarm these moments may be, God esteems them highly (IC II:1:2-3).

It is inconceivable that any soul could advance in holiness without the virtue of humility. It is this virtue that moves us initially to seek mercy from God. We cannot imagine a soul that is full of self-satisfaction and pride over its state of perfection (usually imagined perfection) turning humbly to God and asking for forgiveness of its many transgressions. This kind of soul cannot possibly recognize the need to extend a merciful attitude toward all others who it sees struggling with their weaknesses. Rather, this proud soul is more likely to judge others harshly and demand that they be treated appropriately for their weakness and stumbling. Such an attitude is directly contrary to what Christ teaches. We find what Christ teaches regarding humility and mercy in the parable of the *Prodigal Son*, in which Christ demonstrates the willingness of His Father to forgive us our transgressions. Christ also admonishes us to forgive others seven times seventy if necessary. Lastly, we find in *The Lord's Prayer*, the petition to forgive us as we forgive others. There is no doubt about the mind of Christ on this matter of extending mercy to others as a pre-requisite to receiving mercy from God, either in the form of forgiveness of sin or in the form of grace to grow toward union with God. St. Teresa expresses this necessity of humility frequently in her writings in order for a soul to progress in the spiritual life.

Well now, it is foolish to think that we will enter heaven without entering into ourselves, coming to know ourselves, reflecting on our misery and what we owe God, and begging Him often for mercy (IC II:1:11).

The journey I am speaking of must be taken with great humility. I believe that there is an obstacle for those who do not go forward. It should seem to us that we have gone but a few steps, and we should believe this to be so, and that those our Sisters have taken are rapid ones; and not only should we desire but we should strive that they consider us the most miserable of all (IC III:2:8).

The Last Four Dwelling Places

Mercy extended to others

In the Fourth Dwelling Place, St. Teresa discusses the transition from the natural way of prayer to supernatural prayer infused by God into the soul. She explains and differentiates between the supernatural forms of prayer which are the prayer of recollection, the prayer of spiritual delight, prayer of quiet and the prayer of union. She emphasizes the need for humility as the soul experiences any of these supernatural forms of prayer granted by God. We focus on the importance St. Teresa places on humility in this dwelling place because humility governs our attitude, not only toward God the giver of gifts; but also toward others who may or may not also be gifted with these higher forms of prayer. We are never safe in assuming that another has or has not received the same graces in prayer that we receive; or that our forms of prayer have greater spiritual value than that of another. Humility requires that we assume that others are probably more advanced in prayer than we are regardless of the outward appearances of piety or lack of piety that they show. In this way, we are acting mercifully to others because we value their piety and spiritual growth more than our own, even though we do not have the means to judge the actual truth of the matter.

After you have done what should be done by those in the previous dwelling places: Humility!

> Humility! By this means the Lord allows Himself to be conquered with regard to anything we want from Him. The first sign for seeing whether or not you have humility is that you do not think you deserve these favors and spiritual delights from the Lord or that you will receive them in your lifetime (IC IV:2:9).

As in every aspect of the spiritual life, what is happening in another soul, one for whom we have no responsibility, is really none of our business. The exception to this indifference is of course to rejoice in the spiritual growth of another because it gives greater glory to God. But measuring others against ourselves or ourselves against them in spiritual matters is an exercise in either pride or envy. Mercy demands that the most favorable opinion possible be applied to the acts and motives of others.

> Therefore, Sisters, let this never happen to you, but believe that God can do far more and don't turn your attention to whether the ones to whom He grants His favors are good or bad; for His Majesty knows this, as I have told you. There is no reason for us to meddle in the matter, but with humility and simplicity of heart, we should serve and praise Him for His works and marvels (IC V:1:8).

In discussing the prayer of quiet, St. Teresa emphasizes that this favor granted to souls is not only for the benefit of the soul receiving it. These spiritual gifts intrinsically carry with them a benefit to others that may even be greater than the benefit to the soul that receives them. The awareness of this and the allowance of the benefit to be spread to others without any effort to contain it within the receiving soul is an expression of merciful love toward others. Also, a favor received from God will never be given in vain. Others will benefit from these favors when a soul receiving the gift of union receives it, as the resulting virtue spreads the grace abroad to others. St. Teresa applies her well-known metaphor of the silk worm to illustrate the effects of God's favors on a soul, and by extension, on other souls in proximity to the favored soul. When the silk worm dies, it turns into a beautiful butterfly. All then are able to enjoy the newly created beauty of the butterfly or, to apply the metaphor, of the blessed soul.

It must always be understood that one has to strive to go forward in the service of our Lord and in self-knowledge. For if, a person does no more than receive this favor and if, as though already securely in possession of something, she grows careless in her life and turns aside from the heavenly path, which consists of keeping the commandments, that which happens to the silkworm will happen to her. For it gives forth the seed that produces other silkworms and itself dies forever. I say, "It gives forth the seed" because I hold that it is God's desire that a favor so great not be given in vain; if a person doesn't herself benefit the favor will benefit others. For since the soul is left with these desires and virtues that were mentioned, it always brings profit to other souls during the time that it continues to live virtuously; and they catch fire from its fire (IC V:3:1).

What I said seems to me very beneficial to help you understand how pleased our Lord is that we know ourselves and strive to reflect again and again on our poverty and misery and on how we possess nothing that we have not received. So, my sisters, courage is necessary for this knowledge and for the many other graces given to the soul, the Lord has brought to this stage. And when there is humility, courage, in my opinion, is even more necessary for this knowledge of one's own misery (IC VI:5:6).

If we understand what St. Teresa is telling us in these passages, and we have some insight into our true poverty before God and our indispensable need for Him to lift us up to Himself; then we cannot but be disposed mercifully toward others. We all have the same need for God's assistance in the spiritual life; we are fellow travelers on the road to heaven with them, and therefore, we are all in pursuit of the same end: eternal life with God. Toward this end, we are presented with opportunities to help them and them to help us. Mercy requires that we extend every possible aid to all souls seeking the one God and union with Him. We must tolerate, forgive, and aid anyone when the occasion presents itself to us. In this way, we are merciful, as God desires us to be merciful toward others.

They shall obtain mercy

I have made the point previously that it is impossible to truly love God and not love your neighbor. In this regard, I am not talking about the emotions of love, the feeling of affection for another. We are all subject to irritations from others. Fr. John Hardon, S.J. of fond memory has said that most of our suffering comes from other people. The love I speak of here is the desire that all souls among our acquaintances and otherwise be brought to eternal union with God. And this result is wished no matter how greatly they irritate us in life. Therefore, given this love of neighbor, we cannot help but extend a merciful attitude to them. This is the disposition desired by the Lord, and is rewarded by Him in many ways, among which are spiritual advancement and spiritual gifts. These rewards are not available to us at will, but are pure gifts of God's providence. St. Teresa discusses many of them in the last four mansions of *The Interior Castle*. In speaking of the spiritual delight of the prayer of quiet, she illustrates that God gives this form of prayer without effort on the part of the soul.

> This spiritual delight is not something that can be imagined, because however diligent our efforts we cannot acquire it. The very experience of it makes us realize that it is not of the same metal as we ourselves but fashioned from the purest gold of the divine wisdom. Here, in my opinion, the faculties are not united but absorbed and looking as though in wonder at what they see (IC IV:2:6).

The ultimate gift of God in this life is the gift of union with Him in prayer. This is the ultimate example of His mercy. Imagine that a soul that has done nothing to earn such a gift becomes eligible for this gift in God's eyes by, among other things, showing mercy to others. If all other things were equal, the absence of an attitude of mercy towards others would be a complete inhibitor to the granting of these gifts by God. The many examples mentioned above of the expression by God of the importance of mercy toward all (*The Lord's Prayer*, scriptural statements and especially this *Beatitude*) confirm this fact. St. Teresa describes the extraordinary beauty of the gift of union in the following way:

> Well then, to return to the sign that I say is the true one, you now see that God has made this soul a fool with regard to all so as to better to impress upon it true wisdom. For during the time of this union it neither sees, nor hears, nor understands, because the union is always short and seems to the soul even much shorter than it probably is. God so places Himself in the interior of that soul that when it returns to itself it can in no way doubt that it was in God and God was in it (IC V:I:9).

In subsequent pages, St. Teresa goes on to describe other gifts of God that are more exotic and rare than those already described. These are locutions, raptures, and ecstasies. It is beyond the scope of our subject to delve into each of these favors in detail. Suffice it to say of them that they are further examples of God's generosity to some souls. Not all receive these favors regardless of the degree of their holiness, and no one should judge themselves or others in matters of holiness by the presence or absence of these extraordinary favors. They are highly selective gifts of God in mercy to some souls for His own unique purposes.

St. Teresa explains the many gifts that God gives these fervent souls. They are in reality different forms of supernatural prayer, but prayer that originates in God. God bestows them on the soul as gifts and rewards for desiring and following His will.

> And thus you will see what His Majesty does to conclude this betrothal, which I understand comes about when He gives the soul raptures that draw it out of its senses...I want to put down here some kinds of rapture that I've come to understand because I've discussed them with so many spiritual persons (IC VI:4:2).

> One kind of rapture is that in which the soul even though not in prayer is touched by some word it remembers or hears about God...Yet it does have interior understanding, for this experience is not like that of fainting or convulsions; in these latter nothing is understood inwardly or outwardly (IC VI:4:3).

But, you will insist, if there is no image and the faculties do not understand, how can the vision be remembered? I don't understand this either; but I do understand that some truths about the grandeur of God remain so fixed in this soul, that even if faith were not to tell it who God is and of its obligation to believe that He is God, from that very moment it would adore Him as God,...(IC VI:4:6).

In a rapture, believe me, God carries off for Himself the entire soul, and, as to someone who is His own and His spouse, He begins showing it some little part of the kingdom that it has gained by being espoused to Him (IC VI:4:9).

There is another kind of rapture – I call it flight of the spirit – which, though substantially the same as other raptures, is interiorly experienced very differently. For sometimes suddenly a movement of the soul is felt so swift that it seems the spirit is carried off, and at a fearful speed especially in the beginning (IC VI:5:1).

These favors are like the waves of a large river in that they come and go; but the memory these souls have of their sins clings like thick mire. It always seems that these sins are alive in the memory, and this is a heavy cross (IC VI:7:2).

All of these extraordinary favors given by God are magnificent extensions of God's mercy to loving souls who have sought earnestly to unite their will with God's will. This unity is always acquired through great suffering as the self dies and is replaced by God alone. When this death of self is achieved by God's help, the mercy experienced by this fortunate soul, at the hand of God, is sublime.

C. St. John of the Cross: The Ascent of Mt. Carmel

Mercy extended to others

The point has been made in several places that advancement in the spiritual life is directly proportional to the degree of death of the self. One cannot be self–centered and God-centered at the same time. Neither can one be self-centered and concerned with the good of others at the same time. St. John of the Cross makes the point, drawing on the teachings of the Greek philosopher Aristotle that two opposites cannot exist in the same subject at the same time. What make a soul self-centered are its attachments and appetites. These are our inclinations that continually cry out for satisfaction. The principal point St. John makes in Book I of *The Ascent of Mt. Carmel* is that in order to begin advancing in holiness toward union with God, a soul must purge itself of its inordinate appetites involving creatures and the things of this world.

> This dark night is a privation and purgation of all sensible appetites for the external things of the world, the delights of the flesh, and the gratifications of the will. All this deprivation is wrought in the purgation of sense (AS I:1:4).

It is not possible for one to nurture inordinate attachments and appetites and at the same time to have a sufficient interest in the welfare of our neighbor to extend to him mercy or sentiments of forgiveness for wrongs committed against our self or those whom we love. The attitudes of self-indulgence and that of concern for our neighbor are opposites that cannot exist in the same subject at the same time. Until we have mortified our attachments and appetites, unselfish concern for our neighbor is impossible.

> ...it is sad to consider the condition of the poor person in whom they (the appetites) dwell. How unhappy he is with himself, how cold toward his neighbor, how sluggish and slothful in the things of God (AS I:10:4).

The point to remember is therefore, that the purgation of the self-absorbing appetites must precede any real love of neighbor. Without a real love for neighbor, the extension of mercy to him will simply not occur. Self interest always operates as an obstacle for concern for others; and self- interest is always tied to our attachments which are those aspects of our life that we fiercely protect from interference from others who would interrupt our self-indulgence.

The whole of this work of St. John is an exposition of what is required of the soul in the active nights of sense and spirit to mortify and purge both the sensory appetites and the spiritual appetites in order to arrive at closer union with God. These appetites serve as the principal obstacles to advancing to union with God. Without their purgation, union with God is impossible.

Near the end of *The Ascent of Mt. Carmel,* in Book III of this work, he discusses the purification of the will and the attitude towards and also the treatment of goods that the soul must adopt. In this connection, he raises several different kinds of goods, some of which should be rejected and in some of which the soul should rejoice. For example, he discusses temporal goods, natural goods, sensory goods and supernatural goods. In his discussion of natural goods, he raises a point that advances our discussion of the disposition of the soul required for the extension of mercy toward others. He describes natural goods as those aspects of a person that would most likely lead to self-absorption: "beauty, grace, elegance, bodily constitution, and all other corporal endowments; and in the soul, good intelligence, discretion, and other talents pertinent to the rational part of man." He then speaks of the denial of joy in natural goods, pointing out the harms resulting from joy in natural goods and also the benefits from not rejoicing in natural goods.

> Many are the benefits derived through withdrawal of the heart from this joy (in natural goods). Besides preparing the soul for the love of God and for other virtues, it directly paves the way for humility toward self and general charity toward one's neighbor. In remaining unattached to everyone in spite of these apparent and deceptive natural goods, a person is unencumbered and free to love all rationally and spiritually, which is the way God wants him to love (AS III:23:1).

They shall obtain mercy

As previously pointed out, there are two principal forms that the mercy of God takes vis-à-vis the soul. The first and most obvious is the forgiveness of sins. This form is contained primarily in the sacrament of Penance. Christ bestowed upon the apostles His own authority to forgive sins when He said, "Receive you the Holy Spirit: Whose sins you shall forgive they are forgiven them, and whose sins you shall retain they are retained (John 20: 21-23)." Christ also gave broader authority to His apostles over and above the power to forgive sins. Contained within this broader authority is also the power to forgive sins: "I will give to you the keys of the kingdom of heaven. And whatsoever thou shalt bind upon earth, shall be bound in heaven; and whatsoever thou shalt loose on earth shall be loosed in heaven (Mt 16:19)."

However, there is even greater mercy available to souls who choose to accept it: holiness and ever increasing closeness to God. These gifts lead to the ultimate mercy of God: the possibility of union with Him. This union with God is the goal toward which St. John of the Cross leads us in all of his writings. Throughout the descriptions of the severe trials and afflictions of the soul in the process of the purification and purgation of all that is not God, St. John shows us the light of God's love shining through these most difficult periods. He calls the movement of the soul toward the narrow gate and the rough way a *sheer grace*.

> The soul, through original sin, is a captive in the mortal body, subject to passions and natural appetites; when liberated from this bondage and submission, it considers its escape, which is unnoticed, unimpeded, and unapprehended by its passions and appetites, a sheer grace (AS I:15:1).

It would take another volume to describe the gifts that God makes available and offers to the soul that wishes to endure the affliction necessary to become disposed and capable of receiving them. As previously pointed out, the prerequisite disposition is humility and an absence of self- indulgence and self- preoccupation. We recall that this disposition grows and becomes perfected as we become more interested in the welfare of our neighbor than in that of ourselves. There is no proportion between what we give to God and what we receive in return from God. He touches our soul in ways that are inexplicable.

> This sublime knowledge can be received only by a person who has arrived at union with God, for it is itself that very union. It consists in a certain touch of the divinity produced in the soul, and thus it is God Himself who is experienced and tasted there (AS II:26:5).

> These touches engender such sweetness and intimate delight in the soul that one of them would more than compensate for all the trials suffered in life, even though innumerable. Through these touches a person becomes so courageous and so resolved to suffer many things for Christ that he finds it a special suffering to observe that he does not suffer (AS II:26:7).

St. John of the Cross uses most of Book III of *The Ascent of Mt. Carmel* to discuss the purification of the will. His emphasis is on the joy in various kinds of goods that the soul experiences. He makes the point that the soul is ill advised to take joy in many of the goods discussed; but may profitably take joy in some goods which have the effect of bringing the soul closer to union with God because they are not obstacles to that union. Those goods that produce positive joy are only positive to the extent they are exaltations of God and are separated from all that is not God. When the will is so withdrawn from all but God, God is thereby exalted, and the soul proceeds by faith alone toward union with God. In this response, the soul is the recipient of pure grace from God's unlimited mercy, and God is thereby glorified by the soul.

> God is truly extolled when joy is withdrawn from all things and centered upon Him, but He receives much more glory when it is removed from these more marvelous goods and applied to Him alone, since by being supernatural they are of higher entity. To leave them behind for the sake of joy in God alone is to attribute greater glory and excellence to God than to them (AS III:32:2).

D. St. John of the Cross: The Dark Night

Mercy extended to others

As St. John begins his most important work describing the purgation and purification of the soul that seeks God and union with Him, he first raises the imperfections that have been exposed in the beginner in the spiritual life. These imperfections have been manifested in the soul as a result of the imperfect way in which all beginners proceed through the early stages of their sojourn toward God. We must realize that these imperfections are an inevitable part of the early efforts of the soul in its spiritual life. All souls experience one or more of these imperfections and no one is to be condemned for having had a struggle with any of them. It is because of this rather natural affliction that the dark passive nights are necessary for all souls in order to advance toward union with God. That advancement cannot occur until the soul is purged of these imperfections and many more besides.

These imperfections of *beginners* (who have in fact become proficient in some aspects of the spiritual life) are also impediments to the attitude of mercy toward our neighbor, the attitude necessary for the reception of mercy from God. The mere listing of them demonstrates how they obstruct the attitude of extending mercy to others: spiritual pride, spiritual lust, spiritual anger, spiritual envy, spiritual sloth, spiritual gluttony, and spiritual avarice. Each in their correspondence to the capital sins turns a soul inward upon the self and the gratification of the self, which is the source of all imperfection and sin. Therefore, these must be purged from the soul before any real advancement in spirituality can occur. St. John of the Cross calls this period in the spiritual life the passive nights. By this, he means that the soul does not, by its activity as in the active nights, accomplish the necessary purgation. It is God who alone can reach deeply enough into the soul to extract the roots of these imperfections. Because of this passivity and dependence upon God and His work in the soul, this is a very difficult period for the soul. But, without it, no progress beyond a spiritual childhood is possible, nor can the soul respond appropriately to God's command to extend mercy to others without the death of self. That is the primary achievement to be hoped for in this difficult period of affliction. The first stanza of *The Dark Night* follows. All of what St. John wants to say of this period of the soul's trial is contained within these words of poetry, and also in the second stanza that comes later.

> *One dark night,*
> *Fired with love's urgent longings*
> *-Ah, the sheer grace!-*
> *I went out unseen,*
> *My house being now all stilled;*

We note that this poetry is the same as that which St. John deals with in *The Ascent of Mt. Carmel*. However, the aspects of these words that he applies in this work reflect the great afflictions of the passive nights, whereas, in *The Ascent* the same words were applied to the active nights.

> In this first stanza, the soul is speaking of the way it followed in its departure from love of self and of all things through a method of true mortification, which causes it to die to itself and to all these things and to begin the sweet and delightful life of love with God (DN: Exp:1).

We must bear in mind that the soul that enters these passive nights will endure great suffering and affliction, both in the spirit and in the senses. The task of denying the self unto the death of self-centeredness in all matters spiritual and sensory is a violent rending of our fallen nature. Without this transformation, it would not be possible for a soul to extend the degree of mercy toward others that is demanded by Christ, the forgiveness of another seventy times seven daily. St. John of the Cross enumerates some of these afflictions which will be experienced in the passive night of sense in chapter 14 of Book I of this work: dryness, anxiety, darkening of the senses, strong and abominable temptations, a blasphemous spirit, and scrupulosity. After a long and painful trial with all of these and more, the soul can say of its sensory nature, "**My house being now all stilled.**"

> Yet we cannot say certainly how long the soul will be kept in this fast and penance of the senses. Not everyone undergoes this in the same way, neither are the temptations identical. All is meted out according to God's will and the greater or lesser amount of

> imperfection that must be purged from each one. In the measure of the degree of love to which God wishes to raise a soul, He humbles it with greater or less intensity, or for a longer or shorter period of time.
>
> Those who have more considerable capacity and strength for suffering, God purges more intensely and quickly (DN I:14:5).

In Book II of *The Dark Night*, St. John enters the realm of the passive night of the spirit. In this phase of the spiritual life, the very depths of the soul are exposed to the divine light in order to enable the soul to see itself, as it never had before. Imperfections come to light that were never seen or suspected by the soul. Each of these imperfections constitutes an obstacle to union with God. This union occurs in the spirit. Therefore, these obstacles residing in the spirit must be removed in order for the desired union to take place. One cannot perform the instructions of Christ to extend mercy to our neighbor from our heart, to be holy as the heavenly Father is holy, unless this annihilation of imperfections in the spirit occurs.

> But since, after all, the sensory part of the soul is weak and incapable of vigorous spiritual communications, these proficients, because of such communications experienced in the sensitive part, suffer many infirmities, injuries, and weaknesses of stomach, and as a result fatigue of spirit…Consequently the communications imparted to proficients cannot be very strong, nor very intense, nor very spiritual – which is a requirement of the divine union – because of the weakness and corruption of the senses which have their share in them (DN II:1:2).

The point here is that in order to truly extend mercy to others as God wishes it to be done, from the heart, a death of self must occur. The true welfare of the other, who we assume is an offending party needing forgiveness, can only be actually preferred and fostered by a soul that has substantially died to self. This death can only be brought about through the afflictions and purgation of these passive nights so completely described by St. John of the Cross.

There is a lesser forgiveness possible to the soul offended by another. That is the resolution, that even though one has been offended or hurt deliberately by another, he will not seek revenge and will either ignore the offense or complain of it to the offender and then let the matter be dismissed. He will not seek to cause harm to the one who has committed a wrong against him. However, he will seek to avoid any relationship with the offender from this point forward. We can readily distinguish these two levels of mercy. The former is an extension of mercy in the manner that God extends it to us. The latter is a limited mercy extended to another that results from our weakened human nature seeking to rise above itself, but failing to reach the mercy desired by God. This limited mercy can only be expanded to the level of imitation of divine mercy by the effects of the passive nights that lead to the death of the self.

> Wishing to strip them in fact of this old man and clothe them with the new which is created according to God in the newness of sense...God divests the faculties, affections, and senses, both spiritual, and sensory, interior and exterior. He leaves the intellect in darkness, the will in aridity, the memory in emptiness, and the affections in supreme affliction, bitterness, and anguish, by depriving the soul of the feeling and satisfaction it previously obtained from spiritual blessings. For this privation is one of the conditions required that the spiritual form, which is the union of love, may be introduced in the spirit and united with it (DN II:3:3).

They shall obtain mercy

This section concentrates on the higher level of mercy mentioned above: the grace to become holy through purification and purgation of the soul of its imperfections. While the experiences that constitute the purgation of imperfections are afflictions and sufferings, they are in fact an enormous grace and extension of mercy by God. There could be no greater absence of divine mercy than to be ignored and forgotten by God, and denied the means necessary to draw closer to Him. So the invitation of God to draw near carries with it not only a sublime grace, but also a bitter aroma. This bitter aroma however, is absolutely necessary to reach into the soul and extract these deep-seated imperfections that stubbornly resist all efforts of the soul to correct. Not only this, the soul fails to even see the imperfections that need purging without the aid of the light of God shining on them to illuminate them so as to be seen by the soul.

> The first and chief benefit that this dry and dark night of contemplation causes is the knowledge of self and of one's own misery. Besides the fact that all the favors God imparts to the soul are ordinarily enwrapped in this knowledge, the aridities and voids of the faculties in relation to the abundance previously experienced, and the difficulty encountered in the practice of virtue make the soul recognize its own lowliness and misery, which was not apparent in the time of its prosperity (DN I:12:2).

The soul that does not see its need for purification will never achieve it because it will never allow the process of purifying itself to begin. In addition to seeing its need for purification, the soul that wishes to grow in holiness must also see its own inability to achieve the goal unaided by God's grace. The surrender to the divine will must be increasingly complete as the purification and purgation goes forward.

Perhaps the most difficult principle to understand and accept regarding the spiritual life and the dynamics experienced in it, is that the worse things seem to be, the better they are in truth. When one has advanced a certain distance in spirituality, the only way to continue advancing is to suffer the pains of purgation. Correctly understood, these pains are a very great grace to the soul. Matters are being addressed in this thick darkness which, if unattended, would permanently block the soul's quest for union with God. Hence, the necessity for time in Purgatory for most souls in order to complete the work that remains undone at death.

> As fire consumes the tarnish and rust of metal, this contemplation annihilates, empties, and consumes all the affections and imperfect habits the soul contracted throughout its life. Since these imperfections are deeply rooted in the substance of the soul, it usually suffers besides this poverty and

this natural and spiritual emptiness an oppressive undoing and an inner torment (DN II:6:5).

The afflictions of a soul in this passive night of the spirit would take many pages to enumerate. Because they are so many and so severe, I must continuously remind the reader that these sufferings are indeed a great mercy from God bestowed on a soul so afflicted. There is a goal being striven for that constantly grows closer to achievement with each painful affliction that assails the soul. In order to avoid discouragement, the soul must understand that the pain of this contemplation does not come from God, but emanates from the soul and its imperfection.

> This war or combat is profound because the peace awaiting the soul must be exceedingly profound; and the spiritual suffering is intimate and penetrating because the love to be possessed by the soul will also be intimate and refined. The more intimate and highly finished the work must be, so the more intimate, careful, and pure must the labor be; and commensurate with the solidity of the edifice is the energy involved in the work (DN II:9:9).

> Let us examine now why this light of contemplation, which is so gentle and agreeable and which is the same light to which the soul must be united and in which it will find all its blessings in the desired state of perfection, produces such painful and disagreeable effects when in these initial stages it shines upon the soul.

> We can answer this question easily by repeating what we already explained in part; that is, there is nothing in contemplation or the divine inflow which of itself can give pain, contemplation rather bestows sweetness and delight. The cause for not experiencing these agreeable effects is the soul's weakness and imperfection at the time, its inadequate preparation, and the qualities it possesses which are contrary to this light. Because of these, the soul has to suffer when the divine light shines upon it (DN II:9:10-11).

E. St. John of the Cross: The Spiritual Canticle

Mercy extended to others

This work of St. John of the Cross is devoid of material that can directly be related to the extending of mercy to others. This work deals exclusively with the soul's march toward completion of union with God: the spiritual betrothal and the spiritual marriage. However, from this work we can draw the general principle that all holiness consists to some extent in the proportionate growth of charity toward our neighbor. This emanates first and foremost from love of God. Love of God cannot exist without a corresponding love of neighbor, who is loved in God and for the sake of God. We cannot imagine that one could claim that he loves God, but yet either despises his neighbor or is indifferent to him. Therefore, one who truly loves God is possessed of humility, and this virtue facilitates his love for his neighbor. Such a humble soul will see itself as inferior to the other, and will have admiration for the other soul rather than contempt. This humble soul will wish only what is good for the other soul, and in doing so will extend merciful assistance to the other at every opportunity.

This work of St. John of the Cross is resplendent with examples of the abundant extension of mercy by God to souls who seek Him and love Him. Within *The Spiritual Canticle* is described the path to and the attributes of the spiritual betrothal and the spiritual marriage, the pinnacles of the spiritual quest for God. We will examine these two milestones in the spiritual life of a soul that has labored long and with great difficulty to reach union with God. Each milestone is an extraordinary manifestation of the limitless mercy God is willing to extend to a soul that seeks Him with its whole self and is willing to endure the trials of purgation to be united with Him. These milestones are the generous reward of God that shows forth His mercy more than any other manifestation of it.

They shall obtain mercy

In stanzas 14 through 19, St. John of the Cross describes a soul entering into the spiritual betrothal. In stanzas 1 through 13, he describes the longings of the soul to find God and its sorrow at failing to discover where He has hidden. However, in stanza 13 the Bridegroom speaks to the soul, which experiences enormous consolation in at last hearing Him speak The poetry of St John is very important to the understanding of what is happening here between the soul and its Beloved, soon to become its Bridegroom. The poetry adds immensely to the beauty of the experience of the soul striving to find its Beloved, and its joy at succeeding in its quest. I will therefore, include some of that poetry that most pertains to our subject: the obtaining of mercy from God in the form of the gift of Himself to the soul in the Spiritual Betrothal and Spiritual Marriage. The lines that are most applicable to our subject will be discussed briefly.

STANZA 1

Where have you hidden,
Beloved, and left me moaning?
You fled like the stag
After wounding me;
I went out calling You, and You were gone.

After wounding me;

This wounding is the effect of divine touches given the soul in its earlier spiritual life, which caused affliction and delight at the same time. This wound is more grievous than the wounds of the pain and suffering endured by the soul in the purgation of its imperfections.

> And these wounds, mentioned here, are properly called wounds of love. They so inflame the will in its affection that it burns up in this flame and fire of love. So intense is this burning, that the soul is seemingly consumed in that flame, and the fire makes it go out of itself, wholly renews it, and changes its manner of being, as in the case of the phoenix which burns itself in the fire and rises anew from the ashes (SC 1:17).

I went out calling You, and You were gone.

As a soul grows in holiness, it leaves behind all that is not God or of God's attributes. It is indifferent to all things and persons that formerly interested it, and to which it was attached in times past.

Finally, it detaches from itself and becomes free to fly unhindered to God. This detachment is a gift of God's mercy that enables the flight of the soul toward God to occur.

> When the love of God really touches the soul, as we are saying, it so raises her up that it not only impels her to go out from self in this forgetfulness, but even draws her away from her natural supports, manners, and inclinations, thus inducing her to call after God (SC 1:20).

STANZA 9

Why, since you wounded
This heart, don't you heal it?
And why, since You stole it from me,
Do You leave it so,
And fail to carry off what You have stolen?

Do you leave it so,

When this soul says that God has left it so, it means that God has removed all attachments to natural things and creatures, and even the attachment to itself and its own will. Yet, He does not carry the soul off to Himself, even though He has stolen its heart. This *stealing* of the heart is evident from the soul's utter disinterest in anything but its Beloved, not even an interest in its own will.

> The reason is that the heart cannot have peace and rest while not possessing, and when it is truly in love, it no longer has possession of self or of any other thing. And if it does not possess completely what it loves, it cannot help being weary, in proportion to its loss, until it possesses the loved object and is satisfied (SC 9:6).

Since this soul has been dispossessed of all that is not God, it is truly ready for the espousal that it hopes for. One thing is now lacking; the response of the Beloved to the cries from the heart of this soul that are expressed in all the stanzas of this poem up to this point. If there is no response, the love of this soul for God is unrequited. The Beloved now is faced with a demand upon His mercy to extend His loving response to this afflicted soul. Its love has sent it into raptures of longing that is not yet satisfied. The soul remains in a state of absence of fulfillment.

STANZA 13

Withdraw them Beloved,
I am taking flight!

The Bridegroom speaks:

Return dove,
The wounded stag
Is in sight on the hill,
Cooled by the breeze of your flight.

I am taking flight:

The effect of a divine touch received by a soul is that these touches are not received in the sensory part of the soul, but in the spiritual part. The soul does not depart from the body, but the sensory aspects of an individual are suspended. They do not take part in the divine touch, and do not experience the normal sensory sensations while the divine touch has transported the spirit.

> However, it should not be thought because of this that the soul forsakes the body, which is its sensory life, but rather that the soul's actions are not in the body. This is why in these raptures and flights the body has no feeling, and even though severely painful things are done to it, it does not feel them....
>
> These feelings are experienced in such visits by those who have not yet reached the state of perfection, but are advancing along in the state of proficient's (SC 136).
>
> *Return, dove,*
> *The wounded stag*
> *Is in sight on the hill,*

> The Bridegroom finds the soul in this state of what we can call *elevated frustration and longing.* The Bridegroom at lasts deems it the proper time to respond to this afflicted soul. And what does He say?

> He now tells the soul that He also has received a wound of love from the soul. He refers to Himself as a wounded stag. And thus, we have the completion of the spiritual espousal. Each has now confessed their love to the other. The immensity of this mercy of God is beyond description in words. It is the totality of mercy that is possible. God has invited the soul to union with Him, the One who is infinitely above the soul; the One without whose willing it all, the end and the means, would be impossible to the soul to achieve. But even more lies ahead.

> > Beholding that the bride is wounded with love for Him, He also, because of her moan, is wounded with love for her...Thus, in other words, He says: Return to Me, My bride, because if you go about like the stag wounded with love for Me, I too, like the stag, will come to you wounded by your wound (SC 13:9).

STANZA 22

> *The bride has entered*
> *The sweet garden of her desire,*
> *And she rests in delight,*
> *Laying her neck*
> *On the gentle arms of her Beloved.*

These are the words of the Bridegroom to the soul. This soul has struggled to overcome its appetites, imaginations, and sensory movements that occur in the lower part of the soul. In stanzas 16, 17 &18, St. John refers to these as foxes, the deadening north wind, and the girls of Judea. Now, having overcome all of these obstacles to the spiritual marriage, the soul may now enter that union with God that will last forever. This gift of God is the epitome of His loving mercy to the soul that has chosen Him completely. It is completely gratuitous, but it must be chosen by the soul. The bride enters the garden of her desire by many fiats along the way. That choice is made along the path of spiritual growth by enduring the afflictions and trials necessary to prepare the soul for this union. This purgation cannot be avoided if the end is to be reached. No description in words can be given to the phenomenon of God condescending to allow a soul to enter into intimate union with Him. It is a matter to be contemplated for a lifetime in order to come to some appreciation of the enormity of such a possibility.

> This spiritual marriage is incomparably greater than the spiritual espousal, for it is a total transformation in the Beloved in which each surrenders the entire possession of self to the other with a certain consummation of the union of love. The soul thereby becomes divine, becomes God through participation, insofar as is possible in this life. And thus, I think that this state never occurs without the soul's being confirmed in grace, for the faith of both is confirmed when God's faith in the soul is here confirmed. It is accordingly the highest state attainable in this life (SC 22:3).

STANZA 35

> *She lived in solitude,*
> *And now in solitude has built her nest;*
> *And in solitude He guides her,*
> *He alone, Who also bears*
> *In solitude the wound of love.*

To conclude this discussion of our subject, God extending mercy to His people, we examine the all-important topic of solitude. The soul described in this stanza has passed far beyond the fundamental mercy extended by God to every willing soul through the sacrament of Penance. Those who have yet to travel the great distance traversed by the soul described here have been provided many avenues for obtaining the mercy of God through the ministry of the Church. Not only the primary means, the sacraments, are available to them, but also the ministry of many people, both clerical and lay. These people have been placed by God in the lives of those striving for a closer relationship with Him in order to aid those souls on the journey toward union with Him.

And in solitude He guides her,

However, the soul described in this stanza has advanced so far in achieving union with God that it now finds that God alone is necessary to it in order to sustain this union. Hence, an atmosphere of solitude is enjoyed, and is very pleasing to God. The essence of the spiritual marriage consists in this solitary reliance on God to preserve this union with Him, and the abandonment of all else for the sake of this union.

The Bridegroom does two things in this stanza:

First, He praises the solitude in which the soul formerly desired to live, telling how it was a means for her to find and rejoice in her Beloved alone, withdrawn from all her former afflictions and fatigues...

Second, He states that, insofar as she desired to live apart from all created things, in solitude for her Beloved's sake, He Himself was enamored of her because of this solitude...(SC 35:2).

In this solitude, away from all things, the soul is alone with God and He guides, moves, and raises her to divine things. That is: He elevates her intellect to divine understanding...He moves her will freely to the love of God...and He fills her memory with divine knowledge...Once the soul disencumbers these faculties and empties them of everything inferior and of attachment to even superior things, leaving them alone without these things, God engages them in the invisible and divine. It is God who guides them in this solitude...(SC 35:5).

F. St. John of the Cross: The Living Flame of Love

This last of the major works of St. John of the Cross can only be discussed as it pertains to the mercy of God extended to the souls who have achieved the high level of the spiritual life called the spiritual marriage. The content of this work does not involve our relationship with others, but only with God. However, I note in passing that the perfection of our relationship with God overflows into our relationships with our fellow human beings. While *The Spiritual Canticle* chronicles the passage of the soul through the spiritual espousal into the spiritual marriage, *The Living Flame of Love* looks into the spiritual marriage to examine the attributes and qualities of that wonderful state. This entire work is a parade of mercy upon mercy from God, that would be, in its most sublime moments, a description of eternal life with God, but for the absence of natural death. Natural death renders the ecstasies that occasionally and for short duration occur in this spiritual marriage to become a permanent state of the soul. It will suffice to take a brief look at some of these profound mercies so gratuitously extended to these advanced souls.

STANZA 1

O living flame of love
That tenderly wounds my soul
In its deepest center! Since
Now You are not oppressive,
Now consummate! If it be Your will:
Tear through the veil of this sweet encounter.

O living flame of love

This living flame is the Holy Spirit that has consumed and transformed the soul. It is not only a fire that burns constantly in the soul, but it is also a fire that flares up into a living flame that bathes the soul in glory. These flares that occur only occasionally in this life cause acts of extreme love for God in the soul, infused by God, and is in fact the work of the Holy Spirit.

> Thus these acts of love are most precious; one of them is more meritorious and valuable than all the deeds a person may have performed in his whole life without this transformation, however great they may have been (LF 1:3).

> Thus in this state the soul cannot make acts because the Holy Spirit makes them all and moves it toward them. As a result, all the acts of the soul are divine,

since the movement toward these acts and their execution stems from God (LF 1:4).

STANZA 2

> *O sweet cautery,*
> *O delightful wound!*
> *O gentle hand! O delicate touch*
> *That tastes of eternal life*
> *And pays every debt!*
> *In killing You changed death into life.*

O sweet cautery,
O delightful wound!

The first thing to be noticed in these verses is that this cautery is sweet. A cautery heals a wound by the application of fire to the wound. If there is no wound, the cautery will cause a fire-inflicted wound. St. John of the Cross calls the wound caused by the cautery delightful. In his imagery, the cautery is the Holy Spirit; and it is the Holy Spirit that inflicts this wound. This *wounding* of the soul is unique and differs from all other touches of the soul coming from God. Its intensity exceeds anything the soul has previously experienced. Unless properly prepared for such a touch, over a very long time, and receiving grace upon grace of a lesser quality, a soul would not be able to bear such a sublime elevation to the divine.

> Since the heat of a cautery is more intense and violent and produces a more singular effect than do other fires, the soul calls the act of this union a cautery in comparison with the others, for it is the outcome of a fire so much more aflame than all the others (LF 2:2).

Since this cautery is unique, so must the wound it causes be unique. What is unique is that this wound is delightful. The deeper the wound, the greater the delight. The more the wound is repeated the greater does the delight become. It is a wound of pure divine love impressed on a soul and is a profound act of divine mercy. While this soul has been prepared by grace for such a sublime gift, the soul has in no respect *earned* the gift. It is a gratuitous manifestation of God's mercy.

As often as the cautery of love touches the wound of love, it causes a deeper wound of love, and thus the more it wounds, the more it cures and heals. The more wounded the lover, the healthier he is, and the cure love causes is to wound and inflict wound upon wound, to such an extent that the entire soul is dissolved into a wound of love. And now all cauterized and made one wound of love, it is completely healthy in love, for it is transformed in love (LF 2:7).

STANZA 3

O lamps of fire!
In whose splendors
The deep caverns of feeling,
Once obscure and blind,
Now give forth, so rarely, so exquisitely,
Both warmth and light to their Beloved.

St. John of the Cross warns us at the outset of his commentary on this stanza that explanation of its meaning will be very difficult. It will be worthwhile for the reader to examine the entire commentary on this stanza in order to gain a firm understanding of its meaning.

O lamps of fire!
In whose splendors

Lamps, in the days of St. John, were oil-fired lamps. He begins by saying that lamps give forth both light and warmth. The light described in his poetry is the light of infused knowledge of the many attributes of God. The many lamps of the attributes of God become one lamp that not only imparts knowledge of God's attributes, but also imparts warmth to the soul. This warmth imparted by God is in turn returned by the soul to God as a response to His mercy manifested by this infusion of knowledge.

> *The light communicated to it from all these attributes together is enveloped in the warmth of love of God* by which it loves Him because He is all these things. In this communication and

manifestation of Himself to the soul, which in my opinion is the greatest possible in this life, He is to it innumerable lamps giving forth knowledge and love of Himself (LF 3:3).

To understand what these splendors of the lamps are, and how the soul is resplendent in them, it should be known that they are the loving knowledge which the lamps of God's attributes give forth from themselves to the soul. United with them in its faculties, the soul is also resplendent like them, transformed in loving splendors (LF 3:9).

STANZA 4

How gently and lovingly
You wake in my heart,
Where in secret You dwell alone;
And in Your sweet breathing,
Filled with good and glory,
How tenderly You swell my heart with love!

Whatever spiritual experiences occur in a soul in this advanced state is the work of God, not the work of that soul. It seems to us that God moves in respect to the soul by giving so much of supernatural experience to it. However, since God is immovable, it is the soul that is moving and God is the cause of the movement. Therefore, the awakening described here by St. John is an awakening caused by God in the soul by moving the soul by His grace to the spiritual delights He wishes to give. The allowance of such a transformation of the soul in this awakening is a mercy of God that defies explanation and understanding. It is nearly the equivalent of granting the soul eternal glory in spite of its natural weakness emanating from original sin and its actual sins.

How this movement takes place in the soul, since God is immovable, is a wonderful thing, for it seems to the soul that God indeed moves; yet He does not really move. For since it is the soul that is renewed and moved by God so that it might behold this supernatural sight, and since that divine life and the being and harmony of every creature in that life, with its movements in God, is revealed to it with such newness, it seems to the soul that it is God Who moves and that the cause assumes the name of the effect it produces…We then ought to say that in this movement it is the soul that is moved and awakened from the sleep of natural vision to supernatural vision. Hence, it very adequately uses the term "awakening" (LF 4:6)

CHAPTER 6

BLESSED ARE THE CLEAN OF HEART, FOR THEY SHALL SEE GOD

The first inquiry in this chapter is to discover what Christ means by *clean of heart*. One interpretation is that He means those who are free from sin and single-hearted.[2] St. John Chrysostom says that the clean of heart are either those who practice every virtue, are conscious of no evil in themselves, or those who are adorned with the virtue of chastity.[3] If we conclude that, our Carmelite saints referenced in this book both emphasize the absolute necessity to separate our wills from all attachments to the things of creatures and of this world, then we must recognize that this detachment requires the control of our passions by right reason. It is inconceivable that a soul can progress in the journey toward unity with God, and at the same time be lax or indifferent to the power of the allurements of the flesh and therefore, fail to tame them completely. These appetites are the feeding grounds of the devil, and more souls are entrapped here by the demon, and led off to perdition by these appetites than any other single cause. Today, in our world, this pit of destruction is more dangerous and powerful than ever before in human history because of the loss of the sense moral rectitude and the sense of sin. Attachment or slavery to these passions forms a wall between the soul and God that can only be penetrated by constancy to this virtue of *clean of heart*.

When we consider the words *shall see God*, it is also important to understand the meaning of those words in the mind of Christ. We know that in the next life, those who have been saved by

---

[2] Editors footnote, THE HOLY BIBLE, Good Counsel Publishing Company, 1962.

[3] "For nothing is as necessary as this purity in such as desire to see God. Keep peace with all and chastity, says St. Paul, for without this none can see God. Many are merciful to the poor and just in their dealings, but abstain not from luxury and lust. Therefore our Savior, wishing to show that mercy was not sufficient, adds that if we would see God, we must also be possessed of the virtue of purity." (St. Chry. Hom. 15)

cooperating with the grace given to them will have a vision of God known as the Beatific Vision. We cannot be sure of the nature of this vision of God, but we can conclude that it will be of a quality unknown in this life. But what about *seeing* God in this life? Are there ways of seeing God in this life that are the result of being *clean of heart*, and do we find that quality of seeing in the writings of our two Carmelite saints?

We shall examine the understandings of Sts. Teresa of Jesus and John of the Cross on these two concepts, and we will discover that this *Beatitude* is also immersed in our saints' writings. We will in this examination adhere to the definition given by St. John Chrysostom regarding the concept of clean of heart, as it is rather complete, covering the many aspects of cleanness that the soul must pursue if it is to see God in its life. The two concepts to be avoided he mentions are luxury and lust. Luxury includes vanity of every kind that reveals an inordinate attachment to the self, and the satisfaction of the self.

A. St. Teresa of Jesus: The Way of Perfection

Clean of heart

In chapter 4 of this work, St. Teresa discusses attachments of affection, and especially affection toward the confessor of her nuns. She of course emphasizes the importance of the moral character of the confessor. She also cautions her nuns regarding the opening of doors to the wiles of the devil. In first speaking of relationships of affection between the sisters, she mentions the distraction of such relationships from the main object of the lives of the sisters.

> These intimate friendships are seldom calculated to make for the love of God; I am more inclined to believe that the devil initiates them so as to create factions within religious Orders. When a friendship has for its object the service of His Majesty, it at once becomes clear that the will is devoid of passion and indeed is helping to conquer other passions (WP 4).

St. Teresa deals extensively with the importance of her sisters evaluating their confessor, especially when they become aware of an attachment to him. She points out that an attachment to a confessor can develop over time and repeated confessions, receiving counseling and consoling advice from him. Therefore, in order to avoid all temptations, the character of the confessor is crucial. If such an attachment grows, it is obvious that what is happening is that creatures are being preferred to God in the practice of spiritual matters. This kind of attachment is an absolute obstacle to union with God and a terrible distraction to a soul that has set out on a serious pursuit of God.

> But if you notice that the confessor is tending in any way towards vanity in what he says to you, you should regard him with grave suspicion; in such a case conversation with him, even about prayer about God, should be avoided – the sister should make her confession briefly and say nothing more (WP Appendix to chapter 4).

The best emphasis on the virtues called for by this *Beatitude*, are contained in chapters 38 and 39 in which St. Teresa discusses the phrases of the *Paternoster*: *Et ne nos inducas in tentationem, sed libera nos a malo.* Her discussion is very general regarding the avoidance of certain faults that are temptations. These temptations include believing one has a virtue that they do not have, the belief that one will never fall back into former faults and sins, and the belief that one is so wretched that the mercy of God will not be granted to such a poor soul. Each of these temptations can be reduced to attachment to the self, since each is a focus on our selves rather than on God in His many aspects. Each of these temptations contains a dangerous disposition that opens the soul to the most serious sins. They each describe a soul that is exposed to being caught off guard because of a presumptuous state of mind, either based in pride or a morbidly negative attitude concerning God's care for the soul. In either case, cleanness of heart is endangered.

> What, then, Eternal Father, can we do but flee to Thee and beg Thee not to allow these enemies of ours to lead us into temptation. If attacks are made upon us publicly, we shall easily surmount them, with Thy help. But how can we be ready for these treacherous assaults, my God? We need constantly to pray for Thy help. Show us, Lord, some way of

recognizing them and guarding against them (WP 39).

For they shall see God

When we speak of seeing God, we of course mean the interior sight that reveals His grandeur and truth. This view of God is granted by Him to a soul that is prepared to receive it. This preparation is long and arduous, and cannot be accomplished by the individual soul. The cleansing of the heart that enables the soul to *see* God is a task that goes deeper than the soul can excavate. It requires divine intervention. But the reward for bearing the trials incident upon this cleansing is to *see* God with the eyes of the soul.

> The faculties rejoice without knowing how they rejoice; the soul is enkindled in love without understanding how it loves; it knows that it is rejoicing in the object of its love, yet it does not know how it is rejoicing in it. It is well aware that this is not a joy which can be attained by the understanding; the will embraces it, without understanding how; but, insofar as it can understand anything, it perceives that this is a blessing which could not be gained by the merits of all the trials suffered on earth put together. It is a gift of the Lord of earth and Heaven, Who gives it like the God He is (WP 25).

The interior *sight* of God is most completely expounded by St. Teresa when she describes the prayer of quiet. This deep prayer is characterized by a complete suspension of the operations of the senses. One becomes aware, without knowing how, that they are very close to God, and are moved to profound acts of love, but without words or concepts formed in the interior faculties. It is only in the spirit that this ineffable union can occur even though the spirit has no power unaided to produce this state of prayer. It is God's work in the soul.

> This is a supernatural state, and, however hard we try, we cannot reach it for ourselves, for it is a state in which the soul enters into peace, or rather the Lord gives it peace through His presence, as He did

to that just man Simeon. In this state all the faculties are stilled...This is not because it sees Him either with its bodily senses or with its spiritual eyes...Just so, though less clearly, (than Simeon) does the soul know who He is. It cannot understand how it knows Him, yet it sees that it is in the Kingdom (or at least is near to the King Who will give it the Kingdom), and it feels such reverence that it dares to ask nothing (WP 31).

Let us now conclude by saying that, when the soul is brought to this state of prayer, it would seem that the Eternal Father has already granted its petition that He will give it His Kingdom on earth (WP 31).

B. St. Teresa of Jesus: The Interior Castle

This entire work of St. Teresa describes the journey of a soul from a heart that is absorbed in the things of the world and the flesh, a heart that is divided, and a heart that is anything but clean, to a heart that is transformed into one that is exceedingly pleasing to God. As grace is increased and accepted by a soul, it sees the things of the world and the flesh decrease in importance, the heart becomes single-minded, and the stains of sin diminish until finally the heart of this soul is cleansed. Setting aside the extraordinary experiences of grace that St. Teresa describes in the latter mansions, the ordinary graces offered to a soul through the early mansions of the castle are sufficient to begin the cleansing of this heart. The extraordinary graces that emanate from the different levels of prayer that the saint describes in the later mansions complete the work of bringing this soul to the blessedness described by the Lord in this *Beatitude*.

The First Three Dwelling Places

Clean of heart

After describing the beauty of the interior castle, that resembles a perfect crystal illuminated from its deepest interior where God dwells, St. Teresa sets forth her horror over a soul that is lost in sin: a soul with a very unclean heart.

> It should be kept in mind here that the fount, the shining sun that is in the center of the soul, does not lose its beauty and splendor; it is always present in the soul, and nothing can take away its loveliness. But if a black cloth is placed over a crystal that is in the sun, obviously the sun's brilliance will have no effect on the crystal even though the sun is shining on it (IC I:2:3).

Through St. Teresa's discussions of all the mansions in this work, she constantly refers to the room of self-knowledge. This *room,* and what can be learned in it, is crucial to every stage of spiritual growth. It is here that the virtue of humility must reign supreme. Without that virtue, a soul will never understand where its goodness comes from, and how one grows in holiness through cooperation with the grace of God, and not from its own efforts. Cleanness of heart is the work of God. The soul, as the receiver of grace, must not resist the gift of God nor set up obstructions that block the flow of grace. Preoccupation with the things of the world is a good example of an obstruction that would inhibit the flow of grace into the soul.

> Even though it (the soul) may not be in a bad state, it is so involved in worldly things and so absorbed with its possessions, honor, or business affairs, as I have said, that even though as a matter of fact it would want to see and enjoy its beauty (a bright room) these things do not allow it to; nor does it seem that it can slip free from so many impediments (IC I:2:14).

The second dwelling place presents a soul with greater and different graces. This soul has begun to practice a regular routine of daily prayer, and has begun to awaken to a desire to approach God more closely. The cleanness of heart necessary to *see* God in this life is progressing. However, this soul has not escaped the wiles of the devil, and therefore is conflicted constantly. While it now desires to come closer to God and His will, its weaknesses not yet overcome, continues to restrict its spiritual growth.

> This stage pertains to those who have already begun to practice prayer and have understood how

> important it is not to stay in the first dwelling places. But they still don't have the determination to remain in this second stage without turning back, for they don't understand the occasions of sin (IC II:1:2).

In this dwelling place, the voice of the Lord is beginning to be heard by this soul. However, it is not the only voice that this soul hears. The voice of the devil with all his temptations and urgings trying to silence that other voice is very much in evidence. But the voice of the Lord is so sweet that a longing to hear it more and to respond to it is beginning to grow. In spite of this sweetness, the soul is still conflicted regarding which voice to follow. The voice of the Lord will lead to cleanness of heart, while the voice of the devil and the world will lead in the opposite direction.

> O Jesus, what an uproar the devils instigate here! And the afflictions of the poor soul: it doesn't know whether to continue or return to the first room. Reason, for its part, shows the soul that it is mistaken in thinking that these things of the world are not worth anything when compared to what it is aiming after. Faith, however, teaches it about where it will find fulfillment (IC II:1:4).

Souls that enter the third dwelling place have made very substantial progress in spiritual growth. However, it is a stage based primarily on natural responses to grace. Supernatural phenomena in prayer lie ahead for this soul. This soul has achieved a substantial degree of cleanness of heart as a result of the purification of its senses, both interior and exterior. Although the most intense purification lay ahead for this soul, it has to a great degree set aside the things of this world and the satisfaction of the self alone, and wishes to be pleasing to God in all its thoughts and actions.

> They long not to offend His Majesty, even guarding themselves against venial sins; they are fond of doing penance and setting aside periods for recollection; they spend their time well, practice works of charity toward their neighbors; and are very balanced in their use of speech and dress and in the governing of their households-those who have them (IC III:1:5).

A danger exists here that perhaps was not present in earlier stages of spiritual growth: the belief that one has traveled a long way and therefore, can be content with how it sees itself spiritually. A certain pride develops in such a soul that is the antithesis of cleanness of heart described in this *Beatitude*. To clean is to remove all that defiles; and nothing will defile a soul faster than pride. While many souls suffer from this inflated view of self in varying degrees, it is an attitude of mind that must be discarded. This form of pride is an absolute and powerful obstacle to advancing further toward the cleanness of heart desired and required; and it is the occasion for falling backwards into faults of the past and a certain indifference toward God and one's neighbor.

> With humility present, this stage is an excellent one. If humility is lacking, we will remain here our whole life-and with a thousand afflictions and miseries. For since we will not have abandoned ourselves, this state will be very laborious and burdensome (IC III:2:9).

> If there is some lack in humility, they will feel an inner distaste for which they will find no reason. For perfection as well as its reward does not consist in spiritual delights but in greater love and deeds done with greater justice and truth (IC III:2:10).

For they shall see God

The souls in the first dwelling place do not have any real vision of God, even though He has begun to move them to some little reflection on the realities of life and its purpose. The soul's vision is obstructed by its attachments to worldly things, creatures, and business affairs. Since little or no cleansing of this soul's heart has occurred in this dwelling place, we cannot talk about seeing God in any real sense.

However, in the second dwelling place, the soul begins to catch glimpses of God through its interior spiritual eyes:

> So these persons are able to hear the Lord when He calls. Since they are getting closer to where His Majesty dwells, He is a very good neighbor. His

mercy and goodness are so bountiful; whereas, we are occupied in our pastimes, business affairs, pleasures, and worldly buying and selling, and still falling into sin and rising again...Yet this lord desires intensely that we love Him and seek His company, so much so that from time to time He calls us to draw near Him. And His voice is so sweet the poor soul dissolves at not doing immediately what He commands (IC II:1:2).

The third dwelling place marks the beginning of the opening of the eyes to a clear vision of God. Having negotiated the difficulties of the first two dwelling places, the soul is now on a path that should lead to its salvation. God has granted it many graces and the result has been a significant elevation of the awareness of God in everything this soul does. Fear of the Lord forms an important part of all of this soul's motivation. A pattern of regular prayer has been developed and made a somewhat firm habit by this soul. Real cleansing of this soul's heart is now taking place. This soul has advanced so far that it will now experience trials, some related and some unrelated to its spiritual life. The cleansing resulting from these trials allows the soul to see God more and more clearly. It is only through these trials, and the accompanying humility that the view of God in the soul will increase and clarify.

The Last Four Dwelling Places

Clean of heart

We know that the work of perfection in a soul is ultimately the work of God, and not of the soul. It is true that the soul must be disposed to the graces and movements that God bestows, but the active agent here is God. St. Teresa recognizes this, and at the outset of her discussion of the fourth mansion, she calls upon the Holy Spirit to speak for her. The reason she seeks this assistance from the Holy Spirit is because supernatural experiences begin here, and they are very difficult to communicate from one to another in an understandable way. We know that after a soul has, by the efforts of its own will cooperating with the graces given, advanced a certain amount in perfection, it reaches a point at which it can advance no further. The task of advancing further is now too great to be performed by the soul's own efforts. God must take over from this point on if the soul is to arrive not only at cleanness of heart, but also at union with God. The soul must now be in a passive state receiving from God what He wishes to give in order to perfect the soul further.

> It will seem that to reach these dwelling places one will have had to live in the others a long while. Although it is usual that a person will have to have stayed in those already spoken about, there is no certain rule, as you will have often heard. For the Lord gives when He desires, as He desires, and to whom He desires. Since these blessings belong to Him, He does no injustice to anyone (IC IV:1:2).

In this fourth mansion, a soul receives many favors from God. Among these St. Teresa describes spiritual delights, of which the and the prayer of recollection are examples, and they are bestowed by God when the soul least expects it. The effect of these favors in prayer is to move the soul closer to God by eradicating all attachment to the things of the world and to creatures. As a result, the soul converts more of itself to attachment only to God, to the exclusion of all other attachments. In consequence of this conversion of the heart, that heart is rendered clean and very pleasing to God. These favors are then cleansing agents for the heart and they can only be supplied by God. Because of their supernatural origin and nature, these favors cleanse the heart far more than any effort of the soul could do.

> This spiritual delight (the prayer of quiet) is not something that can be imagined, because however diligent our efforts we cannot acquire it. The very experience of it makes us realize that it is not of the same metal as we ourselves but fashioned from the purest gold of the divine wisdom (IC IV:2:6).

> It is a recollection that also seems to me to be supernatural because it doesn't involve being in the dark or closing the eyes, nor does it consist in any exterior thing, since without first wanting to do so, one does close one's eyes and desire solitude. It seems that without any contrivance the edifice is being built, by means of this recollection, for the prayer that was mentioned (prayer of recollection).

> The sense and exterior things seem to be losing their hold because the soul is recovering what it has lost (IC IV:3;1).

> In the case of this recollection, it doesn't come when we want it but when God wants to grant us the favor. I for myself hold that when His Majesty grants it, He does to persons who are already beginning to despise the things of the world... So I believe that if we desire to make room for His Majesty, He will give not only this but more, and give it to those whom He begins to call to advance further (IC V:3:3).

In the fifth mansion, St. Teresa examines a soul that is highly purified and purged of all attachments to creatures. This is a soul whose heart has been cleansed rather thoroughly by the extraordinary favors granted to it by God in prayer during its tenure in the fourth mansion. So cleansed is this heart, that we can now begin to talk about episodes of union with God.

> This union is above all earthly joys, above all delights, above all consolations, and still more than that. It doesn't matter where those spiritual or earthly joys come from, for the feeling is very different, as you will have experienced. I once said that the difference is like that between feeling something on the rough outer covering of the body or in the marrow of the bones. And that was right on the mark, for I don't know how to say it better (IC V:1:6).

In this fifth mansion, St. Teresa introduces her well known metaphor of the silk worm in order to illustrate the effects of the prayer of union that is granted by God at this level of spiritual development. This metaphor describes the life cycles of the silk worm, ending in the coming forth of a beautiful butterfly. The silk worm spins the cocoon in which it will die, and St. Teresa likens this cocoon to Christ. When the stage of the silk worm is completed, the beautiful butterfly is free to emerge from the cocoon. The metaphor describes the death of the silk worm as the death of the soul to creatures and to itself.

It is in the last two mansions that the cleansing of the heart is completed. However, in the sixth mansion there are great sufferings to endure while God cleanses the heart. The remedy for attachments to the things of the world and to the self is severe afflictions amidst extraordinary favors in prayer. The soul is at one time exalted in prayer, and at another time is humbled and afflicted by torments of doubt and its awareness of its sinfulness. And added to the affliction, dryness is present frequently.

> Since the soul sees clearly that if it has anything good this is given by God and is by no means its own – for just previously it saw itself to be very poor and surrounded by great sins – praise is an intolerable burden to it, at least in the beginning. Later on, for certain reasons, praise is not so intolerable (IC VI:1:4).

> In sum, there is no remedy in this tempest but to wait for the mercy of God. For at an unexpected time, with one word alone or a chance happening, He so quickly calms the storm that it seems there had not been even as much as a cloud in that soul, and it remains filled with sunlight and much more consolation (IC VI:1:10).

The seventh mansion should be dealt with only in the following section because it deals with a soul whose heart has been fully cleansed.

For they shall see God

The spiritual seeing of God is represented by the many descriptions of St. Teresa in *The Interior Castle* of the favors granted by God: the spiritual delights of the prayers of quiet, of recollection, and of union. The result of these favors is to remove from the soul its attachments to creatures, the world and of attachment to itself. When those detachments are accomplished, the soul's seeing of God is unobstructed.

> Would to heaven that we would do what we know we must; and we are instructed about what we must do. Let it die; let this silkworm die, as it does in

> completing what it was created to do! And you will see how we *see* God, as well as ourselves placed inside His greatness, as is this little silkworm within its cocoon. Keep in mind that I say, "see God," in the sense of what I mentioned (in *Life*) concerning that which is felt in this kind of union (IC V:2:6).

The seventh dwelling place illustrates completely the kind of *seeing* of God that comes to the clean of heart. In this dwelling place, the perfecting of the soul has reached the highest point possible in this life. The afflictions of the former mansions are gone, and they are replaced by a loving desire to suffer for the Beloved. This soul has forgotten the self, because now all its efforts and desires are employed in securing the honor of God. This is the goal that has been sought for such a long time and with such effort and perseverance.

> The difference in this dwelling place is the one mentioned (great detachment from everything). There are almost never any experiences of dryness or interior disturbance of the kind that were present at times in all the other dwelling places, but the soul is almost always in quiet...His Majesty reveals Himself to the soul and brings it to Himself in that place where, in my opinion, the devil will not dare enter, nor will the Lord allow him to enter. Nor does the Lord in all the favors He grants the soul here, as I have said, receive any assistance from the soul itself, except what it has already done in surrendering itself totally to God (IC VII:3:10).

C. St. John of the Cross: The Ascent of Mt. Carmel

St. John of the Cross in all his writings examines the acts and efforts of a soul, in cooperation with grace, that are necessary to transform the soul into one that is prepared and disposed to arrive at union with God. The whole scheme of his spiritual doctrine addresses the detachment of the soul from all that is not God. First, he addresses the attachments related to the senses and second, the attachments of the spirit to supernatural phenomena. The entire process of detachment that he describes is, in effect, a cleansing of the heart in the sense meant by Christ in this *Beatitude*. St. John imitates Christ when he insists that a soul cannot reach union with God, or, in other words, cleanse its heart, if that heart is divided. A heart intent on the things of this world cannot be a heart that truly *sees* God in the depths of its spirit. The vision that is necessary to *see* God is clouded, distracted, and obstructed by the divisions in its heart, its attachments to the things of the world, and its distractions; and it will remain so until these things are extinguished.

Clean of heart

The Ascent of Mt. Carmel is an exposition of the beginnings of a soul's movement toward God and union with Him. Therefore, the discussion in this work centers on the removal of attachments of the senses to all that is not God or of God. He begins with the senses because that aspect of our humanity is the lower functions of the rational being, the higher one being matters of the spirit, the aspect of our nature that is created in the image and likeness of God. The interior senses of the intellect and the imagination feed the spirit by presenting images to it upon which judgments are made by the will of the goodness or evil of the images presented.

The poetry that constitutes the basis for *The Ascent of Mt. Carmel* begins with the words: "One dark night…"

> This dark night is a privation and purgation of all sensible appetites for the external things of the world, the delights of the flesh, and the gratifications of the will. All this deprivation is wrought in the purgation of sense (AS I:1:4).

> We are using the expression "night" to signify a deprival of the gratification of man's appetite in all things. Just as night is nothing but the privation of light and, consequently, of all objects visible by means of the light – darkness and emptiness, then, for the faculty of sight – the mortification of the appetites can be called a night for the soul (AS I:3:1).

These two quotes bring us immediately to an understanding of the pattern St. John will follow to illustrate the manner in which the heart is cleansed in the sense meant by Christ in this *Beatitude*.

In fact, St. John teaches that progress to union with God is impossible unless the soul starts with the purification and purgation of the senses. Without accomplishing this purgation of the senses, the soul cannot progress to the purification of the spirit, either active or passive. Union with God is only possible in the spirit and therefore, if the spirit is not purged of all attachments to what is not God, union will never occur.

> The road and ascent to God, then, necessarily demands a habitual effort to renounce and mortify the appetites; the sooner this mortification is achieved, the sooner the soul reaches the top (of the mountain). But until the appetites are eliminated, a person will not arrive, no matter how much virtue he practices. For he will fail to acquire perfect virtue, which lies in keeping the soul empty, naked, and purified of every appetite (AS I:5:6).

In Book II of *The Ascent of Mt. Carmel,* St. John deals with the purification of the spirit through faith, which he states is the only proximate means to union with God. In this Book II, St John treats of the active purification of the spirit, an effort in which the soul is intimately involved, with the assistance of grace, in purging the spirit of attachments to spiritual and supernatural phenomena that are less than God. The passive nights of purgation of the senses and the spirit are dealt with in *The Dark Night*, which we will discuss in the next section of this book.

In order to understand St. John's doctrine of the cleansing of the heart by the soul's detachment from all that is not God, we must have a grasp of the significance of faith in his doctrine as it applies to the active purification of the spirit. And we must have an understanding of why faith is the only proximate means to union with God. I will explain this as briefly as possible because it is tangential to our main subject, but important to understanding the cleansing of the heart that must occur in the spirit in order to *see* God.

Because the transformation required for union with God and the union itself is beyond all human capability, the soul must be devoid of understanding because what it believes it can understand about God cannot have anything to do with the real nature of God.

Not only this, but it must empty itself of those things of the spirit that are less than God. If it fails in this, the soul will wind up seeking union with some phenomena that is not God. Then the whole effort will end in failure. Therefore, this emptiness that is gained by detachment must be filled with something that is a proportionate means to the union being sought, and that something is faith. The object of faith is above and beyond all human capacity, and therefore there is no possibility of arriving at the truth about God if the soul relies on the use of human faculties, either interior or exterior.

> Passing beyond all that is naturally and spiritually intelligible or comprehensible; a person ought to desire with all his might to attain what in this life is unknowable and unimaginable. And parting company with all he can, or does, taste and feel, temporally and spiritually, he must ardently long to acquire what surpasses all taste and feeling (AS II:4:6).

> In relation to our discussion here, this means that faith is the substance of things to be hoped for and that these things are not manifest to the intellect, even though its consent to them is firm and certain. If they were manifest, there would be no faith. For though faith brings certitude to the intellect, it does not produce clarity, but only darkness (AS II:6:2).

Some persons will have difficulty with the teaching of St. John of the Cross on the importance of negating and rejecting supernatural phenomena and experience, in either the senses or in the spirit. The difficulty results because some souls are so attached to sensible and/or spiritual phenomena that their spirituality would be threatened if these phenomena were to be taken from them. St. John advances the proposition of negation of these phenomena for two reasons related to our subject of cleansing the heart. First, because these experiences and the faculties that receive them cannot be the proximate means to union with God. Second, that the possibility of deception by the devil in these matters is very great and the devil wishes to lead us away from the cleansing of the heart required in order to see God.

If you ask me why the intellect must be deprived of those truths, since the Spirit of God illumines it through them, I answer: the Holy Spirit illumines the intellect that is recollected, and He illumines it according to the mode of its recollection, and the intellect can find no better recollection than in faith and thus the Holy Spirit will not illumine it in any other recollection more than in faith (AS II:29:6).

Thus a person should not strive after this knowledge (which comes from the senses or intellect), nor be desirous of admitting it, lest the intellect begin to form the knowledge on its own, or the devil find an entrance for his other various and false knowledge. The devil can easily affect false knowledge, either by means of these feelings or by others which he himself can bestow on the soul that is attached to this knowledge. A person's attitude toward this knowledge should be one of resignation, humility, and passivity (AS II:32:4).

The last book of *The Ascent* deals with the purification of the memory and the will. The purification of these faculties is integral to the cleansing of the heart that seeks to be cleansed. Much of what has been said about the purification of the intellect through faith is also true of the cleansing of the other two faculties, and need not be repeated here. But we should look briefly, at what is peculiar to the purification of these other two faculties in order to comprehend the extent to which the heart must be cleansed in these two faculties in order to *see* God.

The memory is the faculty by which we store experience and knowledge previously learned. Since experience and knowledge can never constitute the means to union with God, the soul cannot draw on this faculty's natural objects to obtain union with God. However, the experience and remembrance of failure by the memory or the knowledge gained from that failure can precipitate a movement to the right approach to union with God: faith, and as we shall soon see love. To this extent, the memory can make a valuable contribution to the quest for union with God by not allowing the repetition of failure.

> The annihilation of the memory in regard to all forms is an absolute requirement for union with God. This union cannot be wrought without a complete separation of the memory from all forms that are not God...Since, as Christ affirms, no man can serve two masters (Mt 6:24), and the memory cannot at the same time be united with God and with forms and distinct knowledge, and since God has no form or image comprehensible to the memory, the memory is without form, figure, or phantasy when united to God; and in great forgetfulness, without the remembrance of anything, it is absorbed in a supreme good (AS III:2:4).

St. John, in Book III of *The Ascent of Mt. Carmel,* discusses many harms that result from failure to purify the memory and purge it of objects that are not God. Without elaborating on his discussion, we can list them as follows: The things of the world, the works of the devil, and the knowledge of these things. It is the knowledge of the first two insofar as we make that knowledge a factor in our motivations that is the impediment and hindrance to the divine union. The third harm he lists is supernatural imaginative knowledge, which comes from supernatural apprehensions that impress themselves upon the memory. None of these things leads to union with God. Finally, he presents a proposition that summarizes his doctrine on purification of the memory.

> Our aim is union with God in the memory; the object of hope is something unpossessed; the less other objects are possessed, the more capacity and ability there is to hope for this one object, and consequently the more hope; the greater the possessions, the less capacity and ability for hope, and consequently so much less of hope; accordingly, in the measure that a person dispossesses his memory of forms and objects, which are not God, he will fix it upon God and preserve it empty, in the hope that God will fill it (AS III:15:1).

To become clean of heart, the will must also be purified of objects that are not God. This is the faculty by which we love the good or what is perceived as good. The will cannot love what the intellect perceives as evil, whether the thing is evil in itself, or is only perceived as evil. People hate the Church, when they should love her, because they perceive her as evil as she pertains to them or to the world. Therefore, error can produce love or repulsion on one level, depending on how the object is perceived, regardless of its real nature.

> The strength of the soul comprises the faculties, passions, and appetites. All this strength is ruled by the will. When the will directs these faculties, passions, and appetites toward God, turning them away from all that is not God, the soul preserves its strength for God, and comes to love Him with all its might (AS III:16:2).

To approach the purgation of the will of all that is not God, St. John of the Cross enumerates the four passions, and then proceeds to explain how they must be purified of all objects less than God. Unfortunately, he never completes this discussion, but only treats incompletely the first of the four passions. The four passions are as follows: joy, hope, sorrow, and fear. He does, however, give us a fine summary of the results in the will of purifying these passions as part of becoming clean of heart.

> It should be known that, in the measure that one of the passions is regulated according to reason, the others are also. These four passions are so brother-like that where one goes, actually the others go virtually; if one is regulated actually, the other three in the same measure are recollected virtually. If the will rejoices over something, it must in the same degree hope for it, with the virtual inclusion of sorrow and fear. And with the removal of satisfaction in this object, fear, sorrow, and hope will also be removed (AS III:16:5).

> The entire matter of reaching union with God consists in purging the will of its appetites and feelings, so that from a human and lowly will it may be changed into the divine will, made identical with the will of God (AS III:16:3).

For they shall see God

St. John of the Cross begins immediately to point out the great rewards of cleansing the heart by purification of the senses. In his poetry, in the first stanza of *The Ascent of Mt. Carmel,* he gives us the verse: "– Ah, the sheer grace." All grace of God is a gift. It is an invitation to do what our human nature cannot do unaided. Here St. John refers to the urgent longings that came to the soul in a dark night as a "sheer grace"; a grace without blemish and not in any way earned. This grace was the movement of the soul to go out from itself to meet the Lord, and the grace was possible because the house of the soul was stilled of its appetites and attachments. He thus describes the beginnings of *seeing* the Lord in the way meant by Christ in this *Beatitude*.

> One is not freed from the sufferings and anguish of the appetites until they are put to sleep. So it was a sheer grace, the soul declares, to have gone out unseen, without encumbrance from the appetites of the flesh, or from anything else. It was also fortunate the departure was at night; that is, that God took from the soul all these things through a privation that was a night to it (AS I:1:4).

In Book II of *The Ascent,* St. John once again repeats the phrase "– Ah, the sheer grace." But this time that phrase refers to the previous verses of stanza 2 which state that the soul, "in darkness and secure" by "the secret ladder, disguised" advances. He is now speaking about the purification of the spirit and that this purification can only occur through faith, the virtue that exists in darkness in the soul, and for that reason renders the soul secure because those aspects of the human spirit that would be obstacles to union with God are plunged into spiritual darkness. The faith required for this purgation and purification of the spirit is the sheer grace received by the soul.

> Faith, manifestly, is a dark night for man, but in this very way it gives him light. The more darkness it brings upon him. The more light it sheds. For by blinding it illumines him . . . (AS II:3:4).

> We can gather from what has been said that to be prepared for this divine union the intellect must be cleansed and emptied of everything relating to sense, divested and liberated of everything clearly apprehensible, inwardly pacified and silenced, and supported by faith alone, which is the only proximate and proportionate means to union with God. For the likeness between faith and God is so close that no other difference exists than that between believing in God and seeing Him (AS II:9:1).

In his discussion of the purification of the will by charity, St. John refers to the greatest grace of all: the grace to love God above all else. The soul that recognizes God as the greatest good and that He must be chosen above all other possible goods is well on the way to purification of the will. By rejecting joy in all other possible goods: temporal, natural, sensory, moral, supernatural, and spiritual the soul is never diverted from the path to union with God. This love of God is a grace that propels the soul into all the beauties and consolations of the later stages of the spiritual journey that are the subject matter of *The Spiritual Canticle* and *The Living Flame of Love.* That is where the soul really begins to *see* God in a manner that is ineffable. Suffice it here to state St. John's principal thesis regarding the purification of the will through the theological virtue of charity.

> The less strongly the will is fixed on God, and the more dependent it is upon creatures, the more these four passions combat the soul and reign in it. It then very easily finds joy in what deserves no rejoicing, and hope in what brings no profit, and sorrow over what should perhaps cause rejoicing, and fear where there is no reason for fear (AS III:16:4).

D. St. John of the Cross: The Dark Night

Clean of heart

I have said above that the cleansing of the heart in the way that phrase was meant by Christ means the extraction of the objects of all appetites from both the senses and the spirit so that there are no competing objects and desires that divert the soul from God. Thus far, we have discussed the kind of cleansing of the heart in which the soul participates, with the assistance of grace, in order to rid itself of sin and sensible and spiritual objects that are obstacles to its desired relationship with God. In this work, *The Dark Night,* St. John of the Cross enters into an analysis of a much deeper and more severe cleansing of the heart. In this stage, the soul is merely a passive receiver of the trials and afflictions that God brings upon the soul. In His infinite wisdom and mercy, God afflicts the soul with trials that He deems necessary for the complete cleansing of the heart. These trials are more severe than anything the soul would or could enter into itself by its own choice and efforts. No soul is able to excavate and remove the roots of its imperfections resulting from our fallen nature. In order to cleanse the soul of these roots it is required that the work be undertaken by God. Therefore, St. John calls these nights passive because the soul is no longer involved actively in this deep level of purification. It is now the receiver of whatever God sends it in order to propel the soul forward toward union. Again, St. John returns to the first stanza of his poem, but this time with a quite different meaning. *One dark night* now signifies something far deeper than it did in *The Ascent of Mt. Carmel.*

> In this first stanza, the soul is speaking of the way it followed in its departure from love of self and of all things through a method of true mortification which causes it to die to itself and to all these things and to begin the sweet and delightful life of love with God. And it declares that this departure was "a dark night." As we shall explain later, this dark night signifies here purgative contemplation, which passively causes in the soul this negation of self and of all things (DN I:Exp:1).

The first passive night is that of the senses. It begins after a somewhat long interval between it and the active nights. During this interval, the soul is able to make progress against its basic imperfections and sins over which it can exercise some control through an act of its will and cooperation with grace. St. John gives us three signs that a soul is beginning to move out of this interval and into the more severe cleansing of the passive night of sense, and all of these signs must exist at the same time. First, the soul does not get satisfaction or consolation from the things of God or of creatures.

Second, the memory ordinarily turns to God solicitously and with painful care, but thinks it is not serving God. Third, is the powerlessness, in spite of one's efforts, to meditate or make use of the imagination in prayer, as one was previously able to do. This soul is still possessed of many of the problems of beginners that St. John discusses at length in the early chapters of this work. These problems can only be purged by the action of God in these passive nights. Until this purging is completed, the soul will not have cleansed its heart to the point that it will be enabled to *see* God in the way Christ meant in this *Beatitude*. In fact, the result of the purgation and purification that takes place in these passive nights is the intimate vision of God and His attributes that would be impossible without passing through these passive nights. We must keep in mind that these are passive nights.

> The attitude necessary in the night of sense is to pay no attention to discursive meditation, since it is not the time for it. They should allow the soul to remain in rest and quietude, even though it may seem very obvious to them that they are doing nothing and wasting time, and even though they think this disinclination to think about anything is due to their laxity (DN I:10:4).

The first benefit that flows from the passive and dark night of sense is self-knowledge. The vice of pride is put to flight by the imposed humility that results from seeing ourselves as God sees us. This result is an immense cleansing of the heart, for it removes the greatest obstacle to advancing to union with God: pride. It firmly establishes the relative positions of the parties, Creator and creature, without which union would be impossible. The chasm between creature and Creator must always be maintained because the desired union is based on reality. God remains God, and man, remains man, and the union is affected by love: God for man, and man for God.

> The first and chief benefit that this dry and dark night of contemplation causes is the knowledge of self and of one's own misery. Besides the fact that all the favors God imparts to the soul are ordinarily enwrapped in this knowledge, the aridities and voids of the faculties in relation to the abundance previously experienced, and the difficulty

encountered in the practice of virtue make the soul recognize its own lowliness and misery, which was not apparent in the time of its prosperity (DN I:12:2).

In addition to pride, all of the other problems of beginners related to the seven deadly sins are purged from the soul: spiritual avarice, gluttony, lust, anger, envy, and sloth. From time to time, God encourages weaker souls in this dark night with sweet consolations that are ineffable. These interludes of spiritual serenity encourage these weaker souls to keep going forward through the trials and afflictions without which its heart cannot be cleansed.

> Although they do not advance, God exercises them for short periods and on certain days in those temptations and aridities to preserve them in humility and self-knowledge; and at other times and seasons He comes to their aid with consolation, lest through loss of courage they return to their search after worldly consolations (DN I:14:5).

The most difficult experiences the soul will encounter in its journey toward union with God follow the passive night of sense, usually after another rather lengthy interval. This very difficult period is called the passive night of spirit. It is in this night that St. John gives us the description of the most severe afflictions of the soul and they occur at its very core. These trials are the hard scrubbing required to cleanse the soul to the point that it will *see* God as never before. Unless a soul permitted to enter this night is sustained and supported by grace, it could not survive this period. These afflictions are similar to those endured by the souls in Purgatory near the end of that purgation.

> In this night that follows both parts are jointly purified. This was the purpose of the reformation of the first night and the calm that resulted from it: that the sensory part, united in a certain way with the spirit, might undergo the purgation and suffering with greater fortitude. Such is the fortitude necessary for so strong and arduous a purgation that if the lower part in its weakness is not reformed first and afterwards strengthened in God through the

> experience of sweet and delightful communion with Him, it has neither the fortitude nor the preparedness to endure it (DN II:3:2).

We can clearly see the intensifying of the cleansing of the heart of this soul. St. John couches his descriptions in ever more severe language in order to convey this increase in affliction that accompanies this deeper purification. Notice the use of the words *supreme affliction, bitterness, and anguish* in the following quote. He also raises his descriptions of the level of consolations and touches that come from Christ, as we shall see later, as the soul progresses ever forward.

> God divests the faculties, affections, and senses, both spiritual and sensory, interior and exterior. He leaves the intellect in darkness, the will in aridity, the memory in emptiness, and the affections in supreme affliction, bitterness, and anguish, by depriving the soul of the feeling and satisfaction it previously obtained from spiritual blessings. For this privation is one of the conditions required that the spiritual form, which is the union of love, may be introduced in the spirit and united with it (DN II:3:3).

When the divine light shines on this soul, the result is an extreme darkness to it. The reason that this light produces darkness is because of the soul's baseness and darkness. The divine light at first blinds it. The afflictions in the soul from this light come from its own imperfections; and until those imperfections are removed by the light of God purifying them, darkness prevails in the soul. The soul cannot *see* God until the imperfections cease to cloud and darken divine truth. It is the process of removing these imperfections through the intervention of the divine light that shines on them that causes the soul so much pain in this night.

> Since this divine contemplation assails him somewhat forcibly in order to subdue and strengthen his soul, he suffers so much in his weakness that he almost dies, particularly at times when the light is more powerful. Both the sense and the spirit, as though under an immense and dark load, undergo

such agony and pain that the soul would consider death a relief (DN II:5:6).

Such a description as this and those that follow in the next chapters of Book II show us the extreme measures needed to cleanse a soul to the point that it can *see* God. One cannot see out of a window until all dirt and smudges on that window that obstruct or distort vision are removed. So it is with the afflicted soul in this night.

This war or combat is profound because the peace awaiting the soul must be exceeding profound; and the spiritual suffering is intimate and penetrating because the love to be possessed by the soul will also be intimate and refined. The more intimate and highly finished the work must be, so the more intimate, careful, and pure must the labor be; and commensurate with the solidity of the edifice is the energy involved in the work (DN II:9:9).

For they shall see God

We have seen that a soul does not *see* God until its interior vision is developed by the cleansing of its heart through the trials and afflictions of the dark nights of sense and spirit, both active and passive. We also know from the spiritual doctrine of St. John of the Cross that a certain *seeing* of God, in the spirit, is possible in this life. God reveals Himself in the consolations and divine touches given to the souls that are undergoing the great afflictions and agonies of the dark nights. He also reveals Himself to the soul in severe trials and afflictions that convince the soul that God's light is shining on them causing the suffering they are experiencing. The suffering does not come from the divine light, but from the imperfections of the soul that the divine light is illuminating. Gradually, as the soul struggles for many years in these nights, its union with God grows, and the soul catches glimpses of God in the divine touches He allows the soul. The consolations and afflictions in the active nights are quite different than the dark contemplation of the passive nights. In *The Ascent of Mt. Carmel,* St John has this description:

> The soul uses as a metaphor the wretched state of captivity. It is a sheer grace to be released from this prison without hindrance from the jailers. The soul, through original sin, is a captive in the mortal body, subject to passions and natural appetites; when liberated from this bondage and submission, it considers its escape, which is unnoticed, unimpeded, and unapprehended by its passions and appetites, a sheer grace (AS I:15:1).

> "My house being now all stilled" means that the house of the appetites, the sensitive part of the soul, is now stilled, and the desires conquered and lulled to sleep. Until slumber comes to the appetites through the mortification of sensuality, and until this very sensuality is stilled in such a way that the appetites do not war against the spirit, the soul will not walk out to genuine freedom, to the enjoyment of union with its Beloved (AS I:15:2).

In *The Dark Night,* the affliction and consolations that lead to the *stilled* house are described differently. The phrase is used both in the first and second stanza, but refer to different aspects of the soul's purification in each of these stanzas. The first stanza in both *The Ascent of Mt. Carmel* and in *The Dark Night* refer to the sensory purification of the soul, the former to the active night of sense, and the latter to the passive sensory night. But in the second stanza, the *stilled house* is the result of the deeper purgation of the spirit.

> The sensory and spiritual parts of the soul, in order to go out to the divine union of love, must first be reformed, put in order, and pacified, as was their condition in Adam's state of innocence. This verse, which in the first stanza refers to the quiet of the lower and sensory part, refers particularly in this second stanza to the superior and spiritual part, and consequently the soul has repeated it (DN II:24:2).

It would be inaccurate to say that the stilling of the house of the soul occurs during the severe and torturous afflictions and deep sufferings of the passive night of the spirit. The very core of this night is the depth of the suffering required to complete the purgation of the spirit, although serene divine touches are sometimes granted by God during these afflictions in order to encourage the soul to continue forward. It is truly Purgatory, and it will occur either during this life or after death. But something else occurs during this passive night of spirit, and especially at its conclusion. The extent of the soul's love and its union with God exceeds anything it has ever experienced. It now *sees* God to a near ecstatic degree. We will see in *The Spiritual Canticle* and particularly in *The Living Flame of Love* the profound intimacy that the purified spirit enjoys with God after the purification of the spirit. There are no words to describe this gift. It can only be understood if it is experienced.

> The soul obtains habitually and perfectly (insofar as the condition of this life allows) the rest and quietude of the spiritual house by means of the acts of substantial touches of divine union which, in concealment and hiding from the disturbance of the devil and of the senses and passions, are received from the divinity. With these touches the soul is purified, quieted, strengthened, and made stable that it may be able to receive permanently this divine union, which is the divine espousal between the soul and the Son of God (DN II:24:3).

> One cannot reach this union without remarkable purity, and this purity is unattainable without vigorous mortification and nakedness regarding all creatures…Whoever refuses to go out at night in search for the Beloved and to divest and mortify his will, but rather seeks the Beloved in his own bed and comfort, as did the bride (Ct. 3:1), will not succeed in finding Him; as this soul declares, it found Him when it departed in darkness and with longings of love (DN II:24:4).

E. St. John of the Cross: The Spiritual Canticle

Clean of heart

In this work, the first twelve stanzas are devoted to the trials and sufferings of the soul because it cannot yet possess God in the loving union it seeks. The curious thing in the dynamic between

God and the soul is that God *wounds* the soul with divine touches that console it and then withdraws from it causing it great longing and pain. We see such expressions in St. John's poetry as "Where have You hidden, Beloved, and left me moaning?" in the first stanza; and "seeking my love" in the third stanza. In the fourth stanza, St. John enumerates many elements of creation and then he adds, "Tell me, has he passed by you?" Then in the sixth stanza the suffering soul says, "Do not send me any more messengers, they cannot tell me what I must hear." In stanza ten, the pleading of the soul becomes even more sorrowful: "Extinguish these miseries, since no one else can stamp them out." All of these verses point to the fact that something is incomplete in the relationship of the soul to union with God. This can only be a deficiency in the cleansing of the heart of this soul that prevents the union with God that it so desires. There is some condition of the soul that remains as an obstacle to the desired union. The union of course, cannot be perfect until after natural death. But there is still an obstacle that remains on the part of the soul preventing the union that is possible in this life. Let us look at what St. John of the Cross suggests that it could be.

In the first stanza the soul asks, "Where have you hidden?" This question must be asked because the soul in its early spiritual journey does not comprehend that God is hidden deeply within it. It does not know this because it is not yet itself hidden from the world and from creatures, and consequently is not yet in the place where God has hidden Himself.

> Yet you inquire: Since He Whom my soul loves is within me, why don't I find Him or experience Him?
>
> The reason is that He remains concealed and you do not conceal yourself in order to encounter and experience Him. Anyone who is to find a hidden treasure must enter the hiding place secretly, and once he has discovered it, he will also be hidden just as the treasure is hidden....Remaining hidden with Him, you will experience him in hiding, and love and enjoy him in hiding, and you will delight with Him in hiding, that is, in a way transcending all language and feeling (SC 1:9).

> Some call the Bridegroom beloved, whereas He is not really their beloved because their heart is not wholly set on Him. As a result, their petition is not of much value in His sight. They do not obtain their request until through perseverance in prayer they keep their spirit more continually with God, and their heart with its affectionate love more entirely set on Him (SC 1:13).

In the third stanza, the soul states, "Seeking my Love." What St. John examines here is how and where the soul is seeking its Love, God. First, we assume that the soul must seek God. The soul that is indifferent or lukewarm in its search for the ultimate meaning and purpose of its existence will never find the answers. The goal of the creature must be a unity with its creator. This concept forms a core theme of all of Christ's teaching. Every soul must mature into a correct ordering of reality or it will be lost. When it realizes that its goal must be to unite with its creator, then that effort must supersede all else in its life. The duty of discovery then falls to the soul. It must learn how to find its Bridegroom by exercising its own effort to the greatest extent possible in all stages of growth. An inadequate effort to do so will result in floundering and stumbling around and figuratively running headlong into brick walls and getting nowhere, and eventually giving up the effort altogether.

> That is, seeking my Beloved. She points out here that for the attainment of God it is not enough to pray with the heart and the tongue and receive favors from others, but together with this a soul must through its own efforts do everything possible...Many desire that God cost them no more than words, and even these they say badly. They scarcely desire to do anything for Him that might cost them something (SC 3:2).

> He who seeks God and yet wants his own satisfaction and rest seeks Him at night and thus will not find Him. He who looks for him through the practice and works of the virtues and gets up from the bed of his own satisfaction and delight, seeks Him by day, and thus will find Him. What is not found at night appears during the day (SC 3:3).

In the fourth stanza St. John of the Cross tells us that the order of advancing in the spiritual life is first, self-knowledge, and second the knowledge of God's excellence manifested in His creatures. The soul here asks, "Has He passed by you?" This means; have your perfections and qualities of both substance and accidents been given to you by God? Becoming clean of heart is a process of learning all one can about God's attributes through His works and His revelation regarding Himself, and which includes the inner-most secrets of our own hearts.

> The soul has made known the manner of preparing oneself to begin this journey: to pursue no longer delights and satisfactions, and to overcome temptations and difficulties through fortitude. This is the practice of self-knowledge, the first requirement for advancing to the knowledge of God. Now, in this stanza, she begins to walk along the way of the knowledge and consideration of creatures which leads to the knowledge of her Beloved, the Creator (SC 4:1).

In the sixth stanza, the soul expresses its frustration over having so little and such a piecemeal knowledge of God; greater knowledge would solidify the union it desires. Its knowledge comes from what it can glean from the perceptions of the senses, the inspirations of the spirit, and the touches given by God deep within the spirit. However, no essential knowledge of God is received by the soul, and it longs for this consummating union of intellects and wills. The soul bemoans that the small injections of divine wisdom that it receives from time to time are insufficient, calling these limited communications *messengers*. It is however, by virtue of the gains from these *messengers* that cleanness of heart gradually develops in the soul. It is in the dichotomy of consolation and desolation that the scrubbing of the heart to the cleanness desired by Christ occurs.

> My Lord, my Spouse, You have given Yourself to me partially; now may You give me Yourself more completely. You have revealed Yourself to me as through fissures in a rock; now may You give me that revelation more clearly. You have communicated by means of others, as if joking with

> me; now may You truly grant me a communication of Yourself by Yourself. In Your visits, at times, it seems You are about to give me the jewel of possessing You; but when I become aware of this possession, I discover that I do not have it, for You hide this jewel as if You had given it jokingly. Now wholly surrender Yourself by giving Yourself entirely to all of me, that my entire soul may have complete possession of You (SC 6:6).

What the soul is really asking for in this stanza is the Beatific Vision. This degree of completeness of union must await natural death for its realization. We will see further on in this work, however, greater satisfaction of many of these longings here expressed by the soul.

Finally, in stanza ten, the soul laments its miseries that can only be extinguished by its Beloved. This soul has a constant longing for God and union with Him, and it has distaste for everything that is not God or is less than God, and finds all things other than God to be burdensome and annoying. This is the misery of which the soul speaks. This soul's heart has been cleansed to the degree that it is bound and tied to its love for God. Everything else has faded into oblivion: love of creatures, self-satisfaction, and dependence on consolations are all things of this soul's past.

> To further urge and persuade her Beloved to grant her petition, she declares that, since He alone suffices to satisfy her need, He must be the one to extinguish these miseries. It is noteworthy that God is very ready to comfort and satisfy the soul in her needs and afflictions when she neither has nor desires consolation and satisfaction outside of Him. The soul possessing nothing that might withhold her from God cannot remain long without a visit from the Beloved (SC 10:6).

For they shall see God

The entirety of this work is aimed at two climactic events in the life of the soul: the spiritual espousal and the spiritual marriage. St. John, as he has done in all his works, uses the imagery of the

Canticle of Canticles, sometimes called *The Song of Solomon,* or *The Song of Songs,* the latter two titles coming from the opening verse of this book of *The Old Testament.* So much does St. John of the Cross borrow from the language of *The Canticle of Canticles* that he adopts almost verbatim the language of chapter 2 (Ct. 2:16) of the Canticle for use in stanza 16 of *The Spiritual Canticle.* In the *Canticle of Canticles* (Ct. 2:16), the author refers to foxes that must be caught to prevent damage to the vineyards, the vineyards being the security of love. The author then states that the vineyards are in bloom. St. John of the Cross, in stanza 16 of *The Spiritual Canticle,* tells us to catch the foxes for the vineyard is now in flower. To St. John the foxes are the appetites and sensory movements used by the devil to hinder the love between the soul and God, and the vineyard is the nursery of all the virtues.

Continuing his reliance on *The Canticle of Canticles,* St. John of the Cross expresses the relationship developing between God and the soul as reflective of the relationship of a man and woman that leads to marriage, and therefore, he uses language appropriate to that natural relationship. Thus, we have him speaking of the spiritual betrothal and the spiritual marriage as the culmination and perfection of the soul's unity with God, and He with the soul. God here becomes the Bridegroom or the Beloved. The *seeing of God* that is stated by Christ in this *Beatitude* then becomes, in the words of St. John, the entering of the spiritual betrothal first, and then the spiritual marriage. These states of the soul are the reward for the clean heart, purified by all the afflictions and consolations experienced earlier.

As the soul enters the spiritual betrothal, it begins to have rapturous experiences of God that are not permanent. These raptures are so intense that they cause the soul great pain: both while they are felt, and after they subside. The soul even asks that they be withdrawn. But within these ecstasies, the seeing of God is different than ever before. The experience is impossible to describe in any meaningful way; to be understood it must be experienced.

> Although the sensory part suffers, the spirit takes flight to supernatural recollection and enjoyment of the Beloved's Spirit, which is what she desired and sought. Yet, she would not want to receive the Spirit in the body, for there she cannot receive Him fully, but only in a small degree and with

considerable suffering. But she would want to receive Him in the flight of the spirit, outside the body, where she can freely rejoice with Him (SC 13:5).

In stanza 22, St. John of the Cross begins his description of the soul that has entered the spiritual marriage, the highest state possible for a soul in this life. This last state of a soul is incomparably greater than anything that has gone before it, including the spiritual betrothal. The transforming union is complete and all that is not God has been left behind by the soul. The Bridegroom is delighted because He has desired this union even more than the soul. He announces that the bride has entered the garden of her desire and rests in delight. The soul now *sees* God as clearly as possible in this life.

> This spiritual marriage is incomparably greater than the spiritual espousal, for it is a total transformation in the Beloved in which each surrenders the entire possession of self to the other with a certain consummation of the union of love...

> This union resembles the union of the light of a star or candle with the light of the sun, for what then sheds light is not the star or the candle, but the sun, which has absorbed the other lights into its own (SC 22:3).

> The union wrought between the two natures and the communication of the divine to the human in this state is such that even though neither changes its being, both appear to be God. Yet in this life, the union cannot be perfect, although it is beyond words and thoughts (SC 22:4).

Stanza 38 contains very important insights into what Christ probably meant in this *Beatitude* by the expression *shall see God*. St. John first points out that the soul has been seeking a love that is comparable to God's love for the soul. The soul's will, infinitely weaker than God's will is not of itself capable of loving to the same extent that God loves. This dilemma is solved by the unity of the soul's will with God's will, which is the definition of holiness. The love by which the soul loves is itself the gift of God to the soul. Having resolved the problem of inequality of wills, St. John poses an even more difficult one. If the soul's delight is in loving God and the glory of the Beatific Vision is in seeing God, then why does the soul say here that it is seeking a love comparable to God's love rather than to see God? St. John gives us the correct interpretation of the first two verses of this stanza in his commentary on these verses. I do not think the language of the stanza without the commentary clearly reveals his interpretation. The meaning of these two verses is so important to our subject that I will conclude this section by quoting extensively from St. John's commentary.

> But before proceeding we ought to resolve a doubt: Why, since essential glory lies in seeing God and not in loving, does the soul declare at the beginning of the stanza that she was seeking this love and not the essential glory, and afterwards request, as something of less importance, essential glory?
>
> There are two reasons; First, just as the ultimate reason for everything is love (which is seated in the will) whose property is to give and not to receive, whereas the property of the intellect (which is the subject of essential glory) lies in receiving and not giving, the soul in the inebriation of love does not put first the glory she will receive from God, but rather puts first the surrender of herself to Him through true love without concern for her own profit. Second, the desire to see is included in the desire to love and already presupposed in the preceding stanzas, for it is impossible to attain to the perfect love of God without the perfect vision of God. Thus, the force of this doubt is resolved in the first answer. With love, the soul pays God what she owes Him; with the intellect, on the contrary, she receives from Him (SC 38:5).

What a magnificent insight St. John of the Cross has given us here into the meaning of this *Beatitude*, an insight that can be and should be the subject of constant meditation on what is illumined for us by St. John.

F. St. John of the Cross: The Living Flame of Love

St. John of the Cross states at the outset of this work that he has been hesitant to comment on the poetry of *The Living Flame of Love* because it deals with matters so interior and spiritual for which words are inadequate. Therefore, he feels that his explanations will be less than adequate for what is being explained. The content of the work describes the intimacy between God and the soul that results from the transforming union of the spiritual marriage. No one could address this immense grace, as it exists in another. Therefore, St. John must draw on his own experience of this union and perhaps some aspects of the union as he observed them in those to whom he gave spiritual direction. There is no need to discuss cleanness of heart as it relates to this work of St. John because the soul described here has successfully arrived at the cleanness of heart desired by Christ in this *Beatitude*. Therefore, let us look at some of the ways St. John describes the interior *seeing* of God in the verses of this poem.

For they shall see God

STANZA 1

O living flame of love
That tenderly wounds my soul
In its deepest center! Since
Now You are not oppressive,
Now consummate! if it be Your will:
Tear through the veil of this sweet encounter!

As we examine these verses it will become very clear why, in the middle chapters of Book II of *The Ascent of Mt. Carmel,* namely chapters 11, 12, and 13, that St John admonishes the reader to reject and dismiss all apprehensions that are less than God, even those received in the spirit and presumed to have a divine origin. They are not the means to union with God as here, described by St. John. If these apprehensions less than God are pursued and possessed by a soul, that soul will never arrive at where the soul described in these verses finds itself: intimately in union with God. This is a grace that takes place in the spirit. Hence, we must understand this intimate union as something wholly spiritual devoid of physical characteristic or sources.

O living flame of love
That tenderly wounds my soul
In its deepest center!

St. John describes the flame of these verses as one that smolders constantly, and then at moments chosen by God flares up causing unspeakable sentiments and acts of love between the soul and its Beloved. The sight of God in these ecstasies that the soul is given, although not perfect and complete, is ineffable.

> This flame of love is the Spirit of its Bridegroom, which is the Holy Spirit. The soul feels Him within itself not only as a fire which has consumed and transformed it, but as a fire that burns and flares within it, as I mentioned. And that flame, every time it flares up, bathes the soul in glory, and refreshes it with the quality of divine life (LF 1:3).

> Hence, we can compare the soul in its ordinary condition in this state of transformation of love to the log of wood that is ever immersed in fire, and the acts of this soul to the flame that blazes up from the fire of love. The more intense the fire of union, the more vehemently does this fire burst into flames (LF 1:4).

The word wound is used in many of the books of St. John of the Cross to describe various experiences of the soul at different stages of the spiritual life. First, a wound of great pain is inflicted on the soul in the midst of purification and purgation of the soul as described in *The Dark Night*. Without citing endless examples, we can say that the soul is severely wounded when the light of God shines upon its imperfections causing it immense suffering and affliction during its trials in the dark contemplation of both nights of the spirit. In stanza 1, of *The Spiritual Canticle* the soul asks where God has hidden after wounding her. This wound is one caused by love.

> It is something splendid that since love is never idle, but in continual motion, it is always emitting flames everywhere like a blazing fire, and since its duty is to wound in order to cause love and delight, and it is

present in this soul as a living flame, it dispatches its wounds like most tender flames of delicate love (LF 1:8).

STANZA 2

O sweet cautery,
O delightful wound!
O gentle hand! O delicate touch
That tastes of eternal life
And pays every debt!
In killing You changed death to life.

O sweet cautery,
O delightful wound

A closer look at the nature of the wound St. John of the Cross describes here is in order. This wound is the essence of the exchange between the soul that has been purified, whose heart is clean, and its Beloved. We recall again that the wounds suffered by the soul in its dark and passive nights were oppressive and caused the soul much suffering. This wound, spoken of here, is however, of a much different character. It is called delightful. And most remarkable of all, it is shared by the soul and God.

> To understand the nature of this wound the soul is addressing, it should be known that the cautery of material fire always leaves a wound where it is applied. And it possesses this property: If applied a wound not made by fire, it converts it into a wound caused by fire. Whether a soul is wounded by other wounds of miseries and sins or whether it is healthy, this cautery of love immediately affects a wound of love in the one it touches, and those wounds due to other causes become wounds of love...

> As often as the cautery of love touches the wound of love, it causes a deeper wound of love, and thus the more it wounds, the more it cures and heals (LF 2:7).

STANZA 4

How gently and lovingly
You wake in my heart,
Where in secret You dwell alone;
And in your sweet breathing,
Filled with good and glory
How tenderly You swell my heart with love!

How gently and lovingly
You wake in my heart,

We can conclude our examination of the sixth *Beatitude* by looking at St. John's analysis of what has happened in the soul that achieved cleanness of heart, and how this has affected the soul's ability to see God. We have considered several different meanings to the terms *see God* as they are used in this *Beatitude*. At this point, we are discussing a soul that has arrived at the highest spiritual state possible in this life. Its ability to *see* God is therefore, in a high state of perfection. When St. John says, as he does here, that God wakes in the soul's heart, what movement is meant here and by whom? St. John's conclusion is that since God is immovable, it must be the soul that has moved as a result of its growth spiritually. The change in this soul is so great because the obstacles to union with God have been so diminished or completely eliminated that its vision of God is much enhanced in its clarity and joy.

> How this movement takes place in the soul, since God is immovable, is a wonderful thing, for it seems to the soul that God indeed moves; yet He does not really move. For since it is the soul that is renewed and moved by God so that it might behold this supernatural sight, and since that divine life and the being and harmony of every creature in that life, with its movements in God, is revealed to it with such newness, it seems to the soul that it is God Who moves and that the cause assumes the name of the effect it produces...We then ought to say that in this movement it is the soul that is moved and awakened from the sleep of natural vision to supernatural vision (LF 4:6).

CHAPTER 7

Blessed are the peacemakers,
For they shall be called children of God

To begin with, we must examine the breadth of the meaning of the term *peacemakers* as it relates to the theme of this book: how the *Beatitudes* are reflected in the writings of the two Carmelite Doctors of the Church. First, we can say that the concept of peacemakers goes beyond the elimination or amelioration of strife between others and ourselves or between others among themselves. The concept of peacemakers is in fact a result of the presence of a special peace within any particular soul: the peace of Christ that the world cannot give nor understand. When a soul is possessed of such a peace, humility is always present in that soul. This humility is born of a realization of the right relationship of that soul to God, and its utter dependence upon the mercy of God for its welfare, temporal and eternal. For that reason there is no necessity in such a soul to oppose or combat with others over some presumed right that has been violated or to compete for dominance in any activity. The securing of recognition of some sort to which one assumes he is entitled is a matter of indifference to a soul immersed in the peace of Christ. The desire of a soul to imitate Christ by silent surrender to injustice or an offense against it spreads an aura of peace around that soul. The absence of strife on the part of such a soul with all who would contend with it reduces all to silence and some degree of wonder that has the effect of calming the waters of turmoil. It is this peace that we will look for in the writings of St. Teresa of Jesus and St. John of the Cross. Like all good children, the peacemakers in this *Beatitude* will respond to the will of their Father and seek to become like Him so that they can be truly called *children of God*.

What is most important for a child of God is to surrender his/her will to the Divine Will. This requires the rigorous purification of the soul and the purgation of all that is contrary to the achieving of this unity of wills. This is the only way the resistance to giving up one's will resulting from self-centeredness can be overcome. Self-centeredness must be defeated if a soul is to grow in unity with the will of God. It is true that self-knowledge accomplishes the defeat of self-absorption. We will look into the writings of our Carmelite saints for the manner in which self-knowledge moves us closer to these ends that will allow us to make this *Beatitude* a part of our spiritual life.

A. St. Teresa of Jesus: The Way of Perfection

Blessed are the peacemakers

The first requirement of becoming a peacemaker among men is to have a truly spiritual love for others. Without this element, the inclination to establish peace with others and for others would not occur. Peace is the natural result of love. Love begets peace as surely as hate begets animosity and destruction. Without love, interest in the good of another is absent, and the opposite, bringing evil upon another, thrives. Without love, others are seen as obstacles to my own self-satisfaction. Without the love of others and a sincere interest in their welfare, no community is possible. The result is a destructive and self oriented individualism that bears no fruit. Witness the childless marriages of today that are based on the convenience and comfort of the couple rather than on the self-sacrifice of their own wills for the sake of fulfilling the objects of marriage which is the bringing into being of their offspring. Love is born of sacrifice for the sake of the other and is not based on the satisfaction of one's own desires. A community of people who are only interested in their own gratification is doomed to strife and conflict.

> There are only three things which I will explain at some length and which are taken from our constitution itself. It is essential that we should understand how very important they are to us in helping us to preserve that peace, both inward and outward, which the Lord so earnestly recommended to us. One of these is love for each other (WP 4).

After naming the other two as detachment from all created things and humility, St. Teresa proceeds to explain why the first, love for each other, is so important. Remember that St. Teresa is encouraging members of her community in the manner they must relate to each other and to God in order to have a community that is pleasing to God. It is this unselfish love that makes it possible to bear the faults and irritations from others. In this way conflicts in a community are either non-existence or they never become the reason for weakness in or disintegration of a community of like-minded people. I say like-minded people for the reason that tolerance of those who fundamentally disagree with us is frequently a fault in itself. There are times when one must stand his ground against what is obviously error or evil. In these matters, it is better to keep peace with God than with one's fellows.

> With regard to the first–namely, love for each other– this is of very great importance; for there is nothing, however annoying, that cannot easily be borne by those who love each other, and anything which causes annoyance must be quite exceptional (WP 4).

This love that produces peace between others and ourselves is tolerant of what we see as weakness in others, as I said above. But we must be careful that tolerance does not become the enabling of evil. This idea of tolerance in every case is rampant in the world today, and has led to every manner of mischief and destruction of persons. This we cannot do when there is obvious evil to be reprimanded. St. Teresa makes a special point of recognizing this difference.

> If you are not like this (cast down by small things), do not neglect to have compassion on others; it may be that our Lord wishes to spare us these sufferings and will give us sufferings of another kind which will seem heavy to us, though to the person already mentioned they may seem light. In these matters, then, we must not judge others by our selves, nor think of ourselves as we have been at some time when, perhaps without any effort on our part, the Lord has made us stronger than they; let us think of what we were like at the times when we have been weakest (WP 7).

> Their heart does not allow them to practice duplicity; if they see their friend straying from the road, or committing any faults, they will speak to her about it; they cannot allow themselves to do anything else. And if after this the loved one does not amend, they will not flatter her or hide anything from her. Either, then, she will amend or their friendship will cease;

> for otherwise they would be unable to endure it, nor is it in fact endurable. It would mean continual war for both parties (WP 7).

A clear understanding of this difference between love of others, and intolerance of evil in others is very important to the understanding of the idea of peacemakers being children of God. It is the difference between charity and mercy on the one hand, and tolerance and encouragement of evil on the other. These latter cannot in any sense be called children of God. Their entire orientation is promotion of evil against the law of God that was ordained for all mankind at the time of creation. His law is immutable, as is He. This law doesn't change over time with mutations of society and its mores. God's law is eternal, knowable, and observable. No one may tolerate or accept a violation of that law under any circumstances.

For they shall be called the children of God

When we reflect on what it means to be a child of God, we must understand that we are talking about a heavenly Father, and not an earthly father. A child of an earthly father is not required to abandon all self-interest and self-will in the relationship. Frequently a father and a child in the natural order are at odds over many issues, but the relationship remains in spite of the differences of opinion. This is not so in the case of a soul that desires to become a child of the heavenly Father. Rather there must be one will in common among the two, and it must be the will of the Father. That happy result comes about only after much mortification of the soul's will, and the purgation of much imperfection. The necessity of love in order to be the peacemaker referred to by Christ in this *Beatitude* requires for its realization the same mortification and purgation I refer to here. Eventually such a soul will put aside all other loves and subject them to the one love of God by which it shall become a child of God. In turn, God will bestow great virtue and graces on this child of His.

> Let us now come to the detachment which we must practice, for if this is carried out perfectly it includes everything else. I say "it includes everything else" because, if we care nothing for any created things, but embrace the Creator alone, His Majesty will

infuse the virtues into us in such a way that, provided we labour to the best of our abilities day by day, we shall not have to wage war much longer, for the Lord will take our defense in hand against the devils and against the whole world (WP 8).

It must be remembered that God wishes us to become true children of His even more than we ever could desire that paternity. Christ reveals that to us that we are children of God in the opening words of the *Lord's Prayer*: "Our Father who art in heaven." Christ also brings that desire of the Father to our attention in the parable of *The Prodigal Son*. What words of Christ in all the gospels are more consoling than those of this parable? This father who forgives all immediately upon seeing the repentance of the prodigal son reflects deliberately the attitude Christ wants us to learn about His own Father in the Trinity. St. Teresa sees this sublime mercy and condescension of God in her commentary on the very first words of the *Lord's Prayer*.

> O Son of God and my Lord! How is it that Thou canst give us so much with Thy first word? It is so wonderful that Thou shouldst descend to such a degree of humility as to join with us when we pray and make Thyself the Brother of creatures so miserable and lowly! How can it be that, in the name of Thy Father, Thou shouldst give us all that there is to be given, by willing Him to have us as His children-and Thy word cannot fail (WP 27).

> You have a good Father, given you by the good Jesus; let no other father be known or referred to here. Strive, my daughters, to be such that you deserve to find comfort in Him and to throw ourselves into His arms. You know that, if you are good children, He will never send you away. And who would not do anything rather than lose such a Father (WP 27)?

B. St. Teresa of Jesus: The Interior Castle

The First Three Dwelling Places

Blessed are the peacemakers

St. Teresa describes, in the commentary on the first dwelling place, the absence in the soul of any desire to enter into a relationship with God. This soul is concerned with matters of this world and its own successes in those earthly matters. We know from our own experience that strife and conflict are always connected to competition for prominence and prestige above others in worldly matters. This is so whether the area of conflict is wealth, power, or fame. As a result, there is no peace in such a soul, either within itself or in its dealings with others. In fact, this soul sees every other soul as an adversary that must be conquered or at least bested in every endeavor. Since one cannot give what he does not have, this soul is far from being a peacemaker. We must return to our original theme that it is only through love that one can become a peacemaker: love of God and love of neighbor in God. This attitude is the antithesis of the soul in the first dwelling place. Remember that contraries cannot exist in the same subject at the same time. If one is to become the peacemaker desired by Christ in this *Beatitude*, he must empty himself of the characteristics of the beginner described above.

> Thus, there are souls so ill and so accustomed to being involved in external matters that there is no remedy, nor does it seem they can enter within themselves. They are now so used to dealing always with the insects and vermin that are in the wall surrounding the castle that they have become almost like them...If these souls do not strive to understand and cure their great misery, they will be changed into statues of salt, unable to turn their heads to look at themselves, just as Lot's wife was changed for having turned her head (IC I:1:6).

We begin to see in this quote the introduction of the element most necessary for spiritual growth according to St. Teresa: self-knowledge. In fact, a soul cannot grow spiritually toward becoming the peacemaker desired by Christ without this most painful element. Its effects are salutary in so many ways: insight that leads to perfection, knowledge that leads to humility, the removal of obstacles to love of neighbor, and an understanding of the immensity of God's mercy to us.

> Sometimes they do put all these things aside, and the self-knowledge and awareness that they are not proceeding correctly in order to get to the door is important. Finally, they enter the first, lower rooms (IC I:1:8).

In the second dwelling place, St. Teresa discusses the soul that is entering into prayer, albeit with imperfection and weakness. This soul is ambivalent about whether it wants to go forward or backward. Because of this ambivalence, this soul begins to suffer conflict and indecision in its spiritual endeavors. There is anything but peace in such a soul. Nor can it extend peace to others in any consistent way because its own interior struggles prevent it. But grace is beginning to pour out upon this soul. God is now showing Himself to this soul in small doses.

> I say that these rooms involve more effort because those who are in the first dwelling places are like deaf-mutes and thus the difficulty of not speaking is more easily endured by them than it is by those who hear and cannot speak...Yet this Lord desires intensely that we love Him and seek His company, so much so that from time to time He calls us to draw near to Him And His voice is so sweet the poor soul dissolves at not doing immediately what He commands. Thus, as I say, hearing his voice is a greater trial than not hearing it (IC II:1:2).

As we go through the progress of a soul moving toward God, as described in the writings of St. Teresa on the third dwelling place, we must keep in sight our premise. It is love of God and of our neighbor in God that brings a soul to be a peacemaker in the meaning intended by Christ in this *Beatitude*. St. Teresa emphasizes that two qualities are necessary in order to reach the possibility of being such a peacemaker: humility and perseverance. These two virtues, if put into practice, lead inevitably to the unselfish love required to invest one's self in others to the extent necessary to bring them peace in their struggles and trials. This is even true in a soul that is at a somewhat low level of spiritual perfection. The presence of some degree of humility will over-shadow the remaining self-interest in this soul sufficiently to avoid dealing with another soul for the sake of the soul offering help rather than the soul needing help.

> I believe that through the goodness of god there are many of these souls in the world. They long not to offend His Majesty, even guarding themselves against venial sins; they are fond of doing penance and setting aside periods for recollection; they spend their time well, practicing works of charity towards their neighbors; and are very balanced in their use of speech and dress and in the governing of their households-those who have them. Certainly this is a state to be desired (IC III:1:5).

The soul that wishes to advance to great perfection must be willing to conform its will to God's Will, regardless of what that requires. There is much more that lies ahead for a soul that is just beginning to develop the virtues of humility and perseverance. There is a quality of love that must be learned without which no soul can claim to be a disciple of Christ. We frequently believe that we have developed that quality of love, only to find when it is tested that we are found lacking. This love is not an emotion. It is an act of the will that is able to reject all else but God and His will, no matter what is asked. It is here that one has become a peacemaker among men.

> If, like the young man in the Gospel, we turn our backs and go away sad when the Lord tells us what we must do to be perfect, what do you want His Majesty to do? For He must give the reward in conformity with the love we have for him. And this love, daughters, must not be fabricated in our imaginations but proved by deeds. And don't think He needs our works; He needs the determination of our wills (IC III:1:7).

> For little things happen, even though not of this kind, (examples of spiritual weakness) in which you can very well test and know whether or not you are the rulers of your passions. And believe me the

whole affair doesn't lie in whether or not we wear the religious habit but in striving to practice the virtues, in surrendering our will to God in everything, in bringing our life into accordance with what his Majesty ordains for it, and in desiring that His will not ours be done (IC III:2:6).

For they shall be called the children of God

Now let us see how St. Teresa describes the slow moving path along which a soul struggles to become truly a child of God. In the first three dwelling places, she is examining a soul in its beginning stages of spiritual growth. But these first hesitant steps of a soul are necessary to experience, because, like climbing a ladder, each step leads to the next until the top is reached. No one leaps several steps at a time and arrives at the top quickly. What is more likely to happen if that approach is attempted, is that the soul will tumble backwards to the spiritual ground and have to start over to cover the steps missed.

> Sometimes they do put all these things (of the world) aside, and the self-knowledge and awareness that they are not proceeding correctly in order to get to the door is important. Finally, they enter the first, lower rooms. But so many reptiles get in with them that they are prevented from seeing the beauty of the castle and from calming down; they have done quite a bit just by having entered (IC I:1:8).

The soul that advances to the second dwelling place is progressing nicely toward the goal of becoming a child of God. Even though the ambivalence described in the previous section is a continuing problem, there is a discernible step forward here. There is a sense of interior listening that was not there before, and this soul begins to feel the urge to respond to what it is hearing. Prayer is leading it to trust in God's love for it, and this is the beginning of converting the love of God for it into its love for God. The voice of God is becoming discernible to the soul and it sounds in that soul with a small degree of sweetness to the listening soul.

> I don't mean that these appeals and calls are like the ones I shall speak of later on. But they come

through words spoken by other good people, or through sermons, or through what is read in good books, or through the many things that are heard and by which God calls, or through illness and trials, or also through a truth that He teaches during the brief moments we spend in prayer; however lukewarm these moments may be, God esteems them highly (IC II:1:3).

When the soul enters the third dwelling place by the grace of God, the relationship of Father and child really begins to develop. We know that God is always disposed toward us as Father, but we are not always disposed toward Him as His child. To the extent that we are so disposed, it is usually as a child focused on itself and its wants and needs. The Father is there only to satisfy the child's desires. God is seen as a provider of gifts and relief from unpleasant realities. If God fails to conform to our wishes, well then listen to the howling and complaining that God has abandoned me and cares not for me at all. This is the immature view of God that most of us start with. But the soul that has advanced as far as the third dwelling place is beginning to change that view of God. What God wills begins to take on some degree of importance to this soul. Offending God becomes a horror to avoid, sometimes at all costs.

I believe that through the goodness of God there are many of these souls in the world. They long not to offend His Majesty, even guarding themselves against venial sins; they are fond of doing penance and setting aside periods for recollection; they spend their time well, practicing works of charity toward their neighbors; and are very balanced in their use of speech and dress and in the governing of their households–those who have them (IC III:1:5).

Although these souls have made real advancement, they remain shackled by many faults and self-centered spiritual attitudes. This is a place we all have been. They are disturbed greatly by anything that is seen as a failing or weakness. They rationalize their refusal to surrender completely to God and leave the things of this world behind by many and varied excuses. If tried in a public way so that they are required to defend their faith or the honor and glory of God, they are disturbed for a long period, and have a sense of embarrassment for having gone against the prevailing antipathy toward God that we meet everywhere. But, the relationship of child to the Father has germinated and is growing.

> Love has not yet reached the point of overwhelming reason. But I would like us to use our reason to make ourselves dissatisfied with this way of serving God, always going step by step, for we'll never finish this journey. And since, in our opinion, we are continually walking and are tired (for, believe me, it is a wearisome journey), we will be doing quite well if we don't go astray (IC III:2:7).

> With humility present, this stage is a most excellent one. If humility is lacking, we will remain here our whole life- and with a thousand afflictions and miseries (IC III:2:9).

The Last Four Dwelling Places

Blessed are the peacemakers

The principal change that occurs as a soul moves from the third dwelling place to the fourth dwelling place is that its spiritual life begins to rise from the natural level to the supernatural level. In its relationship with God, the soul adopts a more passive role than the active role it exercised in the first three dwelling places. The love of God that leads to the spiritual childhood of the peacemaker, changes from the emotional approach that desires consolations to the predominance of an act of the will that chooses the ultimate good, regardless of the sentiment of the moment. There begins a great intimacy with God that results in an enhanced understanding of God's ways and an acceptance of His will even when affliction is the order of the day. These afflictions of the soul that occur principally in the natural order of things in the fourth dwelling place are endured with much greater acceptance and patience. As a result, the soul remains in peace through its afflictions, whereas, before it was in turmoil over the same experiences. Therefore, there goes out from this soul to others a manifestation of serenity that has a calming effect on others. These others are influenced by the serenity they observe in this soul and discover that the peace they observe originates in the love of God's Will.

> To return to the verse [*dilatasti cor meum* (from the Rule of St. Albert)], what I think is helpful in it for explaining this matter is the idea of expansion. It seems that since that heavenly water begins to rise from this spring I'm mentioning that is deep within us, it swells and expands our whole interior being, producing ineffable blessings; nor does the soul even understand what is given to it there (IC IV:2:6).

> It seems clear to me the will must in some way be united with God's will. But it is in the effects and deeds following afterward that one discerns the true value of prayer; there is no better crucible for testing prayer (IC IV:2:8).

The key to understanding what it means to be a peacemaker is to realize that the disposition to go out to others in peace requires that the soul itself first be in peace. For the soul to be at peace the usual conflicts that afflict most lives are to be avoided. These conflicts will be removed by this soul when the attachments to worldly success and to the self are defeated. Grace will enable these preoccupations to diminish and eventually disappear. This grace will come in the form of experiences of interior prayer. These forms of interior prayer are the prayer of recollection and the prayer of quiet discussed by St. Teresa at length in this work.

> But one noticeably senses a gentle drawing inward, as anyone who goes through this will observe, for I don't know how to make it clearer…In the case of this recollection, it doesn't come when we want it but when God wants to grant us the favor. I for myself hold that when His Majesty grants it, He does so to persons who are already beginning to despise the things of the world (IC IV:3:3).

> The prayer of recollection is much less intense than the prayer of spiritual delight from God that I mentioned. But it is the beginning through which one goes to the other; for in the prayer of recollection, meditation, or the work of the intellect, must be set aside (IC IV:3:8).

In the fifth and sixth mansions, St. Teresa expands on her explanation of the growth of the soul in the forms of prayer that are now becoming customary for this soul in these dwelling places. Unity with God increases significantly in these two dwelling places. The prayer of union begins to be experienced. It is from this increasing unity with God that the peace within the soul increases, thus enabling it to be at greater peace within itself, and as a result of this peace, to express that serenity in all its dealings with others. This soul now manifests that it is becoming the peacemaker that Christ describes in this *Beatitude*. Agitation and conflict may wage all around it, but this soul remains self-possessed in its unity with God and in its love for His Will. It therefore communicates its peace to others who are caught up in conflicts and this has a very calming effect on all around it.

> When the soul is, in this prayer (the prayer of union), truly dead to the world, a little white butterfly comes forth. Oh, greatness of God! How transformed the soul is when it comes out of this prayer after having been placed within the greatness of God and so closely joined with Him for a little while...(IC V:2:7).

> I don't mean to say that those who arrive here (at the prayer of union) do not have peace; they do have it, and it is very deep. For the trials themselves are so valuable and have such good roots that although severe they give rise to peace and happiness. From the very unhappiness caused by worldly things arises the ever so painful desire to leave this world (IC V:2:10).

> And be certain that the more advanced you see you are in love for your neighbor the more advanced you will be in the love of God, for the love His Majesty has for us is so great that to repay us for our love of neighbor He will in a thousand ways increase the love we have for Him (IC V:3:8).

In the sixth dwelling place, the soul receives extraordinary experiences and favors from God. The usual effect of these divine touches is to cause the soul to withdraw into them, and to temporarily forget all else. This forgetfulness includes the world and all creatures in it. These experiences include locutions, raptures, and flights of the spirit. In order to places these graces in the context of our subject matter, we need to look at their fruits. What effect do they have on the soul that receives them, and how can those effects lead the soul deeper into the practice of peacemaking? First, we can say that they are deep experiences of God that impart knowledge in some cases and in others great love for God. The soul is led by these divine touches away from the petty things of this world that we have described as conflicts and agitation. It is these two properties of the human personality that destroy peace in a soul, and therefore, prevent it from communicating peace to others. These favors are enormous gifts of God outside the realm of the natural, and therefore lead a soul to a level of existence that transcends the natural.

> God gives these souls the strongest desire not to displease Him in anything, however small, and the desire to avoid if possible every imperfection. For this reason alone, if for no other, the soul wants to flee people, and it has great envy of those who have lived in deserts. On the other hand, it would want to enter into the midst of the world to try to play a part in getting even one soul to praise God more (IC VI:6:3).

The seventh dwelling place contains the fruits of all the soul's previous efforts. It contains a peace that is not accelerated or diminished by either the nature of the soul, the circumstances that change around it, nor even by extraordinary supernatural phenomena. The indwelling of the Holy Trinity is experienced without significant interruption, and this reality calms every storm or enthusiasm to which the soul may be subjected. These are the properties of the spiritual marriage on which St. John of the Cross elaborates more fully in *The Spiritual Canticle*. It is this absence of turmoil in this soul that allows it to be the peacemaker at all times for anyone who wishes to take advantage of this offering of the mature soul. In this soul, the virtues reign supreme.

> There is a great detachment from everything and a desire to be always either alone or occupied in something that will benefit some soul. There are no interior trials or feelings of dryness, but the soul

lives with a remembrance and tender love of our Lord (IC VII:3:8).

I repeat, it is necessary that your foundation consist of more than prayer and contemplation. If you do not strive for the virtues and practice them, you will always be dwarfs. And, please God; it will be only a matter of not growing, for you already know that whoever does not increase decreases. I hold that love, where present, cannot possibly be content with remaining always the same (IC VII:4:9).

For they shall be called the children of God

Every soul, by virtue of being a creature of the Creator is a *child* of God. That is undeniable in the supernatural realm. This soul is also a child of its parents in the natural order, and that reality also cannot be denied or modified regardless of what unfortunate circumstances that befall this soul. Every soul is made in the image and likeness of God. That likeness establishes the childhood of every soul in its relationship with God. This paternal relationship to God is not, at least as it begins, a choice of the soul. It exists because it is a created being, coming into existence through a paternal act of love on the part of God. However, this relationship to God can be spoiled and interfered with by the voluntary acts of the soul in committing sin. In mortal sin the soul loses the life of God in it, which is called sanctifying grace. It is this grace that establishes the childhood of the soul in God. The likeness to God is erased by mortal sin; and it can only be re-established by the mercy of God through sacramental confession, or in extraordinary circumstances, by a perfect act of contrition. So the objective of life is to preserve the original image and likeness of God that was given to us at our beginning.

> …there came to my mind what I shall now speak about, that which will provide us with a basis to begin with…I don't find anything comparable to the magnificent beauty of a soul and its marvelous capacity. Indeed, our intellects, however keen, can hardly comprehend it, just as they cannot comprehend God; but He Himself says that He created us in His own image and likeness (IC I:1:1).

> ...His Majesty in saying that the soul is made in His own image makes it almost impossible for us to understand the sublime dignity and beauty of the soul (IC I:1:1).

Souls that enter the second dwelling place are beginning to confirm themselves as children of God. A soul in turmoil and caught in habits of sin does not possess the peace necessary to communicate peace to others. Peace is the result of the conforming of one's will to the will of God. There is no other manner by which peace comes to a soul. A soul living in opposition to the will of God, even though its conscience has been deadened, is not at peace in any real sense of that word. However, as the soul grows in its desire to do the will of God in all things, it grows proportionately in peace. In the same way, its childhood to God grows in this soul as its likeness to God, in love, increases.

> Yet this Lord desires intensely that we love Him and seek His company, so much so that from time to time He calls us to draw near Him. And His voice is so sweet the poor soul dissolves at not doing immediately what He commands (IC II:1:2).

> The whole aim of anyone who is beginning prayer – and don't forget this, because it's very important– should be that he work and prepare himself with determination and every possible effort to bring his will into conformity with God's will (IC II:1:8).

A soul that enters the third dwelling place has truly advanced a great deal in holiness. It has a very serious concern about not offending God. Prayer is now a serious and regular part of its life. As this soul advances in wishing to conform itself to the will of God, its childhood to God advances proportionately, and as it does, so also does its capacity increase for being a peacemaker for others. Humility now becomes an essential component of this soul's spiritual life. Recognition of its dependence on God brings into focus its relationship of child to its heavenly Father. This change cannot help but have an edifying effect on all around it. The resulting peaceful demeanor of this soul is contagious and inspiring to others.

> But His Majesty well knows that I can boast only of His mercy, and since I cannot cease being what I have been, I have no other remedy than to approach His mercy and to trust in the merits of His Son and of the Virgin, His Mother...(IC III:1:3).

Those souls that enter the fourth dwelling place and the dwelling places beyond are involved in a different dimension of the spiritual life. They have left the natural milieu of life and are now in a supernatural spiritual environment. As everything in the spiritual life is transformed here, so also is their childhood to God. This transformation is characterized by the growth of a likeness in love to God. The supernatural atmosphere in which the soul is now beginning to exist enhances the virtues. God has now become the Prime mover of this soul in its spiritual growth. Never before has it been so much a child of God as it is in this dwelling place. In spite of periods of dryness and affliction, its peace is well established here.

> Since these dwelling places now are closer to where the King is, their beauty is great. There are things to see and understand so delicate that the intellect is incapable of finding words to explain them, although something might turn out to be well put and not at all obscure to the inexperienced; and anyone who has experience, especially when there is a lot of it, will understand very well (IC IV:1:1).

In her discussion of this fourth dwelling place, St. Teresa describes several forms of prayer that begin here: the prayer of recollection, and the prayer of spiritual delight, which she also calls the prayer of quiet. These are supernatural forms of prayer. This soul is now beginning to move within the supernatural realm of prayer. Consequently, its relationship to God is becoming more and more supernatural. It is more a relationship of spirits in the form of love than in former times. The submission of the soul to the will of its Creator comes easier, and actually produces a level of delight in this conformity of its will to that of God.

> It must be understood that when something is truly from God there is no languishing in the soul, even though there may be an interior and exterior

> languishing, for the soul experiences deep feelings on seeing itself close to God (IC IV:3:12).

The soul that enters the fifth dwelling place, while expanding on the spiritual growth of the fourth dwelling place, begins to shed its attachments to the world and to its own will and the self. God is now calling forth a more complete surrender of this soul to Him and to His will. This soul is becoming more single minded and attached to God as its Father, a heavenly Father. We can easily understand how such a soul is growing in peace as, on the negative side, it is losing the turmoil of the world, and on the positive side, it is uniting itself intimately with God.

> But reflect, daughters that He doesn't want you to hold on to anything, so that you will be able to enjoy the favors we are speaking of. Whether you have little or much, He wants everything for Himself; and in conformity with what you know you have given you will receive greater or lesser favors (IC V:1:3).

> That which is most valuable in the delightful union is that it proceeds from this union of which I'm now speaking; (union with the will of God) and one cannot arrive at the delightful union if the union coming from being resigned to God's will is not very certain. Oh, how desirable is this union with God's will (IC V:3:3)!

In the sixth dwelling place, the soul experiences afflictions and sufferings that have a corresponding similarity in the natural world to the afflictions a child suffers as it seeks to please its parents, and at the same time struggles with its self-centeredness and self-will. In the supernatural realm of its spiritual life, this soul now has an acute anguish over its past sins. Its desire to please God remains very intense, but it frequently experiences the absence of the Beloved, and knows not what to make of this absence. This anguish over sins and the perceived absence of God can be very severe and cause great suffering. But through it all, the soul is being re-made in a way only God can accomplish. This transformation is far beyond the capability of the soul to produce by its own efforts. In the natural life of the person, afflictions and trials result in a strong integrity and character. The more difficult these trials are, the greater the positive result produced in the character of the individual.

> For this is another one of the terrible trials these souls suffer, especially if they have lived wretched lives; thinking that because of their sins God will allow them to be deceived. Even though they feel secure and cannot believe that the favor (joy in persecution) when granted by His Majesty, is from any other spirit than from God, the torment returns immediately since the favor is something that passes quickly, and the remembrance of sins is always present, and the soul sees faults in itself, which are never lacking (IC VI:1:8).

In this sixth dwelling place, the soul receives favors from God that are so extraordinary that one of their effects is to solidify permanently the Fatherhood of God with this soul. The very intimacy that now envelops this soul also causes it great affliction. This suffering comes from several sources: First, the heightened awareness of its own sins and failings are a torment to this child of God while at the same time it is enjoying the new closeness to God that it is experiencing. The favors themselves carry with them an exquisite pain of longing to be lost in God. The world holds no interest for this soul and it looks only for the desired unity with God that will never end. But this experience is always colored by more than consolations alone.

> Briefly, in one way or another, there must be a cross while we live. And with respect to anyone who says that after he arrived here he always enjoyed rest and delight I would say that he never arrived but that perhaps he had experienced some spiritual delight–if he had entered into the previous dwelling place–and his experience had been helped along by natural weakness or perhaps even by the devil who gives him peace so as afterward to wage a much greater war against him (IC V:2:9).

This soul in the sixth dwelling place is very blessed by what God is willing to give to it by way of supernatural intimacy with

Him. These divine touches that this soul receives have an exquisite mixture of joy, peace, and pain. They are wounds filled with delight.

> And as clearly as it hears a thunderclap, even though no sound is heard, the soul understands that it was called by God. So well does it understand that sometimes, especially in the beginning, it is made to tremble and even complain without there being anything that causes it pain. It feels that it is wounded in the most exquisite way, but it doesn't learn how or by whom it was wounded. It knows clearly that the wound is something precious, and it would never want to be cured (IC VI:6:2).

St. Teresa discusses the phenomena of locutions as an additional favor granted by God to some advanced souls. She, however, sternly cautions such a favored soul to beware of diabolical deceptions in locutions that are not from God. A complete discussion of this danger is beyond the scope of this book. Suffice it to say that one who believes that God is speaking to it in this manner must always exercise caution and discretion. A discussion with one's spiritual director about this is always called for in these situations.

Another favor granted to the soul that manifests God's fatherhood is the suspension of the human faculties of sense, intellect, and imagination. Within the void left by this suspension, God is able to speak to the soul directly on a supernatural level. This exchange is a very great grace that opens lines of communication with the Divine that is unavailable to the soul by its own power.

> When the soul is in this suspension, the Lord likes to show it some secrets, things about heaven, and imaginative visions. It is able to tell of them afterward, for these remain so impressed on the memory that they are never forgotten. But when they are intellectual, the soul doesn't know how to speak of them (IC VI:4:5).

Because these favors are so extraordinary and supernatural, much courage is required to bear them. The reason for this is that with the divine touch comes a heightened awareness of one's own imperfection and misery, and the great need for God's mercy for forgiveness of these remembered transgressions.

> And when there is humility, courage, in my opinion, is even more necessary for this knowledge of one's own misery. May the Lord give us this humility because of who He is (IC VI:5:6).

> Hence the soul doesn't consider itself to be any greater because of this (intimate contact with God through divine touches of many sorts), and it thinks that it is the one who serves God the least among all who are in the world. This soul thinks that it is more obligated to Him than anyone, and any fault it commits pierces to the core of its being, and very rightly so (IC VI:8:6).

In the seventh dwelling place, St. Teresa presents us with a description of the consummation of the spiritual journey, the spiritual marriage of the soul with God. While the soul must always remain a child in its relationship with God, this spiritual marriage unites the soul to God in such a way that this union cannot be broken. In all its previous experiences of God some separation always occurred and the union that was experienced was temporary even when there were lasting effects. But in the spiritual marriage, the union is always present, and the soul experiences the presence of the Most Holy Trinity whenever it turns its mind to God. All it does in its natural life is done in God and with God. This is the complete transformation of the soul into a child of God. The pursuit of peace by this soul is now rewarded by the gift by God of Himself to the soul. In the seventh dwelling place, God fulfills the promise of Christ in this *Beatitude* that the soul that seeks and gives peace will become a child of God.

> In this seventh dwelling place the union comes about in a different way: our good God now desires to remove the scales from the soul's eyes and let it see and understand, although in a strange way, something of the favor He grants it...It knows in such a way that what we hold by faith, it understands, we can say, through sight–although the sight is not with the bodily eyes nor with the eyes of

> the soul, because we are not dealing with an imaginative vision. Here all three Persons communicate themselves to it, speak to it, and explain those words of the Lord in the Gospel: that He and the Father and the Holy Spirit will come to dwell with the soul that loves Him and keeps His commandments (IC VII:1:6).

> In the spiritual marriage the union is like what we have when rain falls from the sky into a river or a fount; all is water, for the rain that fell from heaven cannot be divided or separated from the water of the river (IC VII:2:4).

C. St. John of the Cross: The Ascent of Mt. Carmel

Blessed are the peacemakers

In the first book of this work, St. John of the Cross examines the necessity of ridding the soul of all its inordinate sensory appetites if it is to advance in its quest for union with God. This mortification of the appetites of sense forms the essential beginning of the soul's quest for union with God. This beginning is essential because until the sensory appetites are purged of their objects, the spirit will remain in its rudimentary condition of imperfection, and union with God will be obstructed by too many imperfections. It also begins the development of peace and an absence of turmoil within such a soul. Most experiences of agitation, frustration and anger in an individual can be traced to an attachment, sometimes quite inordinate, to a person, thing or to one's self and one's own glory before men. This lack of peace will remain as a constant infirmity in a soul until these attachments and appetites are mortified and finally purged from a soul.

> For we are not discussing the mere lack of things, this lack will not divest the soul, if it craves for all these objects. We are dealing with the denudation of the soul's appetites and gratifications; this is what leaves it free and empty of all things, even though it possesses them. Since the things of the world cannot enter the soul, they are not in themselves an encumbrance or harm to it; rather, it is the will and

appetite dwelling within it that causes the damage (AS I:3:4).

So therefore, a soul that is a slave to its own appetites and attachments is in torment frequently, and peace cannot be present in that soul at the same times that it is in intense suffering and bitterness. Therefore, these attachments must be purged from the soul or it will never become the peacemaker God desires it to be, because it will never itself be at peace. As pointed out above, one cannot give peace to others if one does not possess it.

> All the delights and satisfactions of the will in the things of the world in contrast to all the delight that is God are intense suffering, torment, and bitterness. He who links his heart to these delights, then, deserves in God's eyes intense suffering, torment, and bitterness. He will not be capable of attaining the delights of the embrace of union with God, since he merits suffering and bitterness (AS I:4:7).

The degree of union with God that a soul obtains will be directly proportional to the detachment from the world and creatures that develops within it. Attachment to the world and to God cannot co-exist in the same soul at the same time. The level of peace that a soul comes to enjoy depends also on its detachment from the causes of torment and turmoil: its appetites. The mortification of the appetites, if this effort is to bear fruit in the future, requires a permanent separation from the attraction of the world and of creatures. While temptations to return to one's former way of pursuing his appetites will continue, the purgation must be firm enough to be lasting.

> If anyone is to reach perfect union with God through his will and love, he must obviously first be freed from every appetite however slight. That is, he must not give the consent of his will knowingly to an imperfection, and he must have the power and freedom to be able, upon advertence, to refuse this consent (AS I:11:3).

> We have witnessed many persons, whom God favored with progress in detachment and freedom,

> fall from happiness and firmness in their spiritual exercises and end up losing everything merely because they began to indulge in some slight attachment to conversation and friendship under the color of good. For by this attachment they gradually emptied themselves of both holy solitude and the spirit and joy of God. All this happened because they did not put a stop to their initial satisfaction and sensitive pleasure, and preserve themselves for God in solitude (AS I:11:5).

This same degree of detachment from sensory objects must also be accomplished in the spiritual or supernatural realm. One who remains deeply attached to supernatural phenomena or religious objects replaces God with these things to some extent. The soul who pursues purgation of all things less than God must do so also in the spirit. These spiritual attachments are the source of the loss of peace every bit as much as the attachments of the soul at the sensory level. Any disturbance of the attachment to these spiritual objects casts the soul into desolation and doubt concerning its faith. The solitude and denudation, so necessary at the sensory level to eliminate the obstacles to peace, is even more necessary at the spiritual level because that is the level at which union with God occurs. One cannot imagine being the peacemaker described in this *Beatitude* if he is constantly struggling to protect and preserve the attachments in his spirit against challenges that come from grace or from others. It is in the spirit that one truly becomes a child of God.

> Similarly, if the soul in traveling this road leans upon any elements of its own knowledge or experience of God, it will easily go astray or be detained for not having desired to abide in complete blindness, in faith which is its guide. For, however impressive may be one's knowledge or feeling of God, that knowledge or feeling will have no resemblance to God and amount to very little (AS II:4:3).

The effort to reach the desirable goal of becoming a peacemaker among others must be preceded by the establishment of peace in our souls. This means that not only conflicts with others must be removed, but also conflicts within us must be resolved and cast out. In many cases, this is a matter of eliminating self-will in our dealing with others and in our acceptance of God's will where it is manifested clearly. This clarity is seen in those matters that are beyond any choice of our own or are absolutely under the authority and control of others, and especially the obvious control of God. The hard work of purification of the will occurs in the spirit. St. John of the Cross discusses at great length the four passions of the will, joy, hope, sorrow, and fear in Book III of *The Ascent of Mt. Carmel*. He insists that these passions must be mortified and purified before the soul can find the peaceful union with God that it seeks.

> The less strongly the will is fixed on God, and the more dependent it is upon creatures, the more these four passions combat the soul and reign in it. It then very easily finds joy in what deserves no rejoicing, and hope in what brings it no profit, and sorrow over what should perhaps cause rejoicing, and fear where there is no reason for fear (AS III:16:4).

For they shall be called children of God

Children imitate their fathers (and mothers) and seek to know and do the will of their parents. The term children, also implies a generational status that is permanently lower than the parental figures. By virtue of this lower station, the children are learners and the parents are teachers. So it is in the spiritual realm in our relationship to God. We strive to be imitators of God's perfect virtues as manifested to us by Christ in order to become His children. Therefore, we must learn the will of our Heavenly Father, the ends He desires for us, and what are the means that He provides for us to reach those ends. One such means is given to us in this *Beatitude*: to be peacemakers. We have discussed the pre-requisites to becoming a peacemaker as intended by Christ in this *Beatitude*. Let us continue to examine *The Ascent of Mt. Carmel* to not only find the ways to establish peace within ourselves so that it may be extended to others, but also to understand how the finding of this peace contributes to our becoming children of God.

St. John of the Cross, very early in this work, proclaims the indispensable nature of the purgation of the senses and spirit to reach union with God.

> The necessity of passing through this dark night (the mortification of the appetites and the denial of pleasure in all things) for the attainment of the divine union with God arises from the fact that all of man's attachments to creatures are pure darkness in God's sight. Clothed in these affections, a person will be incapable of the enlightenment and dominating fullness of God's pure and simple light, unless he rejects them (AS I:4:1).

This theme is carried forward throughout *The Ascent of Mt. Carmel.* St. John also establishes a sequence of purification: first, the sensory part of the soul must be purged and purified and then the spirit must be perfected. Both purgations, are accomplished by the elimination of the objects of our senses and spirit that are, first of all voluntary attachments that constitute obstacles to union with God.

> To achieve this liberation it was advantageous for the soul to depart in the dark night, that is, in the privation of all satisfactions and in the mortification of all appetites, as we mentioned. "My house being now all stilled" means that the house of all the appetites, the sensitive part of the soul, is now all stilled, and the desires conquered and lulled to sleep (AS I:15:2).

Remembering that becoming a child of God means that the union with Him must be complete, we know that the union occurs in the spirit. Because of this, the spirit must be purified of all that is less than God. The proximate means of this purification is faith that eliminates the danger of the inadequacies of the human faculties of intellect and memory from leading us to the wrong ends and conclusions. Faith is given by God to the soul in order for it to move ahead toward union with God without falling into errors that in fact block the desired union. This reliance on faith is the only means of becoming children of God, because that end requires the union with the will of God we are speaking of.

> There is no advancing in faith without the closing of one's eyes to everything pertaining to the senses and to clear, particular knowledge...This place (the intellect–the holder on which the candle of faith is

placed) must remain in darkness until the day, in the next life, when the clear vision of God dawns upon the soul; and in this life, until the daybreak of transformation in and union with God, the goal of a person's journey (AS II:16:15).

In the measure that a man approaches spirit in his dealings with God, he divests and empties himself of the ways of the senses, of discursive and imaginative meditation. When he has completely attained spiritual communion with God he will be voided of all sensory apprehensions concerning God (AS II:17:5).

D. St. John of the Cross: The Dark Night

Blessed are the peacemakers

If we accept the proposition that a peacemaker must have a genuine interest in the good of others equal to or greater than he has in his own benefit and self–centered satisfactions, then we will immediately see that the problems of beginners discussed by St. John of the Cross in chapters 1 through 7 of Book I of *The Dark Night* are serious obstacles to becoming the peacemaker that Christ desires us to be. This work treats the passive nights of purification of both the sensory and spiritual natures of man. It is within these passive nights that the beginner's spiritual defects are purged and this allows his soul to acquire the freedom to enter into union with God. It is in the results of this passive purgation that the soul finds itself able to be a peacemaker. In bringing peace to itself, the soul is able to extend that peace to others in an unselfish manner. The process of purgation is, however long and painful. There is much in all of us that must be excised if we are ever to be the peacemaker that brings us to the status of children of God. We will examine some of the afflictions of the soul in these nights to gain an insight into the intensity of the process of purgation; and then we will see the effects in a soul that perseveres through the trials necessary to accomplish the purification.

During this period of passive purgation, the soul will be in constant darkness, as it proceeds, not knowing where it is going and how it is being moved toward God. All of its own methods and ideas about the spiritual life are, except for the continuation of our religious practices, of little use in these passive nights, and the soul must surrender in blindness to the mercy and wisdom of God, seeking only His will.

> God now leaves them in such darkness that they do not know which way to turn in their discursive imaginings; they cannot advance a step in meditation, as they used to, now that the interior sensory faculties are engulfed in this night. He leaves them in such dryness that they not only fail to receive satisfaction and pleasure from their spiritual exercises and works, as they formerly did, but also find these exercises distasteful and bitter (DN I:8:3).

Within the purgation of the senses, the soul is advancing toward union with God, but the soul is unaware of how it is advancing and to what improvement it has come. It is of the nature of the passive nights that the transformation of the soul is unseen. This lack of awareness, so different from the active nights when the soul was more in charge of how and at what rate its spiritual life advanced (always with the aid of grace, of course) is threatening to the soul that does not understand the dynamics of the spiritual life. This stage is absolutely essential for the soul in gaining the capacity to be a peacemaker, as we understand Christ's use of that word to be. The annihilation of self-interest and narcissism within the soul must occur before enough interest and concern for others can develop, which is the sine qua non to being a peacemaker. Hence, the necessity of the afflictions of these passive nights which bring the soul to the transformation required.

> Since God introduces a person into this night to purge his senses, and accommodate, subject, and unite the lower part of his soul to the spiritual part by darkening it and causing a cessation of discursive meditation (just as afterwards in order to purify the spirit and unite it to Himself, He brings it into the spiritual night), this person gains so many benefits- though at the time this may not be apparent to him- that he considers his departure from the fetters and straits of the senses a sheer grace (DN I:11:3).

After the passive night of sense, if it is God's will that a soul go even further in the spiritual life toward union with Him, He places the soul in the passive night of spirit. In this night, the concept of peacemaker changes, not in degree, but in kind. The capacity for peace increases exponentially and as a result so does the ability to communicate that peace to others. The severe afflictions of the dark and passive night of spirit have the effect of stripping the soul of its self-centeredness. As a result, the capacity for giving to others will become perfected through the trial of self-knowledge and the resulting humility.

> Why, if it is a divine light (for it illumines and purges a person of his ignorance) does the soul call it a dark night?
>
> In answer to this, there are two reasons why this divine wisdom is not only night and darkness for the soul, but also affliction and torment. First, because of the height of the divine wisdom which exceeds the capacity of the soul. Second, because of the soul's baseness and impurity and on this account it is painful, afflictive, and also dark for the soul (DN II:5:2).
>
> The two extremes, divine and human, which are joined here, produce the third kind of pain and affliction the soul suffers here. The divine extreme is the purgative contemplation and the human extreme is the soul, the receiver of this contemplation. Since the divine extreme strikes in order to renew the soul and divinize it (by stripping it of the habitual affections and properties of the old man to which it is strongly united, attached and conformed), it so disentangles and dissolves the spiritual substance-absorbing it in a profound darkness-that the soul at the sight of its miseries feels that it is melting away and being undone by a cruel spiritual death; it feels as if it were swallowed by a beast and being digested in the dark belly, and it suffers an anguish comparable to Jonas's when in the belly of the whale (Jn 2:1-3). It is fitting that the soul be in this sepulcher of dark death in order that it

attains the spiritual resurrection for which it hopes (DN II:6:1).

These two quotes from St. John of the Cross illustrate perfectly the degree of transformation that must take place in the soul in order to become the purveyor of peace that will render the soul a child of God. They do this by describing the harsh and extreme affliction that must befall a soul that desires to move so far forward toward union with God. The descriptions of these afflictions of the soul could be multiplied many times over. St. John describes them in detail in this work that deals with the soul in its most difficult time of purification. Suffice it to say that every soul that enters these passive nights requires oppressive affliction to purge itself of the obstacles to union with God that will, in turn, result in the ability of the soul to convey peace to others.

For they shall be called children of God

Becoming a child of God involves at least to some extent the imitation of the perfections of God by the practice of the virtues. In this way, a soul takes on a certain likeness to God that is founded in love and the response to the love given by God. So we can ask, "What is the result of the afflictions and torments of these passive nights, and how are these results connected to the idea of becoming a child of God?" We can start this inquiry by once again turning to St. John's well-known metaphor of the burning log. In this metaphor, St. John illustrates the transformation of the soul in the dark night of contemplation by comparing this transformation to the transformation of a log that is placed in a fire.

> Fire, when applied to wood, first dehumidifies it; dispelling all moisture and making it give off any water it contains. Then it gradually turns the wood black, makes it dark and ugly, and even causes it to emit a bad odor. By drying out the wood, the fire brings to light and expels all those ugly and dark accidents which are contrary to fire. Finally, by heating and enkindling it from without, the fire transforms the wood into itself and makes it as beautiful as it is itself. Once transformed, the wood no longer has any activity or passivity of its own,

except for its weight and its quantity which is denser than the fire (DN II:10:1).

The most perplexing aspect of perfecting a soul to the extent that it becomes united with God as His child is that the soul's imperfections are so hidden, even from itself, that they can only be uncovered by the work of God and are always accompanied by painful afflictions. God does not cause this affliction directly. It comes from the imperfections themselves. When the imperfections have been removed then the affliction ceases. By applying the above metaphor of the burning log, St. John of the Cross makes it very clear that the passive submission to God's work in the soul is essential to becoming a child of God. The ultimate fruit of the suffering of these afflictions in the soul is a peace that surpasses all understanding. Here is how St. John describes the path the soul must take if it is to become a true child of God.

> First, we can understand that the very loving light and wisdom into which the soul will be transformed is that which in the beginning purges and prepares it...

> Second, we discern that the experience of these sufferings does not derive from this wisdom (into which the soul will be transformed)...but from the soul's own weakness and imperfection.

> Third, we can infer the manner in which souls suffer in purgatory. The fire, when applied, would be powerless over them, if they did not have imperfections from which to suffer.

> Fourth, we deduce that as the soul is purged and purified by this fire of love, it is further enkindled in love, just as the wood becomes hotter as the fire prepares it.

> Fifth...After that manifestation and after a more exterior purification of imperfections, the fire of love returns to act more interiorly on the consumable matter of which the soul must be purified.

> Sixth, we discover the reason it seems to the soul that all blessings are past and that it is full of evil. For at this time it is conscious of nothing but its own bitterness...,
>
> Seventh, we deduce that when the purification is soon to return, even though the soul's joy is ample during these intervals...there is a feeling, if it adverts...that some root remains (DN II:10:3-9).

The divine light that causes the soul so much pain as it is being purified and purged of its imperfections is the same light that imparts great joy to the soul after its purification. The affliction comes from the imperfections that are now illuminated by the divine light. When the imperfections are gone so is the affliction. These passive nights contain within them the most severe trials that a soul will endure in this life. Perhaps the most difficult suffering of a soul in these passive nights is the constantly recurring belief that it has lost God, and that He is angry with the soul because of its imperfections. So much does this soul suffer from this feeling of rejection by God that it believes that it has passed beyond all possibility of forgiveness of its transgressions. We know, however, that such a conclusion is erroneous, and what is really being experienced is the soul's own horror at its misdeeds and is in some way projecting that horror as originating from God. From this state of near despair, God will bring the soul to not only a belief in His mercy, but to an actual experience of that mercy. In the end, it is this purification that has brought the soul into the state of a true child of God, united in every way to His will. The soul's own peace then radiates out from it to all those around it, affecting them in a very positive way, moving them to seek the peace they observe from the purified soul. All of these positive results stem from the union with God that has flowed from the painful purgation the soul has suffered.

> One cannot reach this union without remarkable purity, and this purity is unattainable without vigorous mortification and nakedness regarding all creatures...Whoever refuses to go out at night in search for the Beloved and to divest and mortify his will, but rather seeks the Beloved in his own bed and comfort, as did the bride (Ct 3:1), will not succeed in finding Him; as this soul declares, it found Him

when it departed in darkness and with longings of love (DN II:24:4).

E. St. John of the Cross: The Spiritual Canticle

Blessed are the peacemakers

In this work, St. John presents us with a soul that has advanced at least to the point that it is experiencing very painful longings for God and union with Him. However, the union is incomplete and sporadic. This soul has initiated a search for God, and God has brought the soul into the shallows of the spiritual life where the longings for God are an affliction to it. While we know that movement of the soul in the spiritual life, after the barest beginnings, is the work of God in a willing soul, we must recognize that grace is interior to the soul and moves it interiorly toward God. It is the absorption of this grace in the interior of the soul that will firstly, put it at peace, and secondly turn it into the peacemaker meant by Christ in this *Beatitude*. Let us look at some of the stanzas of *The Spiritual Canticle* wherein we will discover some of the effects of grace that will move the soul to become a true peacemaker.

STANZA 10

Extinguish these miseries,
Since no one else can stamp them out;

The miseries referred to here by St. John of the Cross are things other than God that weary and annoy the soul. The soul is now so enamored of God that He has become the soul's sole object. This single-mindedness discloses a process of separation taking place in the soul from all the conflicts, goods and ideals of the world that always result in strife rather than in peace. The tempering and removal of these motivations represents significant movement in the direction of becoming a peacemaker. This is so because the sources of strife are fading away from this soul. Not only this, but the interior sufferings of the soul that result from its life experiences begin to find a source of patient strength, solace and a reason to persevere in its sufferings from the increasing union of its will with God's will. No one escapes this life without weakness and affliction. The only source of strength to bear the crosses of life is the grace earned by Christ in His life, passion, and death. Hence, our need for a redeemer. The loving union with God makes it possible to endure these maladies of human nature with a degree of equanimity and peace.

> Since the soul has reached this sickness of love of God, she has three traits: in all things that are offered to her or with which she deals, she has ever before her that longing for her health, which is her Beloved...the second trait, arising from this first, is the loss of taste for all things; the third then results, which is that all these things molest her and all dealings with others are burdensome and annoying (SC 10:Intro:1).

> Having a similar yearning (as Mary at the tomb of Christ) to find Him in all things, and not immediately finding Him as she desires-but rather quite the contrary-not only does the soul fail to find satisfaction in these things, but they also become a torment to her, and sometimes a very great one. Such souls suffer much in dealing with people and with business matters, for these contacts hinder rather than help them to their goal (SC 10:Intro:2)

STANZA 16

> *Catch us the foxes,*
> *For our vineyard is now in flower,*
> *While* we *fashion a cone of roses*
> *Intricate as the pine's;*
> *And let no one appear on the hill.*

In this stanza, the foxes are the composite of all the appetites and sensory movements in the soul. These are the obstacles and distractions that keep us from advancing toward union with God. Here St. John describes poetically the desirability of preventing these appetites from interfering with the soul's movement toward the peace that results from the surrender of its will to the will of God. It is these obstacles that have caused all of the soul's afflictions and that have left it in turmoil before and during its movement toward God. It is always our attachments to the appetites and their objects, and the inability to thwart the movements of the sensory part of our nature that causes distress and conflict within us. It is the unity of the entire human being and the reign of reason over the whole, that was lost by original sin. To the degree we are freed from these afflictions and conflicts, we will find peace. Therefore, in this verse of stanza 16, St. John describes the necessity of catching these foxes so that they can do no harm to the soul.

> Desirous that neither the envious and malicious devils, nor the wild sensory appetites, nor the various wanderings of the imagination, nor any knowledge or awareness hamper the continuance of this interior delight of love, which is the flower of her vineyard, the bride invokes the angels, telling them to catch all these disturbances and keep them from interfering with the interior exercise of love, in the delight of which the virtues and graces are communicated and enjoyed by the soul and the Son of God (SC 16:3).

The peace that is required to permeate the soul in order for it to become a peacemaker demands not only that these foxes be captured and contained so that there is unity within the soul in its pursuit of its Beloved, but also that the soul exist in solitude as far as possible. Constant disturbance from the outside, as we know from our own experience, disrupts our peace in many ways. It is either from the fact of disturbance or from the content of the disturbance. So St. John of the Cross says here, "And let no one appear on the hill."

> To attain this divine interior exercise there is also need for solitude and withdrawal from all things presentable to the soul, whether from the lower, sensory portion, or from the higher, rational part. These two parts comprise the entire compound of man's faculties and senses, and she calls this compound a "*hill.*" All the natural knowledge and the appetites dwelling on the hill in this harmonious composite are like prey to the devil, who hunts and catches them in order to harm the soul (SC 16:10).

STANZA 17

Be still, deadening north wind;
South wind come, you that waken love,

Spiritual dryness is also an obstacle to the soul that is constantly at peace. The soul seeks to close the door to aridity by the continual habit of prayer. It also begs the Holy Spirit to banish this aridity and restore its love for the Bridegroom so that it may continuously practice the virtues. The soul is however, subject to and dependent upon the aid of the Bridegroom in this matter because it cannot of itself remove its aridity. So it prays that the dryness be removed and replaced by sentiments of love for the Bridegroom.

> The north wind is very cold, it dries up and withers the flowers and plants, or at least when striking them makes them shrink and close.

> Because the spiritual dryness and affective absence of the Beloved produces this same effect in the soul by extinguishing the satisfaction, delight, and fragrance of the virtues she was enjoying, she calls it a "deadening north wind." It deadens the virtues and affective exercise, and as a result, the soul pleads, "Be still deadening north wind" (SC 17:3).

STANZAS 20 & 21

Swift-winged birds,
Lions, stags, and leaping roes,
Mountains, lowlands, and river banks,
Waters, winds and ardors,
Watching fears of night:

By the pleasant lyres
And the sirens song, I conjure you
To cease your anger
And not touch the wall,
That the bride may sleep in deeper peace.

Here we have in summary form all the obstacles to the enjoyment of union with God in peace. Stanza 21 enumerates these obstacles while stanza 22 proclaims the command of the Bridegroom that all these impediments be put to silence and depart from this soul. In the poetry of St. John of the Cross, these obstacles are represented by colorful imagery, and are as follows:

Swift-winged birds – The wanderings of the imagination
Lions – The impetuosity of the irascible power
Stags and leaping roes – The concupiscible power
Mountains, lowlands, and river banks – Acts that are extreme through excess, defect, or are not level
Waters, winds, and ardors – The emotions of sorrow, hope, and joy
Watching fears of night – The emotion of fear

After identifying the obstacles, St. John proclaims the words of the Bridegroom ordering these impediments to cease their anger, by which is meant to discontinue their disturbance of the soul and allow peace to enter the soul. The Bridegroom then orders these disturbances not to touch the wall that is the enclosure of peace.

> It should be observed that the Bridegroom does not conjure anger and concupiscence to cease, for these powers are never wanting to the soul. But He conjures their disturbance and inordinate actions, signified by the lions, stags, and leaping roes. It is necessary that in this state these inordinate movements be lacking (SC 20:7).

> The Beloved also conjures these four passions of the soul (sorrow, hope, joy, and fear) and makes them cease and be calm insofar as He gives the bride in this state riches, strength, and satisfaction through the pleasant lyres of His sweetness and the siren's song of His delight. He does this so that they may cease not only to reign in her but also to cause her any displeasure (SC 20 & 21:10).

> Finally, the watching fears of night do not reach her, for she is now so clearly illumined and strong and rests so firmly in her God that the devils can neither cause her obscurity through their darknesses, nor frighten her with their terrors, nor awaken her by their attacks. Nothing can reach or molest her now that she has withdrawn from all things and has

entered into her God where she enjoys all peace, tastes all sweetness, and delights in all delight insofar as this earthly state allows (SC 20 & 21:15).

The above words of St. John of the Cross are the description of a soul that has acquired the peace that is necessary if it is to become a peacemaker for others. As I have often repeated in this book, one cannot give what one does not possess himself. Once peace of the kind described above settles upon a soul, all those around it benefit from its presence.

For they shall be called children of God

Just as a child grows by the imitation of its parent's behavior in the natural realm, so also does a soul advance by the imitation of Christ in the supernatural realm. In *The Spiritual Canticle,* St. John of the Cross presents us with not only the strivings of the soul for unity with the Beloved, but he also acquaints us with the wonderful results of that striving. All of these results are indications that the childhood of the soul with God that is found in this *Beatitude* is being achieved. A few examples of these results will suffice to demonstrate some of the characteristics of this childhood with God. St. John of the Cross does not couch these characteristics in terms of childhood, but in terms of espousal and marriage. But there is certain equivalence between the soul that becomes a child of God and by the same means becomes espoused and the bride of the Beloved, Christ. The over-riding common factor is complete submission of the soul's will to the will of God. Each of the states of a child of God and espousal and marriage to the Beloved is reached by the same means and each contains the same characteristics. We will see that these characteristics common to both goals are indeed child-like imitations of the soul's spiritual parent, Christ. But there is more than just imitation of Christ. There is unity with Him in His divinity, and therefore, the soul is not only a child of God, but is also His spouse. We will now look at some of the common characteristics referred to as set forth in *The Spiritual Canticle.*

STANZA 23

Beneath the apple tree:
There I took you for my own,
There I offered you my hand,
And restored you,
Where your mother was corrupted.

There I took you for my own,
There I offered you My hand,

In the imagery of St. John of the Cross, the apple tree represents the cross of Christ. It was there that the Beloved espoused all of mankind and each and every soul by making the grace of the Redemption available to all. St. John further speaks of the restoration of all of human nature, which he refers to as *your mother*. This general espousal of all mankind is an immediate consequence of Christ's life, death, and resurrection. This result does not, without more, render any soul a child of God within the meaning of this *Beatitude*. This childhood is acquired over a somewhat lengthy period of time and with much striving and affliction in the process of the purification of the soul from the effects of original sin (the corruption of our mother, human nature).

> The espousal made on the cross is not the one we now speak of. For that espousal is accomplished immediately when God gives the first grace, which is bestowed on each one at baptism. The espousal of which we speak bears reference to perfection and is not achieved save gradually and by stages. For though it is all one espousal, there is a difference in that one is attained at the soul's pace, and thus little by little, and the other at God's pace, and thus immediately (SC 23:6).

STANZA 34

The small white dove
Has returned to the ark with an olive branch;
And now the turtledove
Has found its longed-for mate
By the green river banks.

The turtledove is rarely if ever seen without its mate. If it is lacking a mate, it takes no delight in anything until a mate is found. Nothing in nature has any attraction for it and it fails to fulfill its desires or follow its instincts while it is without a mate. Once the longed-for mate is found, everything changes. The turtledove is elevated from its misery and its destiny placed in its nature by God is once again pursued and enjoyed. So it is with the soul that seeks God and union with Him. Once the soul finds this union, everything changes. All its activities take on new and wonderful meaning. It is content to enjoy this union in solitude with its Beloved.

> ...the Bridegroom Himself describes in song the end of her fatigues and the fulfillment of her desires, saying that now the turtledove has found its longed-for mate by the green river banks. This is similar to saying: Now the bride alights on the green branch, delighting in her Beloved; now she drinks the clear water of sublime contemplation and wisdom of God, and the cool water of her refreshment and comfort in God; and she also rests in the shade of His protection and favor-which she so longed for-where she is divinely and delightfully consoled, fed, and refreshed... (SC 34:6).

STANZA 35

She lived in solitude,
And now in solitude has built her nest;
And in solitude He guides her,
He alone, Who also bears
In solitude the wound of love.

The key word and central theme of this stanza is "solitude." St. John uses this word in four of the verses, and uses the word *alone* in the other one. The significance of this word for St. John of the Cross is the exclusion of all else but God in this soul's spiritual and natural life. In speaking in terms of espousal and marriage, the exclusivity is necessary in order to adequately express the reality of the relationship that has developed – on both sides of this union. The exclusivity of God's union with each soul is one of the mysteries of the spiritual life that must await eternity for any degree of understanding on our part. The chief characteristic of the union is the unity of wills. The will of the soul is absorbed into the will of the Beloved so that there is but one will: God's.

And now in solitude has built her nest;

> The solitude in which she lived consisted of the desire to go without the things of the world for her Bridegroom's sake-as we said of the turtle dove-by striving for perfection, acquiring perfect solitude in which she reaches union with the Word (SC 35:4).

He alone, Who also bears
In solitude the wound of love.

> The meaning of this is not only that He guided her in her solitude, but that it is He alone who works in her, without any means. This is a characteristic of the union of the soul with God in spiritual marriage: God works in and communicates Himself to her through Himself alone, without the intermediary of angels or natural ability, for the exterior and interior senses, and all creatures, and even the very soul do very little toward the reception of the remarkable supernatural favors which God grants in this state (SC 35:6).

F. St. John of the Cross: The Living Flame of Love

Blessed are the peacemakers

The Living Flame of Love is St. John's descriptions and analyses of the content of the spiritual marriage. It presumes a soul that has risen to the heights of spiritual perfection possible in this life. Because of the nature of this work, the beginning of the couplet of this *Beatitude, Blessed are the peacemakers* cannot be found in this work. Here we find insights into the exclusive work of the Holy Spirit in an individual soul. Since this work of St. John of the Cross examines the interior life of the spiritual marriage, what was said above in our treatment of *The Spiritual Canticle* concerning peacemakers will apply equally here.

This flame of love is the Spirit of its Bridegroom, which is the Holy Spirit. The soul feels Him within itself not only as a fire which has consumed and transformed it, but as a fire that burns and flares within it, as I mentioned. And that flame, every time it flares up, bathes the soul in glory, and refreshes it with the quality of divine life (LF 1:3).

Therefore, we will examine this work in order to find deeper and more explicit descriptions of the second half of the couplet of this *Beatitude*. It is in the second half that we find the results of responding to Christ's desire to have us become peacemakers, rather than the purveyors of strife and conflict.

For they shall be called children of God

In this section, we will examine *The Living Flame of Love* in order to find more profound descriptions of the nature of the spiritual marriage that renders the soul a child of God in all the meanings possible to that phrase.

STANZA 1

O living flame of love
That tenderly wounds my soul
In its deepest center! Since
Now You are not oppressive,
Now Consummate! If it be your will:
Tear through the veil of this sweet encounter

In its deepest center!

We must look at these words of St. John of the Cross in order to understand how this wound of love is different from any other the soul has ever experienced. The soul's deepest center is God. We must advance one caveat here: While the soul here declares that its Beloved has wounded it in its deepest center, there remains one last movement to actually experience: that is natural death that brings on the Beatific Vision. However, there is a center of the soul reachable by the flame of love for the Beloved in this life that wounds it in its deepest center; that is the deepest center of the soul's substance possible to be reached in this life. There is no more deepening movement possible to the soul that would increase the quality or intensity of the loving union with God. We can therefore conclude that the degree of becoming a child of God is directly proportionate to the degree of union with God that has been realized.

> The soul's center is God. When it has reached God with all the capacity of its being and the strength of its operation and inclination, it will have attained to its final and deepest center in God, it will know, love, and enjoy God with all its might. When it has not reached this point (as happens in this mortal life, in which the soul cannot reach God with all its strength, even though in its center-which is God and His communion with it), it still has movement and strength for advancing further and is not satisfied. Although it is in its center, it is not yet in its deepest center, for it can go deeper in God (LF 21:12).

STANZA 2

> *O sweet cautery,*
> *O delightful wound!*
> *O gentle hand! O delicate touch*
> *That tastes of eternal life*
> *And pays every debt!*
> *In killing You changed death to life.*

In killing You changed death to life.

As was said earlier, whatever puts an end to the causes of strife and conflict engenders peace. As this is true in the world of men, so it is also true in the interior of every soul. Further, anyone who wills to become a peacemaker must first be at peace within himself. So we can conclude that the old man imbued with the causes of conflict, such as love of the world and its pleasures, love of money and power, or attachment to sin must experience a death of this man.

As this death progresses, the old man will disappear and a new man will appear whom we can call a peacemaker because that capacity has been acquired along with many other virtues. It is by grace that the killing of the old man is accomplished.

> Let it be known that what the soul calls death is all that goes to make up the old man: the entire engagement of the faculties (memory, intellect, and will) in the things of the world, and the indulgence of the appetites in the pleasures of creatures. All this is the activity of the old life, which is the death of the new spiritual life. The soul is unable to live perfectly in this new life, if the old man does not die completely (LF 2:33).

When the old life is gone, the new life displays a completely different character. It is a life that is impossible to human nature unaided by grace, both actual grace and sanctifying grace. It is indeed the life of God that has entered into the soul and transformed it. If the soul is living the life of God by participation, it has thereby become a child of God. All children in the natural order participate in the life of their parents in the sense that they have received their life as a result of the intervention and cooperation of the parents in the procreation of a new human person. So it is in the supernatural order: they receive the participation in the divine life as children of God through the intervention of God's grace.

> Accordingly, the intellect of this soul is God's intellect; it's will is God's will; its memory is the memory of God; and its delight is God's delight; and although the substance of this soul is not the substance of God, since it cannot undergo a substantial conversion into Him, it has become God through participation in God, being united to and absorbed in Him, as it is in this state…The death of this soul is changed to the life of God (LF 2:34).

STANZA 3

> *O lamps of fire!*
> *In whose splendors*
> *The deep caverns of feeling,*
> *Once obscure and blind,*
> *Now give forth, so rarely, so exquisitely,*
> *Both warmth and light to their Beloved.*

The deep caverns of feeling,
Once obscure and blind,

The deep caverns of feeling are St. John's description of the faculties of the soul. It is these faculties that contain both good and evil attachments. It is within these faculties that the process of purification occurs. As long as they are filled with evil attachments that are the sources of conflict and strife, life as a child of God is impossible. When they are so occupied with the world and its allurements, the life of grace finds no room to flourish. Rather, the soul is then engaged in the conflict and strife that these allurements always bring and no peace can be found in such a soul. However, the spiritual progress of the soul and its increasing understanding of the worthlessness of these voluntary appetites diminish their allurement and they slowly fade away. As they leave the soul, room is provided in the soul for a growing attachment to the things of God. But it must be understood that union with God in the final analysis is given by God and not achieved by the soul. The soul merely is disposed to accept what God is prepared to give and the wise soul accepts the gift. The reason for this is that the transforming union is far beyond the natural capacity of any soul. We can conclude therefore, that becoming a child of God is a grace extended in response to the soul's obedience to the will of God.

> Likewise, when the soul has reached such purity in itself and its faculties that the will is very pure and purged of other alien satisfactions and appetites in the inferior and superior parts, and has rendered its *yes* to God concerning all of this, since now God's will and the soul's are one through their own free consent, then the soul has attained the possession of God insofar as this is possible by way of the will and grace (LF 3:24).

> I reply that it is true that the soul's desire for God is not always supernatural, but only when God infuses it and Himself gives the strength for it. This is far different from the natural desire, and until God infuses the desire there is very little or no merit. Thus when you of your own power have the desire for God, your desire amounts to no more than a

natural appetite, neither will it be anything more until God informs it supernaturally (LF 3:75).

STANZA 4

How gently and lovingly
You wake in my heart,
Where in secret You dwell alone;
And in Your sweet breathing,
Filled with good and glory,
How tenderly You swell my heart with love!

How gently and lovingly
You wake in my heart,

The process of awakening implies movement. One moves from sleep to wakefulness in the rhythm of life and this is always a change in the state of a person. Therefore, it is a movement. In these verses, we must remember that God does not move because He is immovable and unchangeable. Rather, by His grace the soul is moved from unawareness of the grandeur of God to the transforming union with him which is a movement that is beyond the unaided power of any soul. This movement occurs as veils are lifted from the soul and their removal enables the soul to see God as He is. This vision then becomes an irresistible attraction toward God leading ultimately to the transforming union. It is at this point that the soul truly becomes the child of God as meant by Christ in this *Beatitude*. The soul now participates in the life of God by grace. It sees God now as He is. This union is inseparable, as the two wills have become one.

> Yet, since everything in man comes from God, and man of himself can do nothing good, it is rightly asserted that our awakening is an awakening of God and our rising is God's rising…Since the soul was in a sleep from which it could never awaken itself, and only God could open its eyes and cause this awakening, it very appropriately calls this an awakening of God… (LF 4:9).

CHAPTER 8

Blessed are they who suffer persecution for justice sake, for theirs is the kingdom of heaven.

Blessed are you when men reproach you, and persecute you, and speaking falsely, say all manner of evil against you, for my sake. Rejoice and exult, because your reward is great in heaven; for so did they persecute the prophets who were before you.

The last two *Beatitudes* from the Gospel of St. Matthew are treated together in one chapter. The reason for this is that the concepts in the first half of the couplets of both *Beatitudes* are nearly identical. Similarly, the concepts in the second half of the couplets of both *Beatitudes* are only slightly less identical. For instance, the eighth *Beatitude* refers to persecution for justice sake without specifying the nature of the persecution, while the ninth *Beatitude* refers to persecution by reproach and false and evil speaking against one. What can be said about the more specific form of persecution in the ninth *Beatitude* can also be said about the more general form of persecution in the eighth *Beatitude*. However, something must be said about a persecution for justice sake that separates that persecution from all other forms of persecution. We can, as we go along, draw whatever distinctions between the two *Beatitudes* that is helpful to an understanding of each one. Therefore, the form of this chapter will differ somewhat from the forms of the chapters that have gone before it.

The concept of the Kingdom of God (or as sometimes rendered, the *Kingdom of Heaven*) as it is reflected in the writings of St. Teresa and St. John, has been adequately treated in the chapter on the first *Beatitude*, and therefore, it will not be repeated here. The reader is, of course, encouraged to refer back to that treatment whenever understanding requires it. It seems to me that the best way to proceed is to discuss the concept of persecution for justice sake first and primarily. The more specific description of the form of persecution in the ninth *Beatitude* will be examined wherever appropriate, and wherever that will shed more light on the words of Christ. We will then examine how our saints present the great reward in heaven, the Beatific Vision. We will continue, as before, to use each work of our saints separately to discover a reflection of these *Beatitudes* in them. Some reference to the last phrase in the ninth *Beatitude* regarding the persecution of the prophets will be made wherever appropriate, and wherever it will contribute to an understanding of the reflection of these words of Christ in the works of these two Carmelite saints.

Before moving on to the works of St. Teresa, let us say something about persecution for justice sake and how it differs from other forms of persecution. Malefactors may suffer some form of persecution, but that is not persecution for justice sake. It may be that they are persecuted for evil deeds and their persecution itself may in fact be just. Imagine a circumstance regarding a malefactor wherein what might be considered persecution may in fact be an act, not only of justice, but also of charity. One who habitually commits crimes against persons or property will believe attempts to stop him from these transgressions to be persecution. However, in reality those attempts are acts of justice and of charity toward his potential victims.

Persecution for justice sake is however, a much different matter. For as St. Augustine says: "They cannot suffer for justice who have divided the Church; and where sound faith or charity is wanting there cannot be justice."[4] When one is punished for defense of his faith, the good of his neighbor or for some reason related to piety or faith, we have the persecution for justice sake meant by Christ in this eighth *Beatitude*.

In the ninth *Beatitude*, Christ is quite clear that He intends to directly connect the suffering of persecution described there to being done for His sake. It is easier to see in the ninth *Beatitude* that the persecution that will be rewarded is that endured out of loyalty and devotion to Christ. He knows what is coming for his followers. We have much evidence of this kind of persecution throughout history even to our present day.

---

[4] Cont. Epis. Parm. 1. I c. 9. Ep. 50 Ps. 4 Conc. 2. Commentary of Bristow to verse 10 Matt: V., translation of the Latin Vulgate at Rheims, 1582, Haydock's Catholic Bible and commentary, Dr. Husenbeth's edition, 1812.

Lastly, before going forward to the works of our Carmelite saints to find these *Beatitudes* reflected, we should notice that the reward for enduring persecution as described in these two *Beatitudes* occurs in heaven. Therefore, the reward is not temporal, but eternal. Being eternal, it comes directly from God to the soul without His use of an intermediate agent, such as an angel or a saint, to effect His reward for this soul. In light of this, I will examine what St. Teresa of Jesus and St. John of the Cross say about the eternal rewards in the next life, rather than in this life. Lastly, we will keep in mind that persecutions come sometimes directly from the evil one or with his use of his agents and allies in the world.

A. St. Teresa of Jesus: The Way of Perfection

Persecution for justice sake.
Endure reproach, false speaking, and evil for Christ

One who loves God and follows the teachings of Christ and His Church will be unable to avoid persecution. If we are faithful to Him, we know that hardship will come to us from those around us, sometimes from those within our own families. This world belongs to the devil, and he hates Christ. He has convinced many, many people to join him in his hatred. These allies of the devil have only one goal in mind: to defeat Christ and His disciples in the world. These minions seek ways to either defeat the Church, or to entice as many as possible away from the Church and its promulgation of the teachings and doctrines given to it by Christ. A common tactic in these times is to promote and publicize scandals within the Church that are no more egregious than the particular scandalous behavior is in other organizations including Protestant congregations. However, this same behavior outside of the Catholic Church is not publicized or punished. Those who refuse to follow the devil's road out of the Church are persecuted in a multitude of ways. They are excluded, along with Christ, from society and its institutions. They are punished with pain and imprisonment. They are humiliated and ridiculed for their devotion to Christ. In other words, we can say that they are treated exactly as Christ was treated.

> Since worldly people have so little respect for Thee, what can we expect them to have for us? Can it be that we deserve that they should treat us any better than they have treated Thee? Have we done more

> for them than Thou hast done that they should be friendly to us? What then? What can we expect – we who, through the goodness of the Lord, are free from that pestilential infection, and do not, like those others, belong to the devil (WP 1).

When we join Christ in persecution, suffering some of the things He suffered, we can be certain that we are persecuted for justice sake. As disciples of the Just One, hated because of Him, we will be treated as He was. We, as the servants, will not be greater or treated better than the Master was. As repugnant as it is to our nature to suffer persecution, Christ has assured us in this *Beatitude* that such suffering has a beneficial effect for our souls. He says that we are blessed by these trials, and that our reward will be great in heaven: possession of the Kingdom of God. So that as in many, many aspects of Christianity properly lived, what seems repugnant to the world, suffering for justice sake, is in fact a great grace and blessing bestowed by God on a faithful soul.

> When I think of this, (how a weak soul can endure suffering), it amuses me that there should be people who dare not ask the Lord for trials, thinking that His sending them to them depends upon their asking for them! I am not referring to those who omit to ask for them out of humility because they think themselves to be incapable of bearing them, though for my own part I believe that He who gives them love enough to ask for such a stern method of proving it will give them love enough to endure it (WP 32).

> Do not fear that He will give you riches or pleasures or *great* honors or any such earthly things; His love for you is not so poor as that. And He sets a very high value on what you give Him and desires to recompense you for it since He gives you His Kingdom while you are still alive. Would you like to see how He treats those who make this prayer (Thy will be done) from their hearts? Ask His glorious Son, Who made it thus in the Garden. Think with what resolution and fullness of desire He prayed; and consider if the will of God was not

perfectly fulfilled in Him through the trials, sufferings, insults, and persecutions which He gave Him until at last His life ended with death on a cross (WP 32).

It is one of the paradoxes intrinsic to the spiritual life that God manifests His love for souls through the trials that He sends them, one of which is persecution. The Carmelite understands this paradox, and it makes perfect sense to him/her that this is the means by which a soul is enabled to move closer to union with God. It is through these purifications and purgations brought about by suffering that the soul removes the many obstacles to that union.

Your reward is great in heaven

The first reward of heaven is the avoidance of eternal damnation. There are many descriptions by the saints of the state of eternal damnation that is called hell. One thoughtful reading of any one of these descriptions fills the soul with horror. We see in the writings of and about these souls that have seen hell a pleading with God to spare souls on their way to this destination through His great mercy.

On the other hand, we often speculate on the glories of heaven for all eternity. St. Paul says that it has not entered into the mind of man what God has in store for those who love Him. We know from some descriptions by spiritual writers that in heaven, in some mysterious way, we enter into God and participate in His life. We see His glory, love, and mercy as they truly are for the first time. What we experience results in a perfect happiness that is inconceivable in this life. Some things in this life give us some happiness momentarily; but this is a mere speck, and of a different kind, of what awaits us from the glory of God. And this speck of earthly happiness ends quite quickly when events overtake us and return us to our state of affliction that is the norm for this life. In her commentary on the Lord's Prayer, St. Teresa says the following about those who face the loss of their souls.

> As for the unfortunate souls who *will* bring damnation upon themselves and will not have fruition of Him in the world to come, *they are His own creatures, and He did everything to help them*

> *on, and was with them, to strengthen them, throughout the "to-day" of this life,* so it is not His fault if they are vanquished. (Emphasis in the original)...Therefore the Son prays the Father that, since this life lasts no more than a day, He will allow Him to spend it in our service (WP 34).

The economy of salvation requires the payment of our debts before we enter into our reward prepared for us from the beginning of time. The first payment is repentance. The second payment is atonement. When the debt is paid in full, the Master will call us to Him to receive the reward for all that we have done in accordance with His will and for all that we have suffered for His sake.

> Once our debts have been paid we shall be able to walk in safety. We shall not be going into a foreign land, but into our own country, for it belongs to Him Whom we have loved so truly and Who Himself loves us. *For this love of His, besides its other properties, is better than all earthly affection in that, if* we *love Him,* we *are quite sure that He loves us too* (Emphasis in the original)...How sweet will be the death of those who have done penance for all their sins and have not to go to purgatory! It may be that they will begin to enjoy glory even in this world, and will know no fear, but only peace (WP 40).

B. St. Teresa of Jesus: The Interior Castle

The First Three Dwelling Places

Persecution for justice sake.
Endure reproach, false speaking, and evil for Christ

At the beginning of St. Teresa's treatment of the soul as a crystal like castle containing many dwelling places and many rooms within those dwelling places, she also discusses the vermin that inhabit the outer walls. When a soul seeks to enter the first or lowest dwelling place, many of these vermin enter with it. These vermin are the various aspects and sources of evil that roam the world at the behest of Satan. In addition to this, she begins to examine the sorry state of a soul at the beginning of this journey of grace. Since this work considers persecution from others outside the soul very little, I will look at these two factors, the vermin and the sorry state of the beginning soul, as the source of persecution from the evil one. The affliction of self-knowledge that is gained slowly by this soul as it progresses through the various dwelling places is a reproach endured for the sake of Christ. We will encounter, in this work of St. Teresa, some examples of false speaking against the soul striving for perfection that come from either the devil in order to deceive the soul or from other people that must be endured for Christ.

The vermin that accompany the soul just beginning to enter the castle and its first dwelling place are the agents of evil that have attached themselves to this soul. They are not the same for everyone. They are the attachments and weaknesses that the soul will encounter constantly as it progresses spiritually through the various dwelling places of the interior castle. These attachments and weaknesses will obstruct the soul's goal until they are conquered, and consequently will be a constant source of persecution to it. Underlying this struggle will be the ever- increasing self-knowledge that will reproach the soul, but with very desirable results. For it will be from these reproaches that humility will grow in the soul, without which, no progress is possible. Most souls, before any movement toward union with God begins, are unaware of their true misery. They are assailed by their weaknesses and attachments and are unaware of their dismal state, or they erroneously attribute their baneful existence to other causes. When, by grace given, they are moved to seek God, these attachments become a source of strife and affliction; they are then truly persecuted by them from within.

> They are so attached to these things that where their treasure lies their heart goes also. Sometimes they do put all these things aside, and the self-knowledge and awareness that they are not proceeding correctly in order to get to the door is important. Finally, they enter the first, lower rooms. But so many reptiles get in with them that they are prevented from seeing the beauty of the castle and from calming down; they have done quite a bit just by having entered (IC I:1:8).

> For humility, like the bee making honey in the beehive, is always at work. Without it, everything goes wrong. But let's remember that the bee doesn't fail to leave the beehive and fly about gathering nectar from the flowers. So it is with the soul in the room of self-knowledge; let it believe me and fly sometimes to ponder the grandeur and majesty of its God. Here it will discover its lowliness better than by thinking of itself, and be freer from the vermin that enter the first rooms, those of self-knowledge (IC I:2:8).

When the soul enters the second dwelling place, the battle with the devil intensifies. This soul is beginning to show real interest in gaining the union with God to which it is being drawn. The devil, in order not to lose this soul, now begins his assault on the soul in earnest. The persecutions of temptation and deception are experienced more than before. The devil works against this soul, either from within, or enlists the aid of others to persecute the soul from outside for its desire to unite with God. This soul has not progressed far enough to easily or with determination throw off the prompting of the devil to convince the soul to give up the whole effort. There is at this stage a great struggle. Ambiguity in motivation is the characteristic of this dwelling place. The desire to go forward and the constant tug to retreat from the castle and return to the outer walls is a great affliction to this soul. The persecution from the devil is relentless. The only thing that will save this soul's initial progress is to endure the afflictions for the sake of Christ. The supporting grace will be there for those who ask for it.

> O Jesus, what an uproar the devils instigate here! And the afflictions of the poor soul: it doesn't know whether to continue or to return to the first room. Reason, for its part, shows the soul that it is mistaken in thinking that these things of the world are not worth anything when compared to what it is aiming after. Faith, however, teaches it about where it will find fulfillment (IC II:1:4).

> If the devil, especially, realizes that it (the soul) has all it needs in its temperament and habits to advance

far, he will gather all hell together to make the soul go back outside (IC II:1:5).

When a soul enters the third dwelling place, a new affliction is encountered. This soul has advanced quite far from where it started. This progress does not escape the attention of the soul. It now considers itself very proficient in the spiritual life, and seeks to become an adviser to others and to be appreciated by all as a spiritual person. But a new affliction is visited upon this soul. It begins to experience dryness in prayer and a diminishment in its fervor for the things of God. Of course, what is happening is the introduction to this soul of the passive supernatural paths to holiness. Its former fervor and intensity in prayer and matters spiritual was a product of its natural faculties. These tools are inadequate to succeed in arriving at union with God, so they are being put to sleep, so to speak, so that they do not become obstacles to further progress. If a soul clings to them because they are comfortable for it, it will remain stuck in this dwelling place permanently; and this place is still far from union with God. The anxiety that results from the changes the soul is experiencing and doesn't understand because of periods of aridity in prayer is a great trial for this soul, and so a new kind of persecution from within begins. The antidote for this anxiety is humility. Humility will lead to resignation to the way God chooses to advance this soul. Therefore, the goal of complete conformity to the will of God thereby comes closer to this struggling soul.

> After these years (in the third dwelling place), when it seems they have become lords of the world, at least clearly disillusioned in its regard, His Majesty will try them in some minor matters, and they will go about so disturbed and afflicted that it puzzles me and even makes me fearful (IC III:2:1).

> For everything in their minds leads them to think they are suffering these things for God, and so, they don't come to realize that their disturbance is an imperfection (IC III:2:2).

> Oh, humility, humility! I don't know what kind of temptation I'm undergoing in this matter that I cannot help but think that anyone who makes such

an issue of this dryness is a little lacking in humility (IC III:1:7).

The Last Four Dwelling Places

It is in the fourth dwelling place that supernatural experiences begin. These spiritual experiences are radically different from those the soul has in the earlier dwelling places. It is this difference that causes the soul some degree of affliction. The difference is caused, at least in part, by the source of the experience: a divine touch of the soul as opposed to an experience resulting from the exercise by the soul of its natural faculties. Because the source is unfamiliar to the spiritual life of the soul at this stage, anxiety from the initial lack of understanding is always present. Heretofore, the soul has experienced the natural result of its own efforts in matters of the spiritual life: consolations. These pleasant results occur at the natural level of the soul's life. They are natural consequences of natural acts oriented toward God and His will. In the fourth dwelling place, the soul begins to move beyond its own spiritual capacity and God now imposes His method of advancing the soul. This unfamiliarity with a new spiritual environment is quite unsettling to the soul. The consolations it has become accustomed to are now absent. Even though something better is being prepared for the soul, it cannot perceive it at first.

> Terrible trials are suffered because we don't understand ourselves, and that which isn't bad at all but good we think is a serious fault. This lack of knowledge causes the afflictions of many people who engage in prayer; complaints about interior trials, at least to a great extent, by people who have no learning; melancholy and loss of health; and even the complete abandonment of prayer (IC IV:1:9).

Because this state of the soul in the fourth dwelling place involves natural and supernatural influences, the devil can find opportunities for entry into the soul for the purpose of counterfeiting the beginnings of union with God. These efforts by the devil often leave the soul aimless and languishing. A soul being deceived by the devil in this way is prone to being led off in a destructive direction by the deception. In any event, the deception blanks out the beneficial touches of God as long as the soul clings to the subject of the deception. This persecution of a good soul by the devil may require the intervention of an experienced spiritual director to turn the soul away from the devil's counterfeited movements of the soul that lead nowhere.

> I advise them so strongly not to place themselves in the occasions of sin because the devil tries much harder for a soul of this kind than for very many to whom the Lord does not grant these favors. For such a soul can do a great deal of harm to the devil by getting others to follow it, and it could be of great benefit to God's Church....So these souls suffer much combat, and if they go astray, they stray much more than do others (IC IV:3:10).

The soul that enters the fifth dwelling place begins a period of very deep prayer that will extend into the sixth dwelling place with very little change. Because of the nature of this soul's experience of God in prayer, we must see any persecution of this soul for the sake of Christ as coming from the difficulties it encounters in times of deep interior prayer. This affliction is either its lament that the experience is so temporary or the occasional incursions of the devil into the interior of the soul in order to disrupt its prayer. Once the soul gets past its doubts concerning its experiences of God, and its own resistance to them, for these are a carry-over from the previous dwelling places, there is very little trial and affliction at this level of spiritual growth. This soul is beginning to reap the reward of the entry into the Kingdom of Heaven since it has weathered the afflictions of strife and persecution, either from within or from without. However, as long as one lives in this world, trials of some sort never end.

> Briefly, in one way or another, there must be a cross while we live. And with respect to anyone who says that after he arrived here he always enjoyed rest and delight I would say that he never arrived but that perhaps he had experienced spiritual delight – if he had entered into the previous dwelling place – and his experience had been helped along by natural weakness or perhaps even by the devil who gives him peace so as afterward to wage much greater war against him (IC V:2:9).

It is a great paradox that some souls who advance to great heights of spirituality become the recipient of great criticism from those from whom they would least expect it: their confreres in religion. This phenomenon is the work of the devil. He realizes that he cannot move the targeted soul away from its lofty spiritual perch, so he turns his attention to those who surround this soul in order to stimulate envy and criticism in their hearts. These others then proceed to heap persecution upon the lofty soul by showing only contempt and derision toward it. Here indeed is the endurance of persecution for the sake of Christ. The greater the growth in grace of this favored soul, the greater the efforts to defeat it.

> There is an outcry by persons a Sister is dealing with and even by those she does not deal with and who, it seems to her, would never even think of her; gossip like the following: "she's trying to make out she's a saint; she goes to extremes to deceive the world and bring others to ruin; there are other better Christians who don't put on all this outward show." (And it's worth noting that she is not putting on any outward show but just striving to fulfill well her state in life). Those she considered her friends turn away from her, and they are the ones who take the largest and most painful bite at her: "that soul has gone astray and is clearly mistaken; these are things of the devil; she will turn out like this person or that other that went astray, and will bring about a decline in virtue; she has deceived her confessors;"... a thousand kinds of ridicule and statements like the above (IC VI:1:3).

Here St. Teresa, describes and laments her own experiences of suffering, from misunderstanding, and envy. She bore much disdain and hateful dispositions toward her for many years, and speaks here from painful experience. Even the soul that has advanced greatly to the heights of prayer and union with God continues to be tried and afflicted by the effects of its fallen nature: remembrance of its sins, times of extreme weakness in devotion and resistance to sin, and worst of all, the apparent withdrawal of God from its consciousness. These trials however, always result in greater union with the will of God when they are endured with constancy for the sake of Christ and conformity to His will.

> You must not think, Sisters, that the effects I mentioned (in chapter VII:3, n. 2-8, regarding the spiritual effects of highly advanced prayer) are always present in these souls. Hence, where I remember, I say "ordinarily." For sometimes our Lord leaves these individuals in their natural state, and then it seems all the poisonous creatures from the outskirts and other dwelling places of this castle band together to take revenge for the time they were unable to have these souls under their control (IC VII:4:1).

> True, this natural state lasts only a short while, a day at most or a little more. And in this great disturbance, usually occasioned by some event, the soul's gain through the good company it is in becomes manifest (IC VII:4:2).

Your reward is great in heaven

In this section, we will look at the last chapters of *The Interior Castle* to find St. Teresa's references to the rewards that flow from union with God. We remember that these rewards are not temporal, but are eternal. However, St. Teresa gives us an insight into the reward that awaits the faithful soul in her treatment of the seventh dwelling place. The soul that arrives at this dwelling place experiences a loving union with God that contains characteristics that are a foretaste of the rewards of heaven. These favors from God's love are images of heaven in a temporary and miniature way. They result from this soul's entry into the spiritual marriage. Within the union of the spiritual marriage, glimpses of heaven are perceived in the closeness of Christ to this soul.

> You must understand that there is the greatest difference between all the previous visions and those of this dwelling place. Between the spiritual betrothal and the spiritual marriage the difference is as great as that which exists between two who are betrothed and two who can no longer be separated (IC VII:2:2).

> In this seventh dwelling place the union comes about in a different way: our good God now desires to remove the scales from the soul's eyes and let it see and understand, although in a strange way, something of the favor He grants it…Here all three Persons (of the Blessed Trinity) communicate themselves to it (the soul), speak to it, and explain those words of the Lord in the Gospel: that He and the Father and the Holy Spirit will come to dwell with the soul that loves Him and keeps His commandments (IC VII:1:6).

St. Teresa concludes her treatment of the seventh dwelling place with a simple prayer for her community and those who will read this manuscript later. In this prayer, she beseeches God that something of this writing will benefit her and her sisters on the road to salvation.

> May it please His Majesty, my Sisters and daughters that we all reach that place where we may ever praise Him. Through the merits of His Son who lives and reigns forever and ever, may He give me the grace to carry out something of what I tell you, amen. For I tell you that my confusion is great, and thus I ask you through the same Lord that in your prayers you do not forget this poor wretch (IC VII:4:16).

C. St. John of the Cross: The Ascent of Mt. Carmel

Persecution for justice sake.
Endure reproach, false speaking, and evil for Christ

The word *persecution* does not appear in the index to *The Collected Works of St. John of the Cross* (Kavanaugh, OCD, and Rodriguez, OCD, translation). In the treatment of *The Interior Castle* of St. Teresa, it was pointed out that the persecution of the soul striving for union with God comes from the three enemies of the soul: the world, the flesh, and the devil. Persecution from others in the world is always present in the life of a soul responding to grace. However, in *The Ascent of Mt Carmel* and in the other works of St. John of the Cross, persecution of the soul, as in the works of St.

Teresa, comes from within from the three enemies of the soul. That is what we will look for in the sections on persecution for the sake of justice and reproaches suffered for the sake of Christ. While we know that persecution from the outside is the common lot of all followers of Christ, that fact is not a major theme in the works of St. John. His goal is to illustrate the manner and the way a soul must travel to reach union with God. As a soul moves along this way it will encounter difficulties and afflictions that are a persecution to it; and it bears these afflictions for the sake of justice, as for the sake of the will of God, and for the sake of Christ.

A soul that begins movement toward union with God first encounters the obstacle of the appetites. These are voluntary inordinate attachments to the objects of the senses. These attachments are a persecution to the soul that seeks God because they are constantly drawing the soul away from God whom, by the nature implanted in all of humanity, it desires. They must be mortified if the soul is to draw nearer to God.

> The road and ascent to God, then, necessarily demands a habitual effort to renounce and mortify the appetites; the sooner this mortification is achieved, the sooner the soul reaches the top. But until the appetites are eliminated, a person will not arrive, no matter how much virtue he practices (AS I:5:6).

The next obstacles along the road to union with God are the interior faculties of the soul: the intellect, the memory, and the will. Each of these faculties must be mortified and purged of their natural objects if the soul is to reach its goal. The reason for this is that they are incapable of affecting the union with God by their own powers and objects. The intellect cannot understand the mysteries of the divinity of God, the memory cannot find the way to God by its own experience, and the will cannot love God unaided by grace. The purgation and purification of these faculties is accomplished by the infusion of the Theological virtues. This is a suffering for the soul because the purgation results in plunging the soul and its interior faculties into darkness by the removal of the natural objects of these faculties.

Similarly, if the soul in traveling this road leans upon any element of its own knowledge or experience of God, it will easily go astray or be detained for not having desired to abide in complete blindness, in faith which is its guide (AS II:4:3).

I should like to persuade spiritual persons that the road leading to God does not entail a multiplicity of considerations, methods, manners, and experiences – though in their own way these may be a requirement for beginners – but demands only the one thing necessary: true self-denial, exterior and interior, through surrender of self both to suffering for Christ and to annihilation in all things (AS II:7:8).

The point to remember here is that the suffering experienced by a soul in the midst of these purgations of the faculties is endured for the sake of Christ and for the sake of justice. True justice requires that all be surrendered to God and His way of leading us on to greater closeness to Him.

The soul that seeks union with God must give up the use of the memory as a reliable tool to help to achieve that union. The reason for this is that nothing in the natural order including the memory is the proximate means of arriving at that union. The means necessary are supernatural; they come directly from God. Failure to realize this fact and act accordingly on this knowledge exposes the soul to all manner of difficulty. If one relies on the world and its pseudo wisdom, one falls into errors of judgment and many falsehoods that will lead the soul farther away from union with God. If one presses on with natural means to find union with God, one is greatly exposed to the devil because the devil's entry into the soul is through the natural senses and faculties. This angel of darkness never tires of suggesting erroneous knowledge and falsehoods designed to move the soul to sins of pride, anger and many delusions. The memory also is a constant activator of temptations and sins committed over and over again if those sins and their occasions are not literally forgotten by a mortification of the memory. What a severe persecution these harms are and what a great effort is required, with the assistance of grace, to rid ourselves of them.

The first (kind of harm), coming from the world, involves the subjection to many evils arising from this knowledge and reflection, such as; falsehoods, imperfections, appetites, judgments, loss of time, and numerous other evils engendering many impurities in the soul.

Manifestly, the spiritual person allowing himself this knowledge and reflection will necessarily be the victim of falsehoods. Often the true will appear false, and the certain doubtful, and vice versa, since we can hardly have complete understanding of a truth. A man frees himself of this if he darkens his memory to all knowledge and reflection (AS III:3:2).

The devil is unable to do anything in the soul save through the operation of its faculties, and principally by means of its knowledge, because almost all the activity of the other faculties depends upon its knowledge. If the memory is annihilated concerning this knowledge, the devil is powerless. For he finds no means of getting his grip on the soul, and consequently can do nothing (AS III:4:1).

The soul is incapable of truly acquiring the control of the passions and the restriction of the inordinate appetites without forgetting and withdrawing from the sources of these emotions. Disturbances never arise in a soul unless through the apprehensions of the memory. When all things are forgotten, nothing disturbs the peace or stirs the appetites (AS III:5:1).

Your reward is great in heaven

St. John of the Cross gives us many descriptions of the benefits to souls and the great rewards they reap if they will endure the afflictions of mortification and purgation encountered in the active nights of the senses and of the spirit. The final reward for the faithful soul will be perpetual union with God in heaven. However, there are many milestones along the road to this perfect existence which, while incomplete, are foretastes of the glory to come if only the soul will persevere. These milestones are indications of progress toward our goal and necessary stages indicating that the path we are on is the right road to our destination. We must bear in mind that nothing imperfect enters the heavenly presence of God in the Beatific Vision. Therefore, every mortification of an inordinate appetite that is an obstacle to union with God and His Will is a step forward toward eternal life with God in heaven. This purgation of the appetites must occur in this life or in Purgatory. Therefore, we can conclude that the benefit of every such purgation of an inordinate appetite, which moves us closer to union with God, is a small part of our ultimate reward.

> If anyone is to reach perfect union with God through his will and love, he must obviously first be freed from every appetite however slight. That is, he must not give the consent of his will knowingly to an imperfection, and he must have the power and freedom to be able, upon advertence, to refuse this consent (AS I:11:3).

A soul moves forward in its preparation for the gifts and rewards to be given to it by God when its prayer approaches contemplation. This early stage of dark contemplation is called the loving knowledge of God. The soul begins to love what it has learned about God and wishes to rest in that love. This stage cannot happen until the senses are substantially purged of the appetite's objects. A soul that is beginning to experience the loving knowledge of God in early contemplation is still in the active nights. In this loving knowledge, it is receiving a morsel of what awaits it if it perseveres to union in the passive nights that are to follow. In speaking of this period of transition out of prayer as an exercise of the faculties and senses, St. John says the following:

> Indeed, they are getting lost, but not in the way they imagine, for they are losing the exercise of their own senses and first mode of experience. This loss indicates they are approaching the spirit being imparted to them, in which the less they understand the further they penetrate into the night of the spirit – the subject of this book. They must pass through this night to a union with God beyond all knowing (AS II:14:4).

A soul that is advancing toward union with God experiences many rewards along the way that give it a hint of what awaits it in heaven. Among the many such gifts, perhaps the greatest to be experienced in this life is peace. This freedom from disturbance and dismay over afflictions or events in and around our lives is indeed a foretaste of heaven. There we will be free of all care, and enwrapped in the love and loving exchanges of God. Temptations to sin cease to exist in heaven. In the soul advancing toward union with God, many temptations to which it was accustomed either cease or diminish greatly.

> In contrast to the first kind of harm, (coming from the world) the spiritual person enjoys tranquility and peace of soul because of the absence of disturbance and change which derives from thoughts and ideas in the memory, and consequently he possesses purity of conscience and soul, which is a greater benefit (AS III:6:1).

> In contrast to the second, (from the devil) he is freed from many suggestions, temptations, and movements which the devil inserts in souls through their thoughts and ideas, thereby occasioning many impurities and sins...When the thoughts are removed the devil has nothing naturally with which to wage his war on the spirit (AS III:6:2).

> Contrary to the third kind of harm, (impediment to moral good) the soul is disposed, by means of this recollection and forgetfulness of all things, to be moved by the Holy Spirit and taught by Him (AS III:6:3).

D. St. John of the Cross: The Dark Night

Persecution for justice sake.
Endure reproach, false speaking, and evil for Christ

It is in this work of St. John of the Cross that we encounter descriptions of intense affliction and suffering of a soul seeking union with God. It is here that we meet our definition of persecution from within in its most difficult form. Reproaches of the soul are multiple and in ever increasing intensity. With regard to these two afflictions of persecution and reproach, we usually expect that such suffering will come from one or more of the enemies of the soul, the world, the flesh, or the devil. Afflictions from one of these sources always lead to consequences that are evil in some manner and to some degree. However, the afflictions described by St. John in this work are not from these three enemies, but have their source in God. The consequences of these afflictions are far from evil. They are the instruments of advancing holiness. Their effect is to bring about the changes in the soul that are necessary for true holiness that the soul could never effect itself no matter how earnestly it desired to do so. Here the soul enters the passive nights and becomes acquainted with spiritual pain that is absolutely new to its experience. The self-knowledge that is acquired here is humbling beyond words. The light of God, that here is so painful, illuminates the interior of the soul to expose imperfections never before even imagined by this soul. Superficial and partial commitment to the pursuit of unity with God is exposed as inadequate to that end, and an interior struggle between the self's goals and unity with God is joined.

> This going out (unseen) bears reference to the subjection the soul had to its senses, in seeking God through operations so feeble, limited, and exposed to error as are those of this lower part, for at every step it stumbled into numerous imperfections and much ignorance as was noted above in relation to the seven capital vices. This night frees the soul from all these vices by quenching all its earthly and heavenly satisfactions, darkening its discursive meditations, and producing in it other innumerable goods through the acquisition of the virtues... (DN I:11:4).

The primary suffering from an interior form of persecution experienced by the soul is that it feels the weight of its own fallen nature and limitations. Because of this weakness in our nature, it is necessary that the soul experience aridity as it begins to move into the passive nights, which is aridity of the senses and not of the spirit. This is the case, although the aridity in the interior faculties of intellect, will, and memory makes it appear that the aridity is complete and also permanent. The soul is not immediately aware of the fact that the aridity it is experiencing is confined to the senses.

The reason for this is that the senses are being put to sleep so to speak. However, while all this suffering is being endured, intense work is being done by God to purify the spirit. Herein, in this unawareness lies the primary source of the soul's suffering. God induces this aridity for the purpose of removing the soul's desire to work for unity by the use of the senses. They are incapable of accomplishing that unity, and so God wishes to get them out of the way so the desire to proceed by the use of the senses is not an obstacle to further progress toward real unity. This change is a great suffering to the soul because its customary approach to God is squelched and ineffective. Its greatest suffering during this period is the belief that God has turned against it and no longer loves the soul or wishes it to become closer to Himself. Instead of finding relief from this suffering, the soul has in fact embarked on a long and painful period in its spiritual maturity with only minimal consolation and reassurances that it has not lost God forever. St. John of the Cross aptly calls this period of affliction *dark contemplation* or *purgative contemplation*.

> God divests the faculties, affections, and senses, both spiritual and sensory, interior and exterior. He leaves the intellect in darkness, the will in aridity, the memory in emptiness, and the affections in supreme affliction, bitterness, and anguish, by depriving the soul of the feeling and satisfaction it previously obtained from spiritual blessings (DN II:3:3).

> When this purgative contemplation oppresses a man, he feels very vividly indeed the shadow of death, the sighs of death, and the sorrows of hell, all of which reflect the feeling of God's absence, of being chastised and rejected by Him, and of being unworthy of Him, as well as the object of His anger. The soul experiences all this and even more, for now it seems that this affliction will last forever (DN II:6:2).

> God does all this by means of dark contemplation. And the soul not only suffer the void and suspension of these natural supports and apprehensions, which is a terrible anguish (like hanging in midair, unable

to breathe), but it is also purged by this contemplation. As fire consumes the tarnish and rust of metal, this contemplation annihilates, empties, and consumes all the affections and imperfect habits the soul contracted throughout its life (DN II:6:5).

What makes the interior of the soul visible to itself is the divine light that illumines its deepest interior where only darkness and blindness existed before. This light is very painful. However, the pain does not come from the divine light, but from the imperfections of the soul which are now experienced by it consciously for the first time. The soul that believed it had grown very much spiritually is now horrified and afflicted at what it sees within itself. Further growth of the soul requires this painful period. If the soul recoils from this purgation and refuses to go forward, it will never arrive at union with God, and will probably fall back further from God. This interior persecution must be endured for the sake of the justice required from all creatures toward God, which requires expiation for its own sins and the sins of the world. No reproach from outside of the soul could produce a suffering as intense in the soul of good will as a sense of having lost God. Endurance in this suffering is only for the sake of Christ and the soul's search for union with its Beloved. No lesser goal would move the soul to persevere in this affliction.

> I do not want to fail to explain why this divine light, even though it is always light for the soul, does not illumine immediately upon striking, as it will afterwards, but instead causes trials and darknesses...
>
> From the beginning, the divine light illumines the soul; yet at the outset, it can only see through this light what is nearest – or rather within – itself, namely, its own darknesses and miseries. It sees these by the mercy of God, and it did not see them before because this supernatural light did not shine in it (DN II:13:10).

St John of the Cross sets out a magnificent statement on the necessity of the soul to endure this dark contemplation and the reader should read this statement frequently and reflect on it when he is enduring the suffering described in this section of this book.

> Oh, what a miserable lot this life is! We live in the midst of so much danger and find it so hard to arrive at truth. The clearest and truest things are the darkest and most dubious to us and consequently we flee from what most suits us. We embrace what fills our eyes with the most light and satisfaction and run after what is the very worst thing for us, and we fall at every step. In how much danger and fear does man live, since the very light of his natural eyes which ought to be his guide is the first to deceive him in his journey to God and since he must keep his eyes shut and tread the path in darkness if he wants to be sure of where he is going and be safeguarded against the enemies of his house, his senses and faculties (DN II:16:12).

Your reward is great in heaven

All of the trials and afflictions endured by the soul on its path to union with God have a resulting reward for the soul that perseveres. That reward is the preparation of the soul for the Beatific Vision. God is our goal. Unity with him is what animates our will to endure to the end. But to reach this reward the soul must be conditioned and prepared to receive it. As the soul grows in holiness, some faint image of that reward is received in this life. These are the goods that St. John describes as coming from the afflictions of dark contemplation. These effects on the soul and the changes in the soul that they bring about are necessary for the soul to undergo before it can enter the presence of God.

> The first and chief benefit that this dry and dark night of contemplation causes is the knowledge of self and of one's own misery. Besides the fact that all the favors God imparts to the soul are ordinarily enwrapped in this knowledge, the aridities and voids of the faculties in relation to the abundance previously experienced, and the difficulty encountered in the practice of virtue make the soul recognize its own lowliness and misery, which was

not apparent in the time of its prosperity (DN I:12:2).

One cannot over-emphasize the importance and essential place self-knowledge occupies in the ability of the soul to progress in the spiritual life. Before a soul enters the dark contemplation that so afflicts it with pain, it has in reality been proceeding in an environment of self-deception. This self-deception is not intentional and the soul does not incur moral responsibility deserving of punishment for it. This soul is operating with limited knowledge gleaned from the operation of its senses and interior faculties. This unawareness is akin to the first grader who proceeds in class without knowing the multiplication tables. Since he has never been taught the multiplication tables there is no blame for not knowing them to be assigned to him. If he perseveres to the later grades he will be taught the multiplication tables, and the whole world of mathematics begins to open to him. Similarly, God, by the afflictions of dark contemplation instructs the soul in self-knowledge, and the whole of spirituality opens to him, albeit painfully at first. As it does, the soul begins to reap its reward here in this life that will be perfected in heaven, even though it is unaware of the gift it is receiving.

> God esteems this lack of self-satisfaction (from knowledge of self) and the dejection a person has about not serving Him more than all former deeds and gratifications, however notable they may have been, since they were the occasion of many imperfections and a great deal of ignorance (DN I:12:2).

> First, a person communes with God more respectfully and courteously, the way one should always converse with the most High (DN I:12:3).
> In the dryness and emptiness of this night of the appetite, a person also procures spiritual humility, that virtue opposed to the first capital vice, spiritual pride. Through this humility acquired by means of self-knowledge, a person is purged of all those imperfections of the vice of pride into which he fell in the time of his prosperity (DN I:12:7).

> God so curbs concupiscence and bridles the appetites through this arid and dark night that the soul cannot feast on any sensory delight from earthly or heavenly things, and He continues this purgation in such a way that the concupiscence and appetites are brought into subjection, reformed and mortified (DN I:13:3).

We can see from these statements of St. John of the Cross that the soul's first reward for all the affliction it suffers in this dark contemplation is to begin to prepare the soul for heaven. This is a great grace to be given during life in this world. Not only does it insulate the soul from evils of all kinds while it is living in this world, but it also removes the necessity to have this work done after death. We must bear in mind for the sake of our subject matter in this chapter that our reward is God Himself. Whatever prepares our souls for Him is also itself an immense reward. The final reward of union with God comes at the end of the spiritual journey, but there are interim rewards of divine touches that propel the soul forward spiritually. In addition to these, there are rewards within the soul itself that pertain to the condition of the soul. These internal rewards are in the form of fundamental changes without which the final goal of transforming union cannot be reached. This union results in a soul that has acquired a likeness to God in love and now has a detachment from all inordinate affections for creatures, knows the truth about itself, and rightly evaluates the importance of its relationship to God. All of this is accomplished by God, as the soul endures these passive nights of the senses and spirit.

> Oh, then, spiritual soul, when you see your appetites darkened, your inclinations dry and constrained, your faculties incapacitated for any interior exercise, do not be afflicted; think of this as a grace, since God is freeing you from yourself and taking from you your own activity. However well your actions may have succeeded you did not work so completely, perfectly, and securely – owing to your impurity and awkwardness – as you do now that God takes you by the hand and guides you in darkness, as though you were blind, along a way and to a place you know not. You would never have

succeeded in reaching this place no matter how good your eyes and your feet (DN II:16:7).

The soul obtains habitually and perfectly (insofar as the condition of this life allows) the rest and quietude of the spiritual house by means of the acts of substantial touches of divine union which, in concealment and hiding from the disturbance of the devil and of the senses and passions, are received from the divinity. With these touches the soul purified, quieted, strengthened, and made stable that it may be able to receive permanently this divine union, which is the divine espousal between the soul and the Son of God (DN II:24:3).

E. St. John of the Cross: The Spiritual Canticle

Persecution for justice sake.
Endure reproach, false speaking, and evil for Christ

This book of St. John of the Cross raises a new form of affliction for the soul not discussed previously in this section at any length. We find a new interior persecution in the form of privation in the first twelve stanzas of *The Spiritual Canticle*. This new affliction in the soul is a mournful plea for the Beloved to come to the soul and satisfy its longings for union. The soul has endured many sufferings through the passive nights of sense and spirit, and from its purification have arisen an intense love for God and an equally intense desire for union with Him. So the soul goes in search of the Beloved with longings and spiritual wounds that make it feel that it is dying a painful death in the spirit. These spiritual wounds have been inflicted by God, and not only carry a sense of pain with them, but also the pain is coupled with an incomparable delight. This delight and the longing it produces flows from the very painful periods experienced by the soul as it passed through the afflictions of the dark night of contemplation. However, this soul has not yet entered the abode of God within its soul, and therefore, experiences the absence of God and does not yet know where to find Him.

It must be understood that if a person experiences some grand spiritual communication or feeling or knowledge, he should not think that his experiences

> are similar to the clear and essential vision or possession of God, or that the communication, no matter how remarkable it is, signifies a more notable possession of God or union with Him. It should be known too that if all these sensible and spiritual communications are wanting and a person lives in dryness, darkness, and dereliction, he must not thereby think that God is any more absent than in the former case (SC 1:4).

What the soul seeks is union with God that is more proper to eternal life than to this life. Since this soul cannot find the completeness of union that it seeks, it begins to desire this life to end. Because this soul is still tethered to life in this world, the clarity of the desired union with the Beloved is not available to it. But this does not mean that God is absent. It is in fact a case of the soul not knowing where He can be found during this life. His hiding place is actually deep within the soul, and the soul must go there if it is to find Him. To get there, everything that is not of God must be left behind.

> Yet you inquire: Since He Whom my soul loves is within me, why don't I find Him or experience Him? The reason is that He remains concealed and you do not also conceal yourself in order to encounter and experience Him. Anyone who is to find a hidden treasure must enter the hiding place secretly, and once he has discovered it, he will also be hidden just as the treasure is hidden. Since, then, your beloved Bridegroom is the treasure hidden in a field, for which the wise merchant sold all his possessions (Mt 13:44), and that field is your soul, in order to find Him you should forget all your possessions and all creatures and hide in the interior, secret chamber of your spirit (SC 1:9).

A soul that has endured the passive nights, or at least the greater part of them, arrives at such a love for its longed for Bridegroom, that anything that keeps the soul from Him is an intense suffering. The main obstacle before it to union with the Beloved is its own natural life in the body. Its affliction is the conflict between the life of the body and the longings of the soul. It sees its natural life as something to be extinguished in order to fly unhindered to the

Beloved. This dilemma is a major part of its suffering in this advanced period of spirituality.

> The soul lays great stress on this complaint, for she announces here that she suffers from two contraries: natural life in the body, and spiritual life in God. They are contraries insofar as the one wars against the other (Rom 7:23). And living both in the body and in God, she necessarily feels great torment, since the one painful life thwarts the other delightful one, so much so that the natural life is like death to her, because through it she is deprived of the spiritual life in which she has all her being and life by nature and all her operations and affections through love (SC 8:3).

St. John of the Cross likens the condition of a soul so consumed by love for God to one who is suffering from an illness. All that such a person desires is a return to health. No matter what else is offered to such a person, it cannot displace the longing for health to return, or even interest this unfortunate person. Similarly, a soul that is consumed by love for God is devoid of care or interest in any other matter. It is God alone who is its health. When God seems absent to such a soul, there is nothing that can fill the void even to a small extent. In fact, all else that is not God is an irritant to this soul and causes it much pain. This is a unique suffering that passively afflicts a soul and calls for great patience in order to endure it. Of course, we can see that this soul is in fact in an enviable state. It has succeeded in shedding all the useless and worthless distractions of the senses and imagination that have served as obstacles to union with God in the spirit. Actually, isn't this the state to which all the early efforts of the soul and the graces accompanying these efforts in the passive nights have been directed?

> Since the soul has reached this sickness of love of God, she has three traits: in all things that are offered to her or with which she deals, she has ever before her that longing for her health, which is her Beloved (even though she cannot help being occupied with them, she always has her heart fixed on Him); the second trait, arising from this first, is the loss of taste for all things; the third then results, which is that all

these things molest her and all dealings with others are burdensome and annoying (SC 10:1).

Your reward is great in heaven

The soul that endures the pains of love described above is on the threshold of the advanced spiritual state that St. John calls the spiritual espousal. There are delights and divine touches that, although only a speck of what awaits the soul in heaven, nonetheless partake of the eternal reward that awaits such a faithful soul. God's spirit is taking hold of the soul and drawing it to Him by a powerful attraction. This attraction to God smothers all other attractions as the sun smothers the glow of a candle. This invasion of the soul by God does not now cause the pain that it previously caused stemming from the soul's imperfections. The soul is now filled with longings and delights in God, and union with Him is advancing rapidly. The spiritual voice that the soul hears is the effect of these divine touches in the spirit. St. John refers to these sounds as *love-stirring breezes*.

By *love-stirring breezes* is understood the attributes and graces of the Beloved which by means of this union assail the soul and lovingly touch it in its substance.

> This most sublime and delightful knowledge of God and His attributes which overflows into the intellect from the touch these attributes of God produce in the substance of the soul, she calls the whistling of these breezes (stanza 14). This is the most exalted delight of all the soul here enjoys (SC 14:12).

The knowledge of God communicated to the soul in this state of espousal is substantial knowledge of Him. There are no accidents, characteristics, or revealed facts about God that are being communicated to this soul in this state. Rather, what is received by the soul is God as He is to the extent the soul can bear and absorb this divine touch. This substantial knowledge of God is received in the possible intellect, which differs from the active intellect in the following way. The possible intellect is entirely passive, and receives only what is given to it within its capacity to receive. Divine assistance is always a factor in this reception of the substantial knowledge of God. The active intellect, on the other hand, is the faculty by which we reason to the truth about reality, and it makes it possible to accept the truth of what has been revealed to us by God about Himself. The key word here is *about*, which connotes facts beyond our power to decipher or, by the use of our reason, to reach true conclusions concerning the nature of God. The substantial knowledge of God does not involve any of the human faculties except the power of the passive intellect, aided by grace, to receive a divine communication about God and His attributes.

> She calls the knowledge a "whistling" because just as the whistling of the breeze pierces deeply into the hearing organ, so this most subtle and delicate knowledge penetrates with wonderful savoriness into the innermost part of the substance of the soul, and the delight is greater than all others.

> The reason for the delight is that the already understood substance, stripped of accidents and phantasms, is bestowed. For this knowledge is given to that intellect which philosophers call the passive or possible intellect, and the intellect receives it passively without any efforts of its own (SC 14:14).

The soul that enters into the spiritual marriage is in a state never before experienced by this fortunate soul. It is very near to its eternal salvation. But what will its eternal salvation be like to this soul and what properties will it have? Not only does St. John of the Cross struggle with this question, but so also did St. Paul when he said, "Neither eye has seen, nor ear heard, nor has it entered into the heart of man what God has in store for those who love Him" (1 Cor 2:9). Starting with this quote from St. Paul's letter to the Corinthians, St. John of the Cross goes to the words of Christ in order to find some insight into the nature of the glory of the Beatific Vision. In doing so, he points out that from all eternity the existence of the soul was planned by God, and with its existence, its eternal glory was also planned by God. St. John of the Cross uses the following words of Christ, among others, to try to reach a glimpse of eternal glory, which will be the soul's great eternal reward in heaven, as described in this *Beatitude*.

> To him that overcomes I will give to eat of the tree of life which is in the paradise of my God (Ap. 2:7).

> Be faithful unto death and I will give you the crown of life (Ap. 2:10).
>
> To him that overcomes I will give the hidden manna and a white stone, and on the stone a new name will be written, which no one knows save he who receives it (Ap. 2:17).
>
> To him who overcomes I will give to sit with me on my throne, as I also have conquered and sat with my Father on His throne. He who has ears to hear, let him hear etc. (Ap. 3:21-22) (SC 38:7-8).

Even all of these descriptions do not fully explain the *what* that is stated in stanza 38 of *The Spiritual Canticle.* Therefore, we must return to the words of St. Paul and humbly acknowledge that: "it has not entered into the heart of man what God has prepared for those who love Him (I Cor 2:9)."

Lastly, in stanza 40 St. John of the Cross resolves the question: "What has occurred in this soul?" He does so very simply by citing five blessings that have been bestowed on this soul.

> First, her soul is detached and withdrawn from all things.
>
> Second, the devil is conquered and put to flight.
>
> Third, the passions are subjected and the natural appetites mortified.
>
> Fourth and fifth, the sensory and lower part is reformed, purified, and brought into conformity with the spiritual part. The sensory part not only offers no obstacle to the reception of these spiritual blessings, but is even accommodated to them, since it participates according to its capacity in the goods now possessed (SC 40:1).

This soul is now fully spiritualized and the bodily senses, both interior and exterior, are accommodated to the spirit, and have become indifferent to their natural objects, except insofar as they are useful in advancing the soul's unity with God. Using the imagery of the cavalry as the bodily senses and the waters as the spiritual goods and delights given to the soul, St. John ends *The Spiritual Canticle* with these two lines:

> *And the cavalry*
> *At the sight of the waters, descended.*

> The bride declares that in this state the cavalry descended at the sight of the spiritual waters, because in this state of spiritual marriage the sensory and lower part of the soul is so purified and spiritualized that it recollects the sensory faculties and natural strength so that they may thereby share in and enjoy in their own fashion the spiritual grandeurs which God is communicating in the inwardness of the spirit.
> (SC 40:5).

F. St. John of the Cross: The Living Flame of Love

As we have seen in the treatment of some of the other *Beatitudes*, the first part of the couplet that constitutes the full *Beatitude* deals with the activity and afflictions of the soul in this life. This work of St. John of the Cross deals only with the nature of the spiritual marriage and all of its joys, which by definition is the soul's reward for enduring the trials and afflictions that have moved it into the spiritual realm of the spiritual marriage. Therefore, we will look at this work of St. John only to find evidence of the final reward of this soul which is great in heaven. These stanzas deal with the highest state of perfection that a soul can reach in this life. It is within this transformation in love that a hint of the heavenly reward is glimpsed. Remember that this soul has left behind all obstacles to unity with God, except one: natural death. It is this last obstacle that prevents the great reward from being realized to the fullest. However, in this state of transformation in love, the seeds of the great reward are, from time to time, experienced. We find these glimpses most prominently in stanza 4. Let us examine that stanza in order to find these glimpses.

Your reward is great in heaven

How gently and lovingly
You wake in my heart,
Where in secret You dwell alone;
And in your sweet breathing,
Filled with good and glory,
How tenderly You swell my heart with love.

How gently and lovingly
You wake in my heart,

In these verses, St. John of the Cross speaks of an awakening in the heart. The nature of this awakening illumines for us much of what the soul is now enjoying as a result of its long and difficult suffering of the purgation and purification of its being. Heretofore, the soul has viewed all of reality through its natural vision. This extremely limited manner of seeing reality has been the cause of many errors and weaknesses that have now been removed from it. The awakening spoken of here is an awakening to supernatural vision. All things are now seen and understood through the *vision* of God. Instead of knowing a cause through its effects, the soul now knows the effects through their cause. This is the disposition and vision it will have in eternal life. With this supernatural vision, there will no longer be any deceptions or misunderstandings regarding imminent or transcendent realty. All things will be known as they truly are.

> And here lies the remarkable delight of this awakening: the soul knows creatures through God and not God through creatures (LF 4:5).

> That which I understand therefore as to how God effects this awakening and view of the soul (which is in Him substantially as is every creature) is that He removes some of the many veils and curtains hanging in front of it so that it might see Him as He is (LF 4:7).

Where in secret You dwell alone

God dwells in all souls in secret in the sense that He is hidden in the substance of the soul. However, in some fortunate souls He dwells alone. We cannot over estimate the importance of the concept of *alone*. In far too many souls, God dwells amidst the debris of the world and the affections of the divided and disoriented soul. Because there is so much *noise* in such souls, the voice of God is seldom, if ever, heard. He has little or no chance of affecting the life of such a soul. This soul's interest and vision is anywhere and everywhere; the natural world is its sole habitat and the delights and mercies of the divine are never experienced. In this soul, God is far from alone.

But in the soul that has responded to grace and trudged along the path of purgation and persevered to unity with God, God does dwell alone. The clutter of the world, the flesh and the devil have been expunged from this fortunate soul and God is the only occupant in the substance of the soul, and all its movements are made in Him. No longer is this soul divided, but now it is integrated completely in God.

> It is in the soul in which less of its own appetites and pleasures dwell where He dwells more alone, more pleased, and more as though in His own house, ruling and governing it. And He dwells more in secret, the more He dwells alone. Thus in this soul in which neither any appetite nor other images or forms, nor any affection for created things, dwell, the Beloved dwells secretly with an embrace so much the closer, more intimate, and interior, the purer and more alone the soul is to everything other than God (LF 4:14).

Oh how happy is this soul which ever experiences God resting and reposing within it! Oh, how fitting it is for it to withdraw from things, to flee from business matters, and live in immense tranquility, so that it may not even with the slightest mote or noise disturb or trouble its heart where the Beloved dwells (LF 4:15).

St. John of the Cross declines to go any further in attempting to describe the beauty and joys of the soul completely transformed in love and united completely with God. He offers his incapability of doing so because it is so profound that he cannot describe it with words anywhere near what the actual experience is. He does however say the following:

> It is a spiration which God produces in the soul, in which, by that awakening of lofty knowledge of the Godhead, He breathes the Holy Spirit in it in the same proportion as its knowledge and understanding of Him, absorbing it most profoundly in the Holy Spirit, rousing its love with divine excellence and delicacy according to what it beholds in Him (LF 4:17).

Printed in Great Britain
by Amazon